EQUALITY

The second edition of this widely acclaimed book about the Equality Act 2010 by one of its leading architects brings forward the story of how and why this historic legislation was enacted and what it means, to cover the first four years of its implementation by the Coalition government and in the courts. This includes an assessment of amendments to the legislation, the reduction in the powers and budget of the Equality and Human Rights Commission and the imposition of tribunal fees, as well as a discussion of possible future directions of equality law and policy.

Equality
The Legal Framework

Second Edition

Bob Hepple

·H A R T·
PUBLISHING

OXFORD AND PORTLAND, OREGON
2014

Published in the United Kingdom by Hart Publishing Ltd
16C Worcester Place, Oxford, OX1 2JW
Telephone: +44 (0)1865 517530
Fax: +44 (0)1865 510710
E-mail: mail@hartpub.co.uk
Website: http://www.hartpub.co.uk

Published in North America (US and Canada) by
Hart Publishing
c/o International Specialized Book Services
920 NE 58th Avenue, Suite 300
Portland, OR 97213-3786
USA
Tel: +1 503 287 3093 or toll-free: (1) 800 944 6190
Fax: +1 503 280 8832
E-mail: orders@isbs.com
Website: http://www.isbs.com

Hart Publishing is an imprint of Bloomsbury Publishing plc.

British Library Cataloguing in Publication Data

Data Available

ISBN: 978-1-84946-639-4

Typeset by Forewords, Oxford
Printed and bound in Great Britain by
CPI Group (UK) Ltd, Croydon CR0 4YY

Preface to the Second Edition

This second edition, within four years of the first, has been necessitated by changes made to the Equality Act under the Conservative-Liberal Democrat Coalition Government since 2010, including the reduction in the powers of the Equality and Human Rights Commission, and the making of regulations under various provisions of the Equality Act 2010. There are commentaries on the effect on law enforcement of the drastic reduction in the budget and staffing of the Commission, and the imposition in 2013 of tribunal fees. Several important decisions by the Supreme Court and European Court of Human Rights since 2010 which clarify and, in a few cases, confuse equality law, are discussed. I am encouraged by the citation of the first edition of this book in some of these judgments.

As far as possible the law is stated as at 30 June 2014. The Deregulation Bill was carried over from the 2013–14 parliamentary session to 2014–15 and is likely to become law in the near future. Unless otherwise stated, the book has been written as if all parts of the legislation, as amended, are in force, but the reader needs to check whether any particular sections are operative. The basic structure of the book remains unchanged, but there are new sections on developments since 2010, including caste discrimination and intersectional or multiple discrimination, and an expanded section on the public sector equality duty.

I am grateful to all those who have spared the time to provide me with information, and to Joshua Hepple for his efficient research assistance. As always, I have had the inspiration and encouragement of my wife, Mary Coussey, and the benefit of her enormous knowledge and experience of equal opportunities.

EXTRACT FROM PREFACE TO THE FIRST EDITION (2011)

Equality law is a socially important and intellectually challenging subject. It is important because it seeks to use law as a means of changing entrenched attitudes, behaviour and institutions in order to secure the fundamental human right to equality. The subject is a challenging one because it involves the construction and development of novel legal concepts and procedures. It is necessary to understand these concepts and the technical structure of the law in order to appreciate their social significance and to use them effectively in the struggles for equal rights. One cannot simply skirt around the hard professional core of the law and procedure. But equality law is not an intellectual game played in court by clever barristers or in universities by philosophers and academic lawyers. It is shaped by and has a vital impact on people in their everyday lives. One has to understand the historical and social contexts and the values on which the law is based.

I have written this book for anyone who wants to understand the Equality Act 2010 in those contexts. This is not a legal practitioners' textbook, but I hope it will be read by students of law and social sciences, human rights activists, lawyers and others who will use and shape the law in future, and that it will also be comprehensible to the general reader who wants to know more about the subject. With that in mind I have tried, wherever possible, to explain the law without digressing into too much technical detail.

The book is dedicated to all those working for equal rights.

List of Abbreviations

ACAS	Advisory, Conciliation and Arbitration Service
ADR	alternative dispute resolution
BME	Black and Minority Ethnic
BSL	British Sign Language
CABx	Citizens Advice Bureaux
CARD	Campaign Against Racial Discrimination
CBI	Confederation of British Industry
CEDAW	Convention on the Elimination of All Forms of Discrimination Against Women
CEHR	Commission for Equality and Human Rights (now EHRC)
CERD	Convention on the Elimination of All Forms of Racial Discrimination
CFA	conditional fee agreement
CFR	Code of Federal Regulations
CLS	Community Legal Service
CMD	Case Management Discussion (mediation)
CRC	Community Relations Commission
CRE	Commission for Racial Equality
CRPWD	Convention on the Rights of Persons with Disabilities
DBA	damages-based agreement
DDA	Disability Discrimination Act 1995
DRC	Disability Rights Commission
EA	Equality Act (note: 'EA' refers to the 2010 Act except where specified, eg EA 2006)
EAT	Employment Appeal Tribunal
ECHR	European Convention on Human Rights
ECJ	Court of Justice of the European Union
ECNI	Equality Commission for Northern Ireland
EEC	European Economic Community
EHRC	Equality and Human Rights Commission
EN	Explanatory Notes to the Equality Act 2010 (rev edn August 2010)
EOC	Equal Opportunities Commission
EOR	Equal Opportunities Review
EqLR	Equality Law Reports
ERA	Employment Rights Act 1996

ERRA	Employment and Regulatory Reform Act 2013
ERT	Equal Rights Trust
ESC	European Social Charter 1961 (rev 1996)
EU	European Union
FEC	Fair Employment Commission (Northern Ireland)
GAD	Government Actuary's Department
GEO	Government Equalities Office
HC	House of Commons
HL	House of Lords
ICCPR	International Covenant on Civil and Political Rights
ICESCR	International Covenant on Economic, Social and Cultural Rights
ILO	International Labour Organization
IRLR	Industrial Relations Law Reports
JCHR	House of Commons and House of Lords Joint Committee on Human Rights
NDPB	non-departmental government body
OCR	Office of the Chief Rabbi of the United Hebrew Congregation of the Commonwealth
ODI	Office for Disability Issues
ONS	Office for National Statistics
PBC (EB)	House of Commons Public Bill Committee (Equality Bill)
PEP	Political and Economic Planning
RRA	Race Relations Act 1976
RRB	Race Relations Board
SDA	Sex Discrimination Act 1975
TCNs	Third Country Nationals
TFEU	Treaty on the Functioning of the European Union
TUC	Trades Union Congress
UNCRC	UN Convention on the Rights of the Child
UNDHR	Universal Declaration of Human Rights

Contents

Table of Cases

Table of Legislation

UK Statutes

UK Statutory Instruments

EU Legislation

Treaties and Conventions

Secondary Legislation

National Legislation

The Netherlands

International Legislation

1

The Aims of Equality Law

THE EQUALITY ACT 2010

THE EQUALITY ACT 2010 was a major landmark in the long struggle for equal rights. This book tells the story of why and how it came to be enacted, what it means, what changes it can bring about in British society, and—no less important—what the Act will not do. Under the Conservative–Liberal Democrat Coalition Government the legal framework has since 2010 been undermined by a series of amendments to the Act, by the disempowerment of the Equality and Human Rights Commission (EHRC) and by restrictions on access to justice in discrimination cases. The nature and impact of these changes are assessed in this new edition.

The Act has three distinctive features which are largely unaffected by these changes. First, it is *comprehensive*, adopting a unitary or integrated perspective of equality enforced by the EHRC. The Commission was established by Part 1 of the Equality Act 2006 to replace the three former equality commissions,[1] and came into operation on 1 October 2007. The single Commission and the single Act of 2010 mark a decisive shift away from the politics and law of single identities—such as race and religion, gender, sexual orientation, disability and age—towards the politics and law of fundamental human rights. Secondly, the Act of 2010 *harmonises, clarifies and extends* the concepts of discrimination, harassment and victimisation and applies them across nine protected characteristics. Thirdly, it contains some measures, described as *transformative* equality, extending positive duties on public authorities to have due regard to the need to eliminate discrimination, advance equality of opportunity, and foster good relations between different groups. It also clarifies and broadens the circumstances in which positive action may be taken voluntarily in both private and public sectors to further these objectives. The shift of focus from negative duties not to

---

[1] The Commission for Racial Equality (CRE), Equal Opportunities Commission (EOC), and Disability Rights Commission (DRC). Part 1 of the Equality Act (EA) 2006 remains in force with amendments effected by the 2010 Act, and by the Enterprise and Regulatory Reform Act 2013 (ERRA).

discriminate, harass or victimise, to positive duties to advance equality, justify the reinvention of this branch of the law as *equality law*, of which discrimination law is an essential but not exclusive part. The Act replaces nine major earlier pieces of legislation[2] covering gender, race, disability, religion or belief, sexual orientation and age. It also seeks to implement fully the principal EU directives[3] in these fields.

The Act was the outcome of over 13 years of campaigning by equality specialists and human rights organisations. There were numerous reasons why the prevailing framework of anti-discrimination legislation needed to be reformed.[4] There was fragmentation and inconsistency between three separate anti-discrimination regimes (sex, race and disability) and three commissions. There was pressure to extend the grounds of discrimination to include sexual orientation, religion or belief, and age, and to impose duties on the public sector to promote equality. The EU Race Directive and Framework Employment Directive, made under Article 13 of the EC Treaty inserted by the Treaty of Amsterdam, made it necessary for the UK to legislate on these matters, and to revise existing law on sex, race and disability discrimination. There were also several gaps between the rights and obligations guaranteed by EU law and domestic legislation, and international treaties ratified by the UK had not been fully respected.

The CRE, EOC and DRC repeatedly reported on the urgent need for reform of the legislation, and the courts and tribunals pointed out serious defects in legal procedures in areas such as equal pay for women. These were not simply the gripes of lawyers and equality activists. Social research showed that while anti-discrimination legislation had broken down many

[2] Equal Pay Act 1970; Sex Discrimination act 1975 (SDA), Race Relations Act 1976 (RRA), Disability Discrimination act 1995 (DDA), all of which had been amended on various occasions; Employment Equality (Religion or Belief) Regulations 2003, SI 2003/1660; Employment Equality (Sexual Orientation) Regulations 2003, SI 2003/1661; Employment Equality (Age) Regulations 2006, SI 2006/1031; EA 2006, Pt 2; Equality Act (Sexual Orientation) Regulations 2007, SI 2007/ 1263.

[3] Council Directive 2000/43/EC (Race Directive) implementing the principle of equal treatment between persons irrespective of racial or ethnic origin; Council Directive 2000/78/ EC (Framework Employment Directive) establishing a general framework for equal treatment in employment and occupation; Council Directive 2004/113/EC (Equal Treatment Amendment Directive) implementing the principle of equal treatment between men and women in access to and supply of goods and services; European Parliament and Council Directive 2006/54/EC (Recast Equal Treatment Directive) on the implementation of the principle of equal opportunities and equal treatment of men and women in matters of employment and occupation (recast). Also relevant in this context is Art 157 of the Treaty on the Functioning of the European Union (TFEU) (formerly Art 141 (ex 119) of the EC Treaty). In January 2008, the European Commission published a new draft Directive which would prohibit discrimination because of disability, religion or belief, sexual orientation and age in access to goods and services, housing, education, social protection, social security, and social advantage. This draft is still under negotiation.

[4] See Hepple, Coussey and Choudhury (2000) ch 1.

barriers for individuals in their search for jobs, housing and services, and there were fewer overt expressions of discrimination than in the previous generation, women continued to face occupational segregation, concentration in low-paid, part-time work, unequal pay, pregnancy discrimination and sexual harassment, and members of ethnic minorities, disabled persons, gays, lesbians and transsexuals and older people still suffered from prejudice and stereotypes relating to their abilities. Discrimination and exclusion had become more complex and covert than they were when the first anti-discrimination laws were enacted. There were attitudes, policies and practices within organisations of the kind identified as 'institutional racism' by the inquiry into the murder of Stephen Lawrence, a Black teenager.[5] It was becoming ever more obvious that eliminating institutional barriers required greater emphasis on changing organisational culture.

Shortly before the general election in 1997, Lord Lester of Herne Hill QC and I brought together a small group of equality specialists under the auspices of Justice and the Runnymede Trust.[6] Our pamphlet set out what was wrong with the law—including incoherence and complexity, unnecessary differences between Britain and Northern Ireland, the muddled definitions of indirect discrimination, the tortuous nature of equal pay procedures, the inadequacy of provisions on the rights of pregnant women, and ineffective enforcement, as well as the failure to implement international and EU obligations. We canvassed a number of options for reform which could be undertaken by an incoming government. After the election Lord Lester and I had a meeting with the Labour Home Secretary (Jack Straw) and his officials, and proposed that the new government should review anti-discrimination law and practice. He said that the government had too much else to do, but he was sympathetic and supported our application for funding to the Nuffield Foundation and the Joseph Rowntree charitable Trust for a one-year independent review under the auspices of the Cambridge Centre for Public Law and the Judge Institute of Management Studies. This was conducted by Mary Coussey, Tufyal Choudhury and myself, with the guidance of an advisory committee chaired by Lord Lester.[7] We undertook targeted case studies of employers in Great Britain, Northern Ireland and the USA in order to elucidate how employers behaved under different legislative regimes. There were extensive consultations and interviews in different parts of the country, and a consultative conference with key stakeholders. The Report was published in July 2000. This explained the defects in the existing law

---

[5] Stephen Lawrence Inquiry (1999).

[6] Hepple, Lester, Ellis, Rose and Singh (1997).

[7] Hepple, Coussey and Choudhury (2000) (hereafter Cambridge Review). There was also a subsequent research paper on religious discrimination for the Home Office: Hepple and Choudhury (2001).

and made the case for a new framework which would harmonise legislation and institutions. The most important proposals were those that sought to encourage an inclusive, proactive and non-adversarial approach to achieve fair participation and fair access. This included an expanded duty on public authorities to promote equality, including the use of contract and subsidy compliance, and a duty on employers to undertake employment equity and pay equity plans. Detailed suggestions were made for improving procedures in courts and tribunals, and for making the remedies more effective.

The Report was welcomed by the Labour Government as a 'uniquely well-researched guide'.[8] The government recognised the validity of the arguments for comprehensive reform, including harmonisation of all strands and the extension of positive duties to gender and disability, but said it needed time 'to think about how such a framework would be constructed in practice'.[9] The hallowed 'principle of the unripe time'[10] delayed the introduction by the government of single Equality Bill for a further seven years. In order to give a spur to this process and show that a single Act was feasible, the Cambridge Centre for Public Law and the Odysseus Trust published a draft single Equality Bill embodying the main recommendations in the Report and taking account of the Article 13 EU Directives. This was introduced as a Private Member's Bill in the House of Lords in January 2003 by Lord Lester of Herne Hill QC[11] with cross-party and cross-bench support. This Bill passed through all its stages in the House of Lords, and over 200 MPs signed an early day motion requesting the government to introduce such a Bill.

Although the government described the Lester Bill as 'outstanding' (it had been drafted by Stephanie Grundy, an experienced drafter) and promised that it 'will not die the death',[12] there was a change of tack. In 2003, the government decided on a 'salami-slicing' approach. The time was not considered ripe for a unified approach until the Article 13 EU Directives had been implemented. This was done by secondary legislation under the European Communities Act and so avoided controversial amendments which would undoubtedly have been moved in respect of religion or belief, sexual orientation and age. Although the political tactics were understandable, the result was to make the law even more complex and inconsistent than before, with three new sets of regulations on religion or belief, sexual

---

[8] Lord Falconer of Thoroton QC, speaking at the launch of the Report on 25 July 2000.

[9] Hansard HL vol 624 col 1448 (25 April 2001) (Baroness Blackstone).

[10] Cornford (1908): '[P]eople should not do at the present moment what they think right at that moment, because the moment at which they think it right has not yet arrived.'

[11] Hansard HL vol 643 col 1636 (14 January 2003) (1R); vol 645 col 525 (28 February 2003) (2R); vol 645 col 1631 (14 March 2003) (committee); vol 646 col 1629 (4 April 2003) (Report).

[12] Hansard HL vol 645, col 584 (28 February 2003) (Lord Mcintosh of Haringey).

orientation and age, and amendments to existing legislation on sex, disability and race discrimination. But the time was still not ripe for a single Act. In 2004, the government decided that the body of existing law should remain unaltered until a new single Commission had been established. The first task of the new Commission would be to review the legislation. The birth of the EHRC, under the Equality Act 2006, was beset with difficulties and controversy, which complicated the transition process, and delayed the single Equality Act.[13] The 2006 Act added further slices of reform, going beyond the EU Directives by prohibiting discrimination on grounds of religion or belief in the provision of goods and services and education, conferring a power to make regulations for a similar extension in respect of sexual orientation (the Regulations appeared in 2007), and extending the public sector equality duty to gender (from April 2007), as had been done for disability in 2005 (effective from December 2006). There was still no single Act.

In its manifesto for the 2005 general election, the Labour Party pledged to introduce a single Equality Bill. The time was not ripe for another two years, when the government published an Equalities Review[14] and a Discrimination Law Review.[15] The former brought together existing research on persistent inequalities in Britain, and recommended a number of steps to greater equality, including a simpler legal framework and a more sophisticated enforcement regime. The latter made many proposals for harmonising, modernising and simplifying the law, and making it more effective, similar to those set out in the Cambridge Review. However, several proposals were open to criticism, for example not extending indirect discrimination to cover disability discrimination law, not allowing hypothetical comparators in respect of equal pay, and maintaining the distinction between contractual and non-contractual claims in respect of equal pay. Some, but not all, of these defects were remedied following the consultation process. The most serious omission was any kind of requirement to undertake employment equity and pay equity reviews. The government received about 4,000 responses.[16] After prolonged preparations—described by the Conservative front bench MP (later Home Secretary) Theresa May as a period of 'false starts, empty announcements and more delays than I care to remember'[17]—the government's Equality Bill was finally presented in April 2009, by Harriet Harman, Minister for Women and Equalities.

---

[13] See p 177 below.

[14] Department of Communities and Local Government (2007a). The Chair of the Panel that produced the Report was Trevor Phillips, Chair of the CRE, who later became Chair of the EHRC.

[15] Department of Communities and Local Government (2007b).

[16] Government Equalities Office (2008).

[17] Hansard HC vol 492 cols 565–67 (11 May 2009). Theresa May became Home Secretary and Minister for Women and Equalities in the Coalition Government in May 2010.

The Conservatives opposed the Second Reading of the Bill. While claiming to 'welcome many parts of the Bill', they said that the Bill included 'unworkable and overtly bureaucratic proposals' which were 'unnecessarily onerous' to business in a time of deep recession.[18] The Liberal Democrats supported the Bill but thought that it should go further, especially on the subject of equal pay and by incorporating an overarching 'equality guarantee' as proposed by the EHRC.[19] The Act that emerged was the product of intense and detailed scrutiny in Parliament over a period of nearly a year. The House of Commons Public Bill Committee (PBC) heard four days of evidence by interested organisations, and considered over 300 amendments in a further 16 sessions for 38 hours, with another 5½ hours at Report stage. The Bill was also scrutinised by the Joint Committee on Human Rights (JCHR) and the Work and Pensions Select Committee. By the time the Bill reached the House of Lords, their Lordships were being pressed by Lord Lester to be disciplined and to restrict amendments so that the Bill could receive Royal Assent before the pending general election. The House managed to consider numerous amendments over eight days in committee and at the Report stage. The Bill received Royal Assent on 8 April 2010, one of the last measures to do so under the Labour Government, which lost office in May 2010. At this stage, there was cross-party support for the Act.

THE ACT SINCE 2010

The Conservative–Liberal Democrat Coalition Government, which came to power in May 2010, has faced in two directions, one regulatory, the other deregulatory.[20] The first direction maintains continuity with Labour's 'third way' of regulating for social inclusion and competitiveness. This included bringing most of the Equality Act's provisions into operation in stages from October 2010.[21] There were only three sections of the Act that the Conservatives, when in opposition, said that they would not implement. The first was section 1 which created a duty on public authorities when making decisions of a strategic nature to have due regard to the desirability of reducing the inequalities that result from socio-economic disadvantage (the so-called 'Harman clause'). This was never brought into force and was repealed in 2013, on the grounds that 'the remedies and powers to prevent discrimina-

---

[18] Ibid (Theresa May).

[19] Ibid, cols 577–78 (Lynne Featherstone, who became Minister of State for Women and equalities in May 2010).

[20] Hepple (2013) 203.

[21] This book has been written as if all sections of the Act are in force, unless otherwise stated.

tion' are quite different from solutions to 'socio-economic disadvantage'.[22] Some Liberal Democrats also criticised the provision as being 'vague and unworkable'.[23] Secondly, the Conservatives opposed a provision requiring large employers to disclose gender pay gap information,[24] preferring to encourage employers to do so on a voluntary basis. This was not implemented by the Coalition Government. Thirdly, the Conservatives had opposed an exception to the non-discrimination principle that allows the use of a positive action tie-break in recruitment and promotion,[25] but once in office they agreed, under Liberal Democrat pressure, to bring this into force, although it appears to have been little used in practice.

The Coalition Government faced the difficulty of implementing the Act in a time of economic crisis, recession and cuts in public expenditure. However, it showed itself willing to pursue 'family-friendly' policies that promote flexibility and choice at work, for example the extension of the right to request flexible working to all employees, new provisions for shared parental leave, and shared parental pay, a right for the partner of a pregnant woman to accompany her to an antenatal appointment, and rights for employees to paid time-off to attend adoption proceedings.[26] An important concession was made to those campaigning for mandatory equal pay audits by giving employment tribunals the power to order audits by employers who are found to have breached the equality clause in employment contracts or otherwise discriminated in respect of pay on grounds of sex.[27]

In the other direction, at the same time as these extensions of equality rights, the government launched a 'red tape challenge', purporting to remove 'burdens on business' and increase competitiveness. This resulted in many restrictions on employment rights, including raising the qualifying period to claim unfair dismissal from one to two years. One unintended effect of this is to give claimants an incentive to allege that a dismissal was discriminatory for one of the reasons prohibited by the Equality Act,[28] for which there continues to be no qualifying period. Moreover, in response to a ruling by the European Court of Human Rights,[29] the Employment Rights Act 1996 has been amended to remove the qualifying period where the dismissal is

---

[22] PBC (EB), 5th sitting col 129 (11 June 2009) (Mark Harper).
[23] Hansard HL vol 715 col 1416 (15 December 2009) (Lord Lester of Herne Hill QC and to similar effect PBC (EB) 5th sitting (11 June 2009) (Lynne Featherstone). For a critique, see 1st edn of this book, pp 141–3.
[24] EA 2010, s 78.
[25] See p 159 below.
[26] Children and Families Act 2014.
[27] ERRA 2013, s 98. See p 133 below.
[28] ERA 1996, s 108.
[29] *Redfearn v Serco Ltd* [2013] IRLR 51.

alleged to be because of political opinion or affiliation.[30] A number of other deregulatory measures do not apply to discrimination claims, such as the cap on unfair dismissal awards to 12 months' pay, and changing the formula for annual uprating of awards to prevent increases above the rate of inflation.

However, 'burdens on business' were put forward as the reason for repealing some important equality rights which had been introduced in 2010. For example, provisions in the 2010 Act that made the employer liable for harassment of employees by third parties, such as customers or clients, were repealed,[31] as were provisions to deal with intersectional discrimination (ie where two grounds for discrimination, such as age and sex, are inextricably bound together).[32] The questionnaire procedure which replicated the effect of provisions of earlier legislation, for obtaining information by a person who thinks that he or she may have been unlawfully discriminated against or harassed or victimised, has also been removed.[33] The power conferred on employment tribunals by the 2010 Act to make wider recommendations than those affecting the complainant is to be repealed.[34] The Coalition Government pressed ahead with these deregulatory reforms although the evidence for them was largely confined to the subjective perceptions pf employers rather than reality.[35]

The most serious of all the challenges to the new legal framework relate to enforcement. First, access to justice has been made more difficult for victims of discrimination by the introduction of fees for issuing proceedings, and hearings of claims in employment tribunals, and appeals in the EAT.[36] Secondly, the EHRC has been deprived of some of its powers and been reduced to so-called 'core' functions, as well as suffering a cut of about two-thirds in its budget with consequent severe staff losses.[37]

Those resisting the weakening of the vision of the 2010 Act did, however, secure one significant victory. After an effective campaign led by the TUC and Unison, the government failed in its attempt to repeal section 3 of the Equality Act 2006 which gives the EHRC a general duty to encourage and support a society based on freedom from prejudice and discrimination, individual human rights, respect for the dignity and worth of each individual, equal opportunity to participate in society and mutual respect

---

[30] ERRA 2013, s 13, amending ERA 1996, s 108.
[31] ERRA 2013, s 65 repealing EA ss 40(2)–(4).
[32] ERRA 2013, s 65 repealing EA 2010,s 14.
[33] ERRA 2013, s 66, repealing EA 2010, s 138.
[34] Deregulation Bill 2014, cl 2, amending EA, s 124.
[35] See Hepple (2013) at 213.
[36] See p 195 below.
[37] See p 191 below.

between groups based on understanding and valuing of diversity and shared respect of equality and human rights.[38]

The government argued that this 'has no specific legal function' and 'creates unrealistic expectations—both positive and negative—about what the EHRC as an equality regulator can achieve'.[39] It was claimed that the repeal was simply 'legislative tidying up' and the 'removal of gold-plating'.[40] The parliamentary debates about the proposed repeal of section 3 proved to be of great symbolic importance. On the one side stood those who regard broad statements of universal human rights as deceptive rhetoric—a 'noble lie' according to the academic writings of Baroness O'Neill, appointed as Chair of the EHRC by the Coalition Government in 2012, because there is nobody whose duty it is to deliver these rights.[41] It follows from this view that section 3 is not 'of great practical significance'.[42] It was said that the section embodies 'aspirational provisions'[43] which are 'unenforceable'.[44] On the other side of the debate were those[45] who believe that to repeal section 3 would remove the unifying principle which links the right to equality and other fundamental human rights.[46] This link is illustrated in the EHRC's broad-ranging inquiry into the ill-treatment of old people receiving care in their own homes which is both an equality and a human rights issue. The supporters of section 3 also argued that this section serves a specific legal function by providing a useful guide to the interpretation of the Act, enabling those applying the Act to fill gaps and resolve ambiguitities. In a 'ping-pong' between the the House of Commons and the House of Lords, the Commons voted to repeal section 3, the Lords reinstated it, the Commons disagreed, but the Lords refused to budge when the matter returned to them. After this defeat, the government reconsidered its position and withdrew the proposal. Consequently, the general duty remains part of the Act. However, the EHRC's duty to monitor progress has been confined

---

[38] See p 17 below.

[39] Government Equalities Office (2011) at 11–12, para 1.8.

[40] Hansard, HC, 11 June 2013, cols 75–6 (Dr Vince Cable).

[41] O'Neill (2005) at 437, and see Browne (2013) for comment.

[42] Letter by Baroness O'Neill as Chair of EHRC to the Chair of the Joint Committee on Human Rights: see www..parliament.co.uk/documents/joint committees/human rights// Baroness _O'Neill _on _Enterprise_Regulatory_Reform_Bill.pdf.

[43] Hansard HL Deb, 14 November 2012, col 1533 (Lord Lester of Herne Hill QC).

[44] Hansard HL Deb.9 January 2013, col GC51.

[45] Lord Lloyd of Berwick, HL Deb, 22 April 2013, citing Memorandum by Prof Sir Bob Hepple on the proposed repeal of s 3 of the Equality Act 2006 by clause 52 of the Enterprise and Regulatry Reform Bill (7 March 2013).

[46] Hansard HL Deb, 15 June 2005 col 1219 (Lord Falconoer of Thoroton LC), col 1230 (Lord Lester of Herne Hill QC).

to the specific human rights duties set out in sections 8 and 9 of 2006 Act rather than the general duty in section 3.[47]

The two directions of law and policy under the Conservative–Liberal Democrat Coalition—one regulatory, the other deregulatory—reflect the tensions within the coalition between 'social justice liberalism' (or simply 'social liberalism') and market fundamentalism. The common core of these ideologies is the idea of individual liberty. Social liberals support economic liberalism with varying degrees of enthusiasm but also recognise a role for the state to reduce inequality and to correct the unfair distribution of wealth and power that markets produce. This has much in common with one version of New Labour's 'third way', the ideology which claimed to have found a path between unrestrained markets, on the one hand, and the interventionist state and collectivism on the other.

There is an appraisal of the impact of the changes in the legal framework since 2010, and possible alternatives, in chapter 8, below.

Box 1.A
Northern Ireland, Scotland and Wales

The Equality Act covers Great Britain (England, Wales and, with a few exceptions, Scotland) but, apart from a few provisions,[48] not Northern Ireland, which has 'transferred' powers on equal opportunities and discrimination, and appears to be set to continue its own patchwork of anti-discrimination legislation rather than enact a single Act, although the Equality Commission for Northern Ireland (ECNI) has set a number of priorities for reform. This book does not cover the Northern Ireland legislation, but, since that jurisdiction has been the pathfinder in terms of introducing new ways to combat inequality, some of which are reflected in the British Act, these are nevertheless mentioned. There are a number of special provisions relating to Scotland in respect of devolved matters, for example the power of Scottish ministers to impose specific equality duties on Scottish public bodies, and a number of powers for Scottish ministers to make secondary legislation.[49] The subject matter of equal opportunities is not devolved to Wales, but Welsh ministers are given certain powers by the Act, for example in relation to the public sector equality duty.[50]

---

[47] See p 181 below.
[48] See EA, ss 82, 105.
[49] See EA, ss 2, 37, 96, 151, 153, 154, 162, sched 11 para 4, sched 14 para 2, sched 17 para 10.
[50] See EA, ss 2, 151, 152, 153, sched 19.

A HISTORY OF BITS AND PIECES

In order to understand the significance of the Act as a shift from the politics and law of single identities to that of human rights, it is necessary to look briefly at the history of legislation. The Equality Act 2010, together with Part 1 of the Equality Act 2006 setting up the EHRC, is the core of the fifth generation of equality and anti-discrimination law in Britain (see Box 1.B).

The first generation of British legislation, based on the notion of *formal equality*—likes must be treated alike—was rooted in the politics of immigration and race. The Race Relations Act 1965 was the response of a Labour Government to campaigns against the then widespread overt discrimination against recent immigrants from the Caribbean and the Indian subcontinent. The Act was a kind of *quid pro quo* for the Commonwealth Immigrants Act 1962, which had made it more difficult for Black and Asian immigrants to come to the UK. The Labour Government, which came to power in 1964 with a small majority, was committed to maintaining the immigration controls but also to use the criminal law to prohibit direct racial discrimination in places of public resort, such as public houses and hotels. The Campaign Against Racial Discrimination (CARD), whose legal officer was Anthony Lester, persuaded the Labour Home Secretary, Sir Frank Soskice, that civil sanctions were more effective than the criminal law for tackling racial discrimination. Soskice won Conservative support for the Bill by introducing local conciliation committees to investigate and settle complaints. Only if conciliation failed and the discrimination was likely to continue could the Board refer the matter to the Attorney-General to seek an injunction. Essentially, the 1965 Act was conceived as part of the regulation of public order rather than an extension of human rights.

The second generation, the Race Relations Act 1968, was also a measure of *formal equality*. It was limited to direct racial discrimination but extended coverage to employment, housing, goods and services. This was the product of a remarkable 'liberal hour' in British politics.[51] Soskice had been replaced at the Home Office by Roy Jenkins, who with Mark Bonham-Carter, Jenkins' appointee as first chair of the Race Relations Board, participated in a carefully managed campaign to extend the 1965 Act. Political pressure for this new Act was generated by the commissioning of two reports, one by Political and Economic Planning (PEP) on the extent of racial discrimination, after which the existence of racial discrimination could no longer be denied,[52] and the other by Professor Harry Street, Sir Geoffrey Howe QC and Geoffrey Bindman, which was influential in transplanting models of anti-discrim-

---

[51] See Rose and associates (1969) 511–50; Lester and Bindman (1972) 107–49; and Hepple (1970) 156–74 for detailed accounts.
[52] Political and Economic Planning (1967).

ination legislation from the USA and Canada.[53] By the time he left the Home Office at the end of 1967 to become Chancellor of the Exchequer, Jenkins had overcome considerable opposition within government to a new Bill. It was left to his successor, James Callaghan, to steer the Bill through Parliament. The enforcement provisions in the Act were seriously defective. At that time, the Confederation of British Industry (CBI) and the Trades Union Congress (TUC) would have preferred to exclude legal proceedings entirely from the control of racial discrimination in industry, but the challenge of government intervention led them to develop their own voluntary procedures, and the 1968 Act gave these procedures precedence over the Race Relations Board's local conciliation committees. This approach was in tune with the then dominant system of collective *laissez-faire* in industrial relations in Britain, but it meant that victims of discrimination were being asked to submit their complaints to organisations to which the very persons who were discriminating against them were affiliated.[54] Civil proceedings, which only the Race Relations Board could institute, were a little-used last resort. Although supporters of the Act were inspired by the legal victories of the civil rights movement in the USA, the political reality in the British context was that the Act was presented as part of the policy of integration of immigrants, famously defined by Jenkins 'not as a flattening process of assimilation but as equal opportunity, accompanied by cultural diversity, in an atmosphere of mutual tolerance'. The other side of this policy was embodied in the Commonwealth Immigrants Act 1968, which effectively denied the rights of citizenship of British subjects of Asian origin who had fled from East Africa.

The third generation started with the extension of legislation to discrimination on grounds of sex in the Equal Pay Act 1970[55] and the Sex Discrimination Act 1975 (SDA). This had long been fought for by the trade union and feminist movements and by the Labour and Liberal Parties. In 1974, Labour was returned to power and was committed to introducing legislation on sex and race. Roy Jenkins again became Home Secretary. He appointed Anthony Lester as his special adviser. Jenkins shrewdly decided that in order to get political support for new legislation on race equality he would first have to introduce a separate Bill on sex discrimination. The SDA 1975 marked the beginning of a transition from formal equality to *substantive equality*, or what the EU calls 'full equality in practice'. This included the concept of indirect or adverse effects discrimination (borrowed from the USA and translated into rather restrictive statutory language after Jenkins

---

[53] Street Report (1967).
[54] Hepple (1970) 175–95.
[55] For an account of the history of equal pay legislation, see p 116 below.

and Lester had consulted US experts),[56] and provisions permitting positive action. Another part of the strategy was to make compliance with the provisions of the Act a condition of government contracts, but this was never fulfilled. The SDA, for the first time, gave an individual the right to claim compensation for unlawful discrimination. In employment cases this was enforceable in industrial (later called employment) tribunals, and in non-employment cases in county and sheriff courts. An Equal Opportunities Commission (EOC) was created to undertake strategic enforcement and to assist individuals. This model was followed in a new Race Relations Act 1976 (RRA). There was now a separate Commission for Racial Equality (CRE) in place of the Race Relations Board and Community Relations Commission (CRC).

The SDA was enacted two years after the UK joined the European Economic Community (EEC). Article 119 of the Treaty of Rome laid down the principle of equal pay for women and men. This was not then regarded as a human rights provision, but had been inserted into the Treaty because France was the only one of the six founding Member States that had equal pay legislation, and feared that it would be at a competitive disadvantage especially compared to Italy, which also had a large female workforce. This and the Directives on equal treatment of men and women were at first limited to direct discrimination or formal equality. It was only after a series of British test cases on gender equality had been brought with the support of the EOC and references had also been made by the German labour courts to the Court of Justice that the notion of indirect discrimination was brought closer to British anti-discrimination law, and had far-reaching results that profoundly affected the employment conditions of women part-time and temporary workers. Sex equality emerged as a fundamental human right and general principle of Community law.[57]

A further step towards substantive equality occurred with the Disability Discrimination Act 1995 (DDA). Since the 1960s organisations of disabled people have emerged critical of excessive paternalism towards disabled persons and demanding recognition of their rights to equality and independent living. Inspired by the Americans with Disabilities Act 1990, these organisations renewed attempts to obtain similar civil rights legislation in Britain. No fewer than 16 Private Members' Bills were introduced, but as late as 1993, the then Conservative Government of John Major, while acknowledging disadvantages suffered by disabled persons, rejected anti-discrimination legislation, preferring 'education and persuasion'.[58] It was

---

[56] Lester (2001) 88; Hepple (2006b) 607–11.
[57] For this history see Kenner (2003); Ellis and Watson (2012); Barnard (2012).
[58] Doyle (1995) 48.

only in 1995, after intense debate, that the DDA was passed, making it unlawful for employers and the providers of services to discriminate on grounds of disability, and requiring them to make reasonable adjustments for disabled persons. There were significant exceptions, such as education and public transport, and there was no enforcement agency. In 1999, under a Labour Government, the Disability Rights Commission (DRC) was established. By general consent, this Commission did an outstanding job in raising public awareness and supporting individual litigation. The Special Educational Needs and Disability Act 2001 in England and Wales, and the Education (Additional Support for Learning) Act 2004 for Scotland, extended the duty not to discriminate to schools and education authorities and institutions of further and higher education.

The fourth generation is that which marks the start of *comprehensive* equality, but still as separate strands relating to particular identities. This resulted from the Article 13 EU Directives. Article 13 gave the European Council power 'to take appropriate action to combat discrimination based on sex, racial or ethnic origin, religion or belief, disability, age and sexual orientation'. The EU's social action programme saw this as a means of promoting an inclusive European society. This could have remained an 'empty vessel'[59] had it not been for events in Austria when the far-right anti-immigration Freedom Party won a share of power. Europe's mainstream political leaders, including the UK Government, wanted to be seen as opposed to racism and xenophobia. The European Council meeting in Tampere on 15–16 October 1999 asked the European Commission to come forward with proposals to implement Article 13 as part of a strategy to promote human rights and to fight discrimination. Within months the Race Directive covering discrimination on grounds of racial and ethnic origin, and the Framework Employment Directive covering all the other grounds in Article 13, except sex discrimination which was already regulated, had been unanimously adopted. Sex discrimination was to continue along its own path under the enlarged Article 141 (ex 119) (now Article 157 TFEU). There were growing pressures within Britain for an extension of anti-discrimination legislation to the new strands from gay and lesbian organisations, religious groups, particularly Muslims, and those campaigning against age discrimination. However, without the Article 13 EU Directives it is unlikely that any domestic legislation would have been introduced at that time. A series of regulations implemented the Directives between 2003 and 2007.

The fifth generation, represented by the Equality Act, is one in which there is a continuation of the move towards *comprehensive* equality with the significant shift to a regime based on a unitary human rights perspective. It is also

---

[59] Kenner (2003) 393.

the start of a period of *transformative equality*, examples of which are gender mainstreaming, positive measures against institutional racism and reasonable accommodation for disabled persons. These policies are not intended to replace traditional anti-discrimination laws but go further, requiring, for example, equality impact assessments and active labour market policies. This was first sparked by pressures from US and Irish Catholic activists who wanted to promote fair representation in Northern Ireland, and was based on American models. In 1989, the Fair Employment (Northern Ireland) Act imposed positive duties on large employers to achieve fair participation of the Catholic and Protestant communities. The Northern Ireland Act 1998 (implementing the Belfast/Good Friday Agreement) went further, imposing positive duties on public bodies to have due regard to the need to promote equality of opportunity not only between Protestant and Catholic communities, but also in respect of age, disability, race, religion, sex, marital status and sexual orientation. In other words, public bodies had to mainstream equality into the exercise of all their functions. This approach crossed the Irish Sea to Britain in 2000 in respect of race equality, following the Stephen Lawrence inquiry.[60] Amendments to the Race Relations Act not only extended anti-discrimination law to police and similar public functions, but also imposed both general and specific public sector equality duties. Similar public sector positive duties were introduced in respect of disability from December 2006, and gender from April 2007. The Equality Act extended these duties across the board to all protected characteristics.

The cumulative effect of the amendments to the single Act since 2010 is to weaken the fifth-generation structure of comprehensive and transformative equality, though the basic model remains intact, at least for the time being.

There is a question as to how far a single Equality Act can successfully 'simplify' this very complex area of law, and make it more accessible. Lord Lester's Bill in 2003 had 94 clauses and 8 schedules in 111 pages. The 2010 Act consists of 218 sections, organised in 16 Parts and 28 schedules, in 239 pages, and there are also detailed regulations contained in secondary legislation, statutory codes of practice and non-statutory guidance. By contrast, the Dutch Equal Treatment Act of 1994 has only 35 sections, and the Swedish Discrimination Act of 2008 has 71 sections. Both of these measures state broad principles, leaving it to subordinate legislation or the judiciary to fill in the details. The British Act, like the Irish Equality Acts, reflects the different drafting conventions of the Anglo-Saxon common law systems and the continental civil law systems. Within those constraints, the British drafters have provided a model that may influence other jurisdictions. The

---

[60] See p 3 above.

Act is complemented by a very helpful and clearly written set of Explanatory Notes which make the turgid legal language more accessible to the ordinary reader.[61] Guidance and codes of practice have been issued. However, high-quality professional legal advice will still often be needed. With the virtual disappearance of publicly funded legal assistance and the severe cuts in the EHRC's funding and staffing, there are likely to be serious unmet legal needs. Without effective enforcement, the rights set out in the Act will be 'like paper tigers, fierce in appearance, but missing in tooth and claw'.[62]

Box 1.B
Five Generations of Legislation

1. *Race Relations Act 1965*: direct racial discrimination in public places; establishment of Race Relations Board (RRB) which investigated complaints through local conciliation committees; if conciliation failed and discrimination likely to continue, Board could refer to Attorney-General to seek injunction.

2. *Race Relations Act 1968*: direct racial discrimination in employment, housing and services; enforcement through local conciliation committees or voluntary procedures in 40 industries; if conciliation failed RRB itself could bring proceedings in designated county courts.

3. *Equal Pay Act 1970, Sex Discrimination Act 1975, Article 119 [later 141] EEC Treaty [now Article 157 TFEU], EU Council Directives 75/117/EEC and 76/207/EEC as amended, Race Relations Act 1976, Disability Discrimination Act 1995, Disability Rights Commission Act 1999*: direct and indirect discrimination on grounds of sex and race; direct discrimination and duty to make reasonable adjustments for disabled persons; individual right to claim compensation in industrial [employment] tribunals or county court; strategic enforcement and aid to individuals by EOC, CRE and DDA.

4. *Employment Equality (Religion or Belief) Regulations 2003, Employment Equality (Sexual Orientation) Regulations 2003, Employment Equality (Age) Regulations 2006, Equality Act 2006, Part 2, Equality Act (Sexual Orientation) Regulations 2007*: implementation of EU Council Directive 2000/78/EC to extend anti-discrimination legislation to religion or belief, sexual orientation, and age, EU Council Directive 2000/43/EC on racial discrimination, EU Council Directive 2004/113/EC (sex discrimination in goods and services), and European Parliament

---

[61] Explanatory Notes (EN), Equality Act 2010, c 15 (rev edn, August 2010).
[62] Hepple (2002) 238.

and Council Directive 2006/54/ EC (equal opportunities for men and women in employment and occupation).

5. *Fair Employment Act 1989 (NI) and Northern Ireland Act 1998 (NI), Race Relations (Amendment) Act 2000, Equality Act 2006 (positive duties on public bodies, single EHRC), Equality Act 2010*: replacing earlier legislation by single harmonising Act; expansion of public sector equality duty, strengthening of provisions on discrimination, positive action and remedies but weakened by provisions of *Enterprise and Regulatory Reform Act 2013* and *Deregulation Act 2014*.

MEANINGS OF EQUALITY[63]

The government rejected proposals, from many quarters, that the Equality Act should contain a statement of interpretative principles which would help those applying the legislation to promote its purposes, particularly where gaps have to be filled or ambiguities resolved.[64] The government also declined to accept an amendment which would have created a 'right to equality' or 'equality guarantee', as proposed by the EHRC and the Liberal Democrats.[65] The main reason for this legally conservative position was that a purpose clause might conflict with specific provisions of the Act, so leading to litigation, and that a right or guarantee might lead to the widening of equality legislation by the courts and could involve the ratification by the UK of Optional Protocol 12 of the European Convention on Human Rights (ECHR), a step which the government has so far resisted for no good reason.[66]

However, we do not need to look far for the theories of equality upon which the new framework is built. Section 3 of the Equality Act 2006 (which survived the attempt in 2013 to repeal it)[67] states that the general duty of the EHRC is to

encourage and support the development of a society in which—

(a) people's ability to achieve their potential is not limited by prejudice and discrimination;
(b) there is respect for and protection of each individual's Human Rights;
(c) there is respect for the dignity and worth of each individual;
(d) each individual has an equal opportunity to participate in society; and

---

[63] The following sections draw heavily on Hepple (2008) and Hepple (2009).
[64] Cambridge Review (2000) 34–35; cf Government Equalities Office (2008) 175–76.
[65] PBC (EB) 19th sitting col 726 (7 July 2010) (Solicitor-General). Protocol 12 requires States to establish an independent right to equality.
[66] Government Equalities Office (2008) 175–76.
[67] See above p 8.

(e) there is mutual respect between groups based on understanding and valuing of diversity and on shared respect of equality and Human Rights'.[68]

The *Equalities Review*,[69] in words echoed throughout the *Discrimination Law Review*, defines an 'equal society' as one which

> Protects and promotes equal, real freedom and substantive opportunity to live in the ways people value and would choose, so that everyone can flourish.
>
> An equal society recognises people's different needs, situations and goals and removes the barriers that limit what people can do and can be.

If we deconstruct the statutory purposes of the ECHR and the heady cocktail of ambiguous theories of equality espoused in the *Equalities Review* and the *Discrimination Law Review*, we find no fewer than seven meanings of equality: (1) respect for equal worth, dignity and identity as a fundamental human right; (2) eliminating status discrimination and disadvantage; (3) consistent treatment/formal equality; (4) substantive equality of opportunity; (5) equality of capabilities; (6) equality of outcomes; (7) fairness.

Each of these meanings is relevant to an understanding of the Equality Act.

THE UNITARY HUMAN RIGHTS PERSPECTIVE

At the core of the EHRC's general duty, and implicitly underlying the specific rights against discrimination, harassment and victimisation and the positive duty to advance equality as set out in the Equality Act 2010, is respect for and protection of each person's human rights. In the new world order following the Second World War, equality was elevated to a fundamental human right. The first Article of the Universal Declaration of Human Rights (UNDHR), adopted by the new United Nations on 10 December 1948, proclaimed that 'all human beings are born free and equal in dignity and rights'. Article 2 stated:

> Everyone is entitled to all the rights and freedoms set forth in this Declaration without distinction of any kind, such as race, colour, sex, language, religion, political or other opinion, national or social origin, property, birth or other status.

This meant that not only civil and political rights but also the extensive economic and social rights recognised in the UNDHR were to be available without status discrimination. However, in the atmosphere of the Cold War, Western countries, including the UK, became less enamoured of the idea

---

[68] EA 2006, s 3.
[69] *Equalities Review* (2007) 16.

of enforceable social and economic rights because the communist countries claimed supremacy in this respect. Instead, two separate instruments,
which included the right to non-discrimination, were adopted by the UN
in 1966 (in force 1976): the International Covenant on Civil and Political
Rights (ICCPR) and the International Covenant on Economic, Social and
Cultural Rights (ICESCR). Separate conventions were adopted, in 1965, on
the Elimination of all Forms of Racial Discrimination (CERD), in 1979, on
the Elimination of all Forms of Discrimination against Women (CEDAW),
and in 2006, on the Rights of Persons with Disabilities (CRPWD). The most
important and far-reaching international developments affecting equality in
the employment field were not at the level of the UN and the Council of
Europe, but in two ILO Conventions: No 100 on Equal Remuneration of
Men and Women for Work of Equal Value (1951), and No 111 on Discrimination in Employment (1958).

The 1950 European Convention for the Protection of Human Rights
and Fundamental Freedoms (ECHR), confined to civil and political rights
(including the freedom of association), contained a complementary right,
in Article 14, to non-discrimination on grounds of status in the exercise of
convention rights. The much weaker European Social Charter 1961 (ESC)
contained provisions on equal pay for men and women workers for work of
equal value, the right of employed women and of mothers to protection,
the rights of disabled people to vocational training and rehabilitation, and
the rights of migrant workers. But it was not until an additional Protocol
to the ESC was enacted in 1988 that the right to equal opportunities and
equal treatment in matters of employment and occupation without discrimination on grounds of sex was recognised. A revised ESC in 1996 widened
the scope of the original provisions on disadvantaged groups, adding the
elderly and workers with family responsibilities, and specifically declaring
that the rights under the ESC were to be secured without discrimination
on specified grounds of status.

The separation of rights to non-discrimination in respect of economic
and social rights from civil and political ones, and the fragmented approach
to different grounds of discrimination, were to have a lasting negative effect
on the development of equality as a fundamental human right. The separation of discrimination against women in CEDAW from that on racial
grounds in CERD, and the privileged position given to sex discrimination in the EU to the exclusion of other grounds fragmented the struggle
for equality and introduced a hierarchy of rights to equality, with many
inconsistencies. Action against discrimination in employment and other
socio-economic fields was separated from the mainstream struggle for human
rights, weakening both movements. The establishment of the EHRC and a
single Equality Act are an historic reunification of equality and human rights

law, back to its origins in the Universal Declaration of Human Rights. This is not only the well-established right to equality before the law, which, as Tom Bingham, former senior Law Lord, has said is 'a cornerstone of our society',[70] but also a social and economic right to participate in society irrespective of one's race, religion or belief, gender, sexual orientation, disability, age or other status. If the UK ever has its own modern Bill of Rights, the right to equality in the civil, political, social, cultural and economic spheres must surely be its fundamental basis.

RESPECT FOR EQUAL WORTH, DIGNITY AND
IDENTITY AS A FUNDAMENTAL HUMAN RIGHT

Respect for the worth and dignity of each individual has deep roots in the main faiths, and in the philosophy of the enlightenment. It plays a central role in modern discussions of human rights. The Universal Declaration of Human Rights—as a direct response to the holocaust—expressed 'faith in ... The dignity and worth of the human person', and declared that 'all human beings are born free and equal in dignity and rights'. The first Article of the EU Charter of Fundamental Rights too, declares that 'human dignity is inviolable. It must be respected and protected.' in modern constitutions, like that of South Africa, the recognition and protection of human dignity is seen as the 'touchstone' of the political and constitutional order. 'At the heart of the prohibition against unfair discrimination', said Judge Kate O'Regan of the South African Constitutional Court, 'is the recognition that under our constitution all human beings, regardless of their position in society, must be accorded equal dignity. That dignity is impaired when a person is unfairly discriminated against.'[71]

Whether one approaches dignity from a religious or a post-Enlightenment viewpoint, there is consensus that in order to recognise human dignity one must treat everyone with the respect due to our common humanity. This is Dworkin's principle of 'intrinsic value', that each human life has a special kind of objective value.[72] if people belonging to a particular group have not been afforded equal treatment to the rest of the population this is a reflection of the fact that they have not been valued equally. Treating the individual with dignity also means respecting the differences between people that spring from their gender or sexuality or physical or mental abilities or cultural

---

[70] Bingham (2010) 55.

[71] Per O'Regan J in *S v Makawanyane* 1995 (6) BCLR 665 (cc) para 329; Sachs J in *National Coalition for Gay and Lesbian Equality v Minister of Justice* 1998 (12) BCLR 1517 (cc) paras 120–29.

[72] Dworkin (2006) 9–11, 37–38, 160. On the second aspect of dignity, personal responsibility, see below, p 21.

experiences, religion or belief. In fact, each of us has multiple identities. Some of these identities are capable of change, others are not. As Amartya Seen has argued in his book on *Identity and Violence*,[73] there is a great danger in believing that the people of the world can be categorised according to some simple formula. Violence is promoted by cultivating a sense of some unique identity—being a Muslim does not have to mean having the identity of a militant Islamist. Muslims, like Christians, have many potential civic, religious and political affiliations. Multiculturalism is about making it possible for people to have cultural choice and freedom. What is the unifying factor? The Equality Act 2006 speaks of 'mutual respect between groups based on understanding and valuing of diversity and on shared respect of equality and human rights'. A survey in 2005 based on a representative sample from various backgrounds found that the most common British values, shared by all, were the upholding of human rights and freedoms, respect for the rule of law, and tolerance and respect for others.[74] When Gordon Brown, then Prime Minister, suggested an 'English' national day, the public favourite was 15 June, the day when Magna Carta, a symbol of our liberties, was signed at Runnymede in 1215.[75]

Dignity is, however, not uncontested as an ethical and legal value.[76] Interests in dignity are not confined to the prohibited grounds of discrimination. For example, people may be harassed or bullied for many reasons which have nothing to do with protected characteristics, such as gender, ethnicity and religion, disability, age or sexual orientation, and it may be difficult to prove the motivation of the harasser or bully[77] (see chapter 3 below). In other words, limiting the remedies for harassment or bullying to equality law may neglect victims who do not have a protected characteristic.

Some argue that when the protection of human dignity is interpreted as involving a positive duty of the state to provide conditions under which dignity can flourish, this amounts to an unjustified and paternalistic interference with individual autonomy. An approach to equality which focuses solely on human dignity is not sufficiently sensitive to conflicts of equality with individual liberty and autonomy. Let us suppose that Parliament accepted a proposal[78] that anti-discrimination legislation should prohibit discrimination

---

[73] Sen (2006).

[74] Commission for Racial Equality (2005).

[75] Magna Carta was, however, a product of its time; for example, Arts 10 and 11 of the 1215 version sanctioned discrimination against Jewish moneylenders, and the inferior position of women was addressed only so far as it impinged on the property rights of men: see Hindley (1990) chs 8 and 9.

[76] McCrudden (2008) 655; Feldman (1999, 2000).

[77] See p 97 below.

[78] Rubenstein (2007) 31. Weight and height abnormalities may be a 'disability' covered by the EA if they have substantial and long-term effects on one's ability to carry out normal day-to-day activities (see p 43 below).

on grounds of personal appearance ('lookism'), such as obesity. A liber-tarian would clearly object to this invasion of the liberty of the individual, and a classical liberal might argue that there was insufficient evidence of harm to others to justify legal coercion. But legal duties could be supported by those whose values are 'communitarian' or based on notions of soli-darity or social inclusion: we all belong to a society in which each person's welfare and that of the whole community matters to everyone. This does not amount to 'paternalism', usually understood as the 'interference of a state or an individual with another person, against their will, and justified by a claim that the person interfered with will be better off or protected from harm'.[79] A 'third way' between libertarianism and paternalism might take the view that liberal states have responsibilities to look after important needs of people both as individuals and as communities. This entitles public authorities to express value judgements about what is good for their lives, for example to avoid obesity, but then they should leave it to individuals to make their own decisions. This is sometimes called a 'stewardship' model. The difference between paternalism and this stewardship model is that the latter is less likely to support coercive universal measures and is sensitive to respect for individual choice.

To be justified, state intervention through legal rights and duties should be shown by evidence to be proportionate to the legitimate aim of protecting a specific public interest (such as social cohesion, economic efficiency, public health) as well as safeguarding the dignity of individuals. Moreover, the rights and duties should be the result of a transparent and participatory decision-making process, one that relies on evidence, and makes authorities accountable for the reasonableness of actions that reduce individual choice.[80] Instead of treating dignity as an overarching or superior value, more satis-factory conclusions will be reached by applying principles of proportionality.

ELIMINATING STATUS DISCRIMINATION AND PREJUDICE

There are many forms of inequality. The Equality Act is concerned only with *status* equality, that is the association between a limited number of particular characteristics (such as race, gender, age, disability, religion and belief, and sexual orientation) and the treatment afforded to individuals or groups to which they belong.[81]

---

[79] Dworkin (2002).
[80] See Nuffield Council on Bioethics (2007) ch 3.
[81] See McCrudden (2004a) 582–83 for an illuminating analysis of the categories of equality and non-discrimination in English public law.

There is today a European-wide consensus that legislation against status discrimination is proportionate to the legitimate aim of promoting social cohesion and economic efficiency. This is supported by a mass of evidence, including that presented by the *Equalities Review*[82] in 2007, the Report of the National Equality Panel in 2010,[83] and many academic studies.[84]

The social democratic and welfare ideologies that developed in Europe after 1945 proved to be sufficiently strong to resist extreme liberal views that regarded anti-discrimination laws as an obstacle to freedom of contract and efficient market outcomes. Even the Thatcher Government in Britain, despite its neo-liberal agenda, accepted and extended laws on sex discrimination in the 1980s. From an economic viewpoint, it was generally not questioned that the freedom of Black workers and women to search for jobs does not lead inexorably to parity of wages or common terms of employment. There are too many imperfections in the labour market for this to happen.

There can be no doubt that the first four generations of anti-discrimination legislation in Britain have fulfilled the promise of the Race Relations Board, as detailed in its first annual report,[85] of providing an unequivocal declaration of public policy, giving support to those who do not wish to discriminate but who feel compelled to do so through social pressure. It has done more than provide a means of redress for Black and other ethnic minorities, women, disabled persons, the elderly, and gays, lesbians and bisexual and trans people. It has also had an important educative or persuasive function and has helped to reduce prejudice. As the RRB said in its first annual report, 'a law reduces prejudice by discouraging the behaviour in which prejudice finds expression'.[86] Britain is 'a more tolerant society than it was, and there is strong support for equality. ... But we are not yet a nation at ease with our diversity', reported the *Equalities Review*.[87] The impact of the legislation was strengthened, after 1976, by bringing situations of indirect discrimination within the ambit of the law. This led many organisations to examine and redefine those policies and practices that might unintentionally have an adverse impact on the protected groups. However, many barriers remain.

The main obstacles facing women are gender stereotyping, concentration in low-paid, part-time and temporary work, unequal pay, pregnancy discrimination, and harassment. Although younger women now have qualifications equal to or higher than those of men, and have greater expectations

---

[82] *Equalities Review* (2007) 15–18.
[83] National Equality Panel (2010) 1–2.
[84] Hills, Sefton and Stewart (2009).
[85] Race Relations Board (1966–67) para 65.
[86] Ibid; see generally Hepple (1970) 30, 175–76.
[87] *Equalities Review* (2007) 91.

than earlier generations, they continue to be disadvantaged in the labour market. Women from nearly all ethno religious groups are paid less than the least well-paid group of men.[88] Discrimination against ethnic and religious minorities, or indeed anyone who is 'not like me', is perhaps based more on avoidance, or on giving preference to other more socially or culturally familiar people, than on a conscious decision to exclude, although the latter still occurs. People from the same social, cultural or religious background are more favourably considered, because the decision-maker feels more comfortable with them. The effect, however, is the same as old-style racism, as the persistently higher unemployment figures for Black and some other ethnic minorities indicate. The gap between their employment rate and the average employment rate is put at 15.5 per cent, and only one in four Muslim women are in employment. Disabled people are two-and-a-half times more likely to be out of work compared to those with no disability. There is widespread discrimination in particular against those perceived to be mentally disabled or as having learning difficulties.[89] Gay, lesbian and transsexual people suffer homophobic bullying and discrimination at school and work.[90] a central aim of the law is to reduce these inequalities.

CONSISTENT TREATMENT/FORMAL EQUALITY

The early attempts to counter discrimination centred around the liberal concept of formal equality, that likes should be treated alike. The problem with this is that it begs the central question: when are two people sufficiently similar to qualify for equal treatment? 'Why can't a woman be more like a man?' sings Professor Higgins in *My Fair Lady*. 'Equal to what?' is taken to mean 'equal to a man'. Relying in this way on a male norm means taking for granted the existing values in a male-dominated world. For example, women with childcare responsibilities are simply unable to conform to working patterns which assume a male breadwinner and a female housewife. A pregnant woman cannot meaningfully be compared to an ill man.[91] The comparison between a member of an ethnic or religious minority and someone of the dominant culture is in effect a requirement for assimilation or conformity rather than a demonstration of respect for individual dignity and diversity. So too, we cannot simply adjust the paradigm of formal equality to include people with disabilities who do not share the same

---

[88] For details see National Equality Panel (2010) 219–22.
[89] Ibid, 237.
[90] Ibid, 240.
[91] See p 61 below.

capacities as those who are not disabled.[92] Moreover, there is no violation of formal equality if an employer treats all employees equally badly, and a claim to consistent treatment can be satisfied by depriving both persons compared of a particular benefit (levelling down), as well as by conferring the benefit on both of them (levelling up).[93]

The Equality Act retains the principle of formal equality through the wrong of direct discrimination, which involves less favourable treatment of a person than he or she would be treated but for a protected characteristic.[94]

REMOVING BARRIERS TO EQUAL TREATMENT

The criticisms of formal equality led to the development of the principle of *substantive equality*, or what the EU terms 'full equality in practice'. Third-generation British legislation gave effect to a procedural notion of equality of opportunity through the concept of indirect, or adverse impact, discrimination. This was initially defined as a requirement or condition that is applied to both sexes or different racial groups, but the proportion of one sex or racial group who can comply with it is considerably smaller than the proportion of the other sex or racial group who can comply. For example, a requirement to work full-time to earn a higher rate of pay indirectly discriminates against women who, because of family responsibilities, work part time. The duty to make reasonable adjustments for a disabled person also has a vital role in ensuring substantive equality in respect of disability.[95]

The concept of indirect discrimination has been refined in EU case law and legislation and harmonised and extended to all grounds, including disability discrimination, in the Equality Act.[96] It is results-oriented in that 'it is not the equality of treatment meted out to the individual that ultimately matters, but the fact that it has a disparate impact on an individual because of his or her membership of the disadvantaged group'.[97] Despite the focus on outcomes, indirect discrimination suffers from the limitation that, in the absence of exclusionary criteria, or the possibility of appropriate comparisons, or if an economic justification can be made out, no action need be taken by the respondent. The concept brings to mind, in Fredman's words, 'the graphic metaphor of competitors in a race' and 'asserts that true equality cannot be achieved if individuals begin the race from different

---

[92] See p 68 below.
[93] See p 69 below.
[94] See p 67 below.
[95] See p 91 below.
[96] See p 97 below.
[97] Fredman (1999) para 3.10.

starting points'. The aim is to equalise the starting points. This opens up more opportunities but 'does not guarantee that more women or [members of ethnic minorities] will in fact be in a position to take advantage of those opportunities'.[98] Moreover, the indirect discrimination provisions create no obligation to remove the offending criterion or practice unless an individual who was a victim of the discrimination successfully brings an action.

A positive duty to advance equality, because it is proactive, sidesteps many of the limitations of the indirect discrimination provisions,[99] and notions of 'positive action', which allow special measures to be taken in favour of a disadvantaged group as an exception to the prohibition on direct discrimination. The concept of 'affirmative action' was first used in the United States to describe actions that aim at greater inclusion and participation of women and minorities in the workforce. The term was used in Title VII of the Civil Rights act 1964 to describe the power given to judges to remedy unlawful discrimination and in Executive Orders made by President Kennedy in 1961 and President Johnson in 1965[100] to define the obligations of a federal government contractor to remedy the under-representation of minorities and women in the workforce.[101] These provisions have had a significant influence in bringing about substantive equality in employment in large corporations in the United States, and they were followed in Canada, Australia and some other countries.[102] Several justifications have been put forward for such measures, including compensation for past discrimination, achieving substantive equality, and promoting diversity or proportionate representation of all groups in the workforce.

In Europe, the term 'positive action' has been preferred to describe such policies, possibly to avoid any association with 'quotas' or other controversial features of law and policy in the United States. McCrudden[103] has identified no fewer than five different types of action that might fall within the category of 'positive action'. First, there is the eradication of practices that have the effect of disadvantaging a particular group, such as word-of-mouth hiring. This is, in effect, an application of the principle of avoiding indirect discrimination. Secondly, there are policies that seek to increase the proportion of members of a previously excluded or under-represented group. Thirdly, there are outreach programmes, designed to attract candidates from under-represented groups. Fourthly, there are measures which amount to preferential treatment or 'reverse' discrimination in favour of a

---

[98] Ibid, paras 3.12–3.16.
[99] See p 162 below.
[100] McCrudden (2007a) 5.
[101] McCrudden (1986) 220–21.
[102] See Cambridge Review (2000) 65–67.
[103] McCrudden (1986) 223–25.

particular group. Finally, there are attempts to redefine 'merit' by altering the qualifications necessary for a job so as to encourage recruitment or promotion of members of a disadvantaged group. An example is permitting 'genuine occupational qualifications' which might favour a particular group.

Only limited use has been made of each of these forms of positive action in British legislation. The Equality Act has widened the circumstances in which positive action is lawful, but this would not permit reverse or positive discrimination.[104]

EQUALITY OF OPPORTUNITIES, CAPABILITIES, AND OUTCOMES

The Equality Act imposes a positive duty on public bodies to advance 'equality of opportunity' between persons who share a protected characteristic and those who do not.[105] But the meaning of equality of opportunity is not defined.[106] It obviously has both procedural and substantive aspects. 'The central aim of [equal opportunities]', Fredman argues, 'should be to facilitate equal participation of all in society, based on equal concern and respect for the dignity of each individual'.[107] But notions of procedural justice do not guarantee any particular outcome. Sen argues that equality of opportunity includes both (1) the opportunity to pursue one's chosen objectives, and (2) the process of choice itself. The former can be judged either from the viewpoint of outcome (ie what one ends up with) or, more comprehensively, by taking account of the *way* in which a person reaches the outcome (eg whether through his or her own choice or through the dictates of others).[108] Although 'third way' theorists generally welcome equality of opportunity because it fits well with other tenets of this ideology—such as individual responsibility and individual choices—there is much dispute as to when and to what extent redistribution is justified.

The authors of the *Equalities Review* were eclectic in their definition of equal opportunities. First they endorsed the importance of genuine and valuable choices for each individual. Secondly, they acknowledged that that some people may need more and different resources to enjoy genuine freedom and fair access to opportunities. Thirdly, they saw the aim as being to narrow gaps in real opportunities and real freedoms, not by reducing the

[104] See p 156 below.

[105] See p 162 below.

[106] This has been a major concern of political philosophers in recent decades, among them John Rawls (1971), Amartya Sen (1992, 1999, 2009), Ronald Dworkin (2000) and Gerry Cohen (2000).

[107] Fredman and Spencer (2003) 46.

[108] Sen (2009) 228–30.

freedoms of some but by increasing the opportunities of those suffering persistent disadvantage. This perspective views distribution as the outcome of individual choice. This is not equality of welfare in a sense that obliges social institutions to distribute the resources and opportunities over which they have control so there is uniformity regardless of personal choices and individual effort. At the same time, it is not simply merit-based. It recognises that our life chances are determined both by circumstances and by personal choice. Circumstances include our genetic endowments, gender, ethnicity, disabilities, the demand for our skills and other matters beyond our control. Personal choice includes the kind of skills we choose to develop and the effort we put into this. The crucial feature of 'third way' equality of opportunity is that it builds around the ethic of individual responsibility. This principle of personal responsibility is akin to Dworkin's second dimension of dignity, that each person has a special responsibility for realising the success of his or her own life, and this includes exercising judgement about what kind of life is best for him or her.[109] Equality, responsibility and choice are not seen as antithetic. The foundational value is equal concern for all, but this does not mean equality irrespective of people's individual responsibility and choices. In the words of Julian le Grand:

> Our judgments concerning the degree of inequity inherent in a given distribution depend on the extent to which we see that distribution as the outcome of individual choice. If one individual receives less than another owing to her own choice, then the disparity is not considered inequitable; if it arises for reasons beyond her control, then it is inequitable.[110]

While *substantive equality* affords opportunities to people who have in the past been disproportionately excluded, without disturbing the underlying social framework that denies them genuine choice and generates inequitable outcomes, *transformative equality* is aimed at the dismantling of systemic inequalities and the eradication of poverty and disadvantage.[111] This involves ensuring what Amartya Sen has called a 'equality of capabilities',[112] enabling people to have the skills they need to participate in society, to engage in productive activities and to participate in decision-making. The measures needed to achieve this include a positive role for institutions in removing barriers, and in ensuring that those who need more resources than others get them. In other words, it involves an element of redistribution. Transformative equality implies a strong link between substantive equality and

---

[109] Dworkin (2000).
[110] Le Grand (1991) 87.
[111] Albertyn (2006) 257.
[112] Sen (1999).

social and economic rights.[113] However, Sen has emphasised that 'equality of capabilities' does not mean uniformity. For example, there may be a need to reward individual efforts and productivity, and equality has to be weighed with other aspects of justice such as the equity of procedures.[114]

The main criticism of the reliance on choice is that it ignores the existing inequitable distribution of wealth and power in society. It reduces all human choices to the same level. This simply does not correspond with the real world, in which individuals do not have a genuinely free choice, precisely because of differences of wealth, race, gender and social class, and stereotypical assumptions about their roles.[115] The notion that a Black woman refused a job can simply move on to the next job, or choose to improve her educational qualifications, makes some remarkably optimistic assumptions. It ignores the harassment, degradation and humiliation inflicted on Black people and women over generations which may reduce their self-esteem and dignity and their motivation to 'improve' their life chances. This is well recognised in the *Equalities Review,* which explicitly adopts Sen's ideas[116] and sets out an 'equality scorecard' of capabilities which are regarded as central and valuable for people to develop real freedom to choose. These include capabilities to live and be healthy, to have the skills needed to participate in society, to enjoy a comfortable standard of living, to engage in productive activities, to enjoy family life, to participate in decision-making, to express oneself, and to be protected and treated fairly by the law. We may conclude that when the Act refers to 'equality of opportunity' this should be broadly interpreted as including equality of procedures, freedom of individual choice without status-based restraints, and the possibility of acquiring the capabilities necessary for the exercise of choice.

FAIRNESS

What is the relationship of substantive and transformative equality to 'fairness'? This is a word that is mentioned many times in the *Equalities Review* and *Discrimination Law Review.* The former saw their definition of equality as supporting 'the broader, less technical, idea of "fairness" so precious to our society'.[117] The latter said that 'equality is a fundamental part of a fair society in which everyone can have the best possible chance to

---

[113] Fredman (2008) 226–40.
[114] Sen (2009) 296.
[115] See on the effects of male/female stereotypes Browne (2006).
[116] *Equalities Review* (2007) annex a, 125–32.
[117] *Equalities Review* (2007) 15.

succeed in life'.[118] This grounds fairness in freedom to choose based on active promotion of equality of capabilities. It is quite different from the post-war Attlee government's idea that there is an obligation on the state to deliver 'fair shares' and to reduce inequality between rich and poor.[119] Somewhere along the way the interest in economic equality and the redistribution of incomes has all but disappeared, and the gap between rich and poor has grown steadily greater both nationally and globally, and for some groups more than others.[120] Generally, political parties in Britain have been reluctant to take more money off the rich to create greater equality of incomes.

Old forms of collective identity and class conflict have largely been replaced by new individual identities and conflicts of gender, ethnicity, faith and lifestyle. It is in this new social and cultural environment that equal opportunities between persons of different racial groups, gender, marital status, sexual orientation, age, religious or other belief, and between people with disabilities and those without, has considerable attractions. Some who find equal opportunities (either in procedural or substantive terms) inadequate and ineffective as a means for achieving a 'fair' society have suggested alternatives. Hugh Collins argues that 'social inclusion' provides a more satisfactory intellectual basis for anti-discrimination legislation than approaches based on substantive equality.[121] Catherine Barnard suggests that the law needs to be underpinned by the values of 'solidarity' in order to achieve the objectives of integration and participation of disadvantaged groups.[122] She prefers this to the notion of 'social inclusion' because it has a positive as well as a negative dimension. While the negative side of solidarity prohibits discrimination and requires the removal of any measure or practice that constitutes an obstacle to an individual's participation, the positive side of solidarity imposes obligations to take active measures to integrate the individual into society. She draws attention to the way in which the principle of solidarity is already being used by the Court of Justice to help the integration of migrant workers who are EU citizens.

The aims of *transformative equality* that have been outlined above do have much in common with the ideas of 'social inclusion' or 'solidarity': the primary target is to assist disadvantaged people and to facilitate their integration and participation in society. However, the attempts to reconceptualise equality law run the serious risk of unravelling clear and consistent legal principles that have been developed with much thought over the past five decades. The argument of this book is that harmonisation, simplification

---

[118] *Discrimination Law Review* (2007) 8.
[119] For the classic exposition, see Tawney (1931).
[120] See p 226 below.
[121] Collins (2003) 16.
[122] Barnard (2004) 227.

and modernisation of equality law does not require us to resort to vague ideas such as 'fairness'. For the law to make an effective contribution to substantive and transformative equality, at least five conditions are necessary.

(1) The law must be *comprehensive*, covering all disadvantaged status groups, without a hierarchy of equality. This is the subject of chapter 2.
(2) The legal standards, including the definitions of *direct and indirect discrimination, harassment and victimisation*, must be clear, consistent and intelligible, and any departure from the norms must be a *proportionate means* appropriate and necessary to achieve a *legitimate aim*. This is subject of chapter 3.
(3) The legal standards must cover all the main areas of activity and the exceptions must be transparent and objectively justified. This is the subject of chapter 4 (work and equal pay) and chapter 5 (services and public functions, premises, education, associations).
(4) There must be incentives and sanctions to encourage *self-regulation* based on active participation, and the use of *positive action*. Those who comply voluntarily with the standards should be better off than those who do not. The incentives should include positive duties to eliminate discrimination, advance equality of opportunity, and foster good relations, employment equity and pay equity reviews, and compliance with the legal standards in order to enjoy public contracts and subsidies. This is the subject of chapter 6.
(5) There must be effective support for self-regulation with vigorous enforcement by an independent agency against those who disregard the legal standards. There must be individual responsibility and legal liability of wrongdoers with effective and deterrent remedies. This is the subject of chapter 7.

The book ends with an appraisal of how far these conditions have been met in the Equality Act as amended since 2010 (chapter 8).

Box 1.C
Overview of the Structure of the Equality Act

The Act consists of 16 Parts and 28 Schedules. The general arrangement of the Act is as follows:

[**Part 1 which** imposed a duty on certain public bodies to have due regard to socio-economic considerations in making strategic decisions was repealed in 2013.]

Part 2 including Schedule 1 establishes the key concepts on which the Act is based, including:

The characteristics that are protected (age, disability, gender reassignment, marriage and civil partnership, pregnancy and maternity, race, religion or belief, sex and sexual orientation);

The definitions of direct discrimination (including discrimination because of a combination of two relevant protected characteristics), discrimination arising from disability, indirect discrimination, harassment and victimisation. These key concepts are then applied in the subsequent Parts of the Act.

Part 3 including Schedules 2 and 3 Makes it unlawful to discriminate against, harass or victimise a person when providing a service (which includes the provision of goods or facilities) or when exercising a public function.

Part 4 including Schedules 4 and 5 Makes it unlawful to discriminate against, harass or victimise a person when disposing of (for example, by selling or letting) or managing premises.

Part 5 including Schedules 6, 7, 8 and 9 Makes it unlawful to discriminate against, harass or victimise a person at work or in employment services. Also contains provisions relating to equal pay between men and women; pregnancy and maternity pay; provisions making it unlawful for an employment contract to prevent an employee disclosing his or her pay to a colleague; and (the, as yet, unimplemented) power to require private sector employers to publish gender pay gap (the size of the difference between men and women's pay expressed as a percentage) information about differences in pay between men and women. It also contains provisions restricting the circumstances in which potential employees can be asked questions about disability or health.

Part 6 including Schedules 10, 11, 12, 13 and 14 Makes it unlawful for education bodies to discriminate against, harass or victimise a school pupil or student or applicant for a place.

Part 7 including Schedules 15 and 16 Makes it unlawful for associations (for example, private clubs and political organisations) to discriminate against, harass or victimise members, associates or guests, and contains a power to require political parties to publish information about the diversity of their candidates.

Part 8 Prohibits other forms of conduct, including discriminating against or harassing of an ex-employee or ex-pupil, for example: instructing a third party to discriminate against another; or helping someone discriminate against another. Also determines the liability of employers and principals in relation to the conduct of their employees or agents.

Part 9 including Schedule 17 Deals with enforcement of the Act's provisions, through the civil courts (in relation to services and public functions; premises; education; and associations) and the employment tribunals (in relation to work and related areas, and equal pay).

Part 10 Makes terms in contracts, collective agreements or rules of undertakings unenforceable or void if they result in unlawful discrimination, harassment or victimisation.

Part 11 including Schedules 18 and 19 establishes a general duty on public authorities to have due regard, when carrying out their functions, to the need: to eliminate unlawful discrimination, harassment or victimisation; to advance equality of opportunity; and to foster good relations. Also contains provisions which enable an employer or service provider or other organisation to take positive action to overcome or minimise a disadvantage arising from people possessing particular protected characteristics.

Part 12 including Schedule 20 Requires taxis, other private hire vehicles, public service vehicles (such as buses) and rail vehicles to be accessible to disabled people and to allow them to travel in reasonable comfort.

Part 13 including Schedule 21 Deals with consent to make reasonable adjustments to premises and improvements to let dwelling houses.

Part 14 including Schedules 22 and 23 establishes exceptions to the prohibitions set out in the earlier parts of the act in relation to a range of conduct, including action required by an enactment; protection of women; educational appointments; national security; the provision of benefits by charities; and sporting competitions.

Part 15 Repeals or replaces rules of family property law that discriminated between husbands and wives.

Part 16 including Schedules 24, 25, 26, 27 and 28 contains a power for a Minister of the Crown to harmonise certain provisions of the Act with changes required to comply with EU obligations. Also contains general provisions on application to the crown, subordinate legislation, interpretation, commencement and extent. Further contains amendments to the Civil Partnership Act 2004 to allow civil partnership registrations to take place on religious premises that are approved for that purpose.

2

Protected Characteristics

EXTENT OF STATUS PROTECTION

T HERE ARE TWO possible approaches to defining the kinds of status or identity that are protected by law. The first is general and open-ended, and regards all forms of arbitrary exclusion or stereotyping of 'outsiders' as interconnected. This is the approach of Article 2 of the UNDHR and several other international instruments. Article 14 ECHR refers to a number of specific grounds and also to 'other status'. The ECtHR has defined 'status' as a personal characteristic by which persons or groups of persons are distinguished from each other.[1] The second approach treats status inequality as atomised, and restricts legal protection to a defined number of specific characteristics. This is the approach taken in the EU directives and also in the Equality Act; the latter[2] covers only the nine characteristics that featured in earlier legislation: age, disability, gender reassignment, marriage and civil partnership, pregnancy and maternity, race, religion or belief, sex, and sexual orientation. Ministers are under a duty to add 'caste' to this list.[3] As can be seen from Table 2.1, there are at least eight other characteristics covered by either by EU law or the ECHR or UNDHR that fall outside the scope of the Equality Act: birth, genetic features, language, association with a national minority, political or other opinion, property, social origin, and 'other status'.

There are several advantages to a generalised approach. First, it facilitates proof in cases of multiple discrimination where the precise reason for adverse treatment of a person or group is uncertain; for example, was it because she is a woman, or because she is Black, or because she is pregnant, or a combination of these characteristics? Secondly, an open-ended approach recognises the links between different forms of disadvantage and engenders solidarity between different protected groups. Thirdly, it allows courts and

---

[1] Harris, O'Boyle, Bates and Buckley (2009) 584–85.

[2] EA, s 4.

[3] The original EA, s 9(5) gave Ministers the *power* to add caste. This was amended by ERRA 2013, s 9, to make this a *duty*. See p 50 below.

Table 2.1 Protected characteristics

	EA	EU[a]	ECHR	UNDHR[b]
Age	✓	✓		
Belief	✓	✓		
Birth			✓	✓
Colour	✓		✓	✓
Disability	✓	✓		
Ethnic origin	✓	✓		
Gender reassignment	✓	✓		
Genetic features		×		
Irish traveller	✓[c]			
Language			✓	✓
Marriage/civil partnership	✓			
Nationality	✓	×[d]		
National origin	✓		✓	✓
National minority, association with		×	✓	
Other status			✓	✓
Caste	✓			
Political or other opinion	[e]			✓
Property			✓	✓
Race	✓			✓
Racial origin		✓		
Religion	✓	✓		✓
Sex	✓	✓	✓	✓
Sexual orientation	✓	✓		
Social origin			✓	✓

[a]EU: ✓ indicates measures under Article 19(1)TFEU; × indicates additional characteristics under the Charter of Fundamental rights, Article 21.

[b]These characteristics are also protected in the ICCPR, Article 26 (protection against discrimination). ILO C 111 (1958) (discrimination in employment and occupation) covers the same list, with the exclusion of birth, language and property.

[c]Judicial interpretation includes this under race.

[d] Refers only to discrimination against nationals of EU Member States.

[e]ERA 1996, section 108 as amended removes the qualifying period to bring a claim for unfair dismissal on this ground (ERRA 2013, section 13).

tribunals to develop equality law in response to changing social mores—for example, attitudes to homosexuality and transsexualism changed from the 1970s onwards, but it was not until 1999, when Article 13 of the Treaty of Amsterdam came into force and was implemented in the Framework Employment Directive, that these characteristics were brought within the legal framework. In the future, there is bound to be pressure to add characteristics such as social origin, genetic features and language. In the absence of any reference to 'other status' (as in the ECHR), or a general prohibition on any 'unfair' discrimination,[4] the courts and tribunals will not be in a position to expand the protected characteristics. If EU law is the source of a new prohibited ground, this can be implemented in the UK by delegated legislation under the European Communities Act 1972, and the Equality Act can be amended to ensure consistency across the legislation.[5]

AGE

A Response to a 21st-century Challenge

Age became a prohibited characteristic from 1 October 2006 by virtue of the Employment Equality (Age) regulations 2006, which implemented the Framework Employment Directive. The Directive and these regulations were limited to the areas of employment and vocational training. The Equality Act has greatly expanded the reach of the law. First, the Act prohibits age discrimination in the provision of goods and services, the performance of public functions, further and higher education, general qualification bodies and associations. Secondly, there is protection against harassment[6] and victimisation[7] related to age in all these fields, as well as employment. Thirdly, the Act includes age as one of the protected characteristics covered by the public sector equality duty.[8]

Age equality has become a major social demand in the 21st century due to longer life spans, longer periods of retirement, and the decline in pension provision.

'Retirement' from work, and the treatment of 'old' people as a distinct social group, became a cultural and legal norm only after the welfare state made special provision for pensions and other benefits.[9] For centuries before this, old people carried on in paid work for as long as they were able to

---

[4] As in the South African Employment Equity Act no 55 of 1998.
[5] EA, ss 203–04.
[6] EA, s 26. See p 97.
[7] EA, s 27. See p 103.
[8] EA, s 149(7). See p 163.
[9] See Thane (2000) ch 14.

do so. Paradoxically, social security benefits that support old people also became a badge of inferior social status and legitimated age caps on working life and discrimination against those over pensionable age. 'Retirement' for workers as young as 50 became an acceptable way of reducing unemployment among younger workers. By 2020, there are likely to be 41.6 million people of working age in the UK and 12.6 million of pensionable age, an old age support ratio of 3.288; by 2035 this is projected to be 44 million of working age and 15.6 million of pensionable age, an old age support ratio of 2.87. This takes into account a pensionable age of 65 for men and women in 2020, and a staged rise in the pensionable age to 68 between 2024 and 2046.[10] There is an ageing population, partly because the process of senescence is being retarded by medical developments and changes in lifestyle and diet. People are generally able to work longer. Longer working lives will be necessary in order to sustain the rising cost of supporting those in old age. It will also be necessary for there to be a substantial inter-generational transfer to support older people who lack adequate resources. There is a substantial body of evidence to demonstrate that older people suffer discrimination in employment,[11] health care[12] and access to education.[13]

Eliminating this discrimination and advancing equality of opportunity for older workers has become an important social priority alongside the aim of reducing the number of young people who are unemployed and socially excluded. The picture is a complex one so far as socio-economic inequality between and within different age groups is concerned. Income is lowest for those under 16 and over 65, and wealth is highest in the 55–64 age group. But there is also considerable inequality within each group, with a tenth in the 55–64 range having wealth under £28,000 and a tenth having more than £1.3 million.[14] Inequality is not purely a function of age.[15]

Balancing Individual Dignity with the Rights and Interests of Others

The provisions on age discrimination and the public sector equality duty in the Equality Act attempt to reconcile two different conceptions of age inequality. The first sees it as a wrong to individual dignity, choice and participation in society, while the second views age inequality as a social wrong

---

[10] ONS, National Population Projections 2020-based.
[11] Government Actuary's Department (GAD), 2006-based principal population projection.
[12] Hepple in Fredman and Spencer (2003) 74.
[13] Robinson (2003) 103.
[14] Schuller in Fredman and Spencer (2003) 119.
[15] National Equality Panel (2010) 222.

to particular age groups which must be balanced against the rights and interests of others. The first conception focuses on any treatment of individuals as second-class citizens because of their age, and seeks to overcome stereotypes and assumptions that all elderly people share certain negative characteristics, such as being too old to learn ('you can't teach an old dog new tricks'), or being incapable of doing certain jobs ('old people are too slow and forgetful'), or unable to relate to young people ('old people are out of touch'). Those who espouse this conception of age inequality contend that an individual should be treated with equal concern and respect at any particular time. According to this view, it should be regarded as discriminatory to subject a person to a detriment, such as mandatory retirement, because of age, without the need for a comparison with a person of another age, with very limited exceptions.[16]

The starting point of the second approach is that since everyone ages and has different benefits and burdens at different stages of their life, inequality between people needs to be assessed on a 'whole life' basis, rather than at particular ages. It is recognised that there are competing interests between groups. Among these are the interests of government social policy in ensuring longer working lives, lifelong learning, fair distribution of health and other social services, and greater social inclusion, the interests of employers in workforce planning, retention and rewarding of experienced workers, flexibility in the face of global competition, and the interests of other disadvantaged groups such as young workers, women and ethnic minorities.[17]

The Equality Act has adopted the second, group-based approach to unlawful discrimination, harassment and victimisation, and also to the public sector equality duty. Where the Act refers to the protected characteristic of age, it means a person who belongs to a particular age group. An age group includes people of the same age (eg 21 year olds) and people of a range of ages (eg the over 50s). Where people fall within the same age group they share the protected characteristic of age.[18] So the treatment of the age group to which the individual belongs has to be compared with the treatment of those who do not belong to this group. The Act provides a mechanism for balancing competing interests through the defence of justification. Unlike other protected characteristics, there is a defence of justification of direct, as well as indirect, age discrimination.[19] There are also specific exceptions, including derogations in respect of seniority rules.[20]

---

[16] Fredman in Fredman and Spencer (2003) 56.
[17] Ibid, 51–52.
[18] EA, s 5.
[19] See p 78 below.
[20] See p 115 below.

Children

Children are protected when discriminated against because of disability, race, religion or belief, sex and related characteristics, and sexual orientation, but the prohibition on age discrimination in relation to goods and services, and in the performance of public functions, does not apply to persons under the age of 18.[21] The prohibition on discrimination, harassment and victimisation does not apply to age in respect of schools.[22] Children are also excluded in part from the scope of the public sector equality duty.[23] The government's justification for these exceptions, as expressed by the Solicitor-General, was that

> [t]he Government wants to protect special and tailored services for children. Extensions of the age discrimination ban outside the workplace to children could render any service aimed at children, or particular groups of children, vulnerable to challenge under antidiscrimination law.[24]

Examples given included the restrictions on the provision of tobacco products and offensive weapons to children, the provision of special services for young people, such as pregnancy and sexual health screening, and age-related services, such as crèches and child-minding centres.[25] The Joint Committee on Human Rights (JCHR), however, thought that

> [t]he total absence of protection against age discrimination for those under 18 in service provision and the limited protection in respect of the performance of public functions means that children who are subject to unjustified discrimination are left with little or no legal protection. This may prevent children enjoying full protection of their rights as set out in the UN Convention on the Rights of the Child (UNCRC).[26]

The exclusion of children in respect of services, the performance of public functions and the public sector equality duty stands in contrast to their position in work or when seeking work. In principle, the age discrimination provisions apply to employment, but there is special employment legislation for the protection of children (those under the compulsory school-leaving age) and young persons (over compulsory school-leaving age and under 18).[27] There are some exceptions in the Equality Act to the prohibition on

---

[21] EA, s 28(1)(a).

[22] EA, s 84.

[23] EA, s 149 and sched 18 para 1. The provision of education, accommodation, benefits, facilities and services in schools and children's homes is not subject to the requirements of the public sector duty.

[24] JCHR (2008–09) para 42.

[25] Hansard HL vol 716 col 589 (25 January 2010) (Baroness Royall).

[26] JCHR (2008–09) para 44.

[27] Children and Young Persons Act 1933 as amended; Children (Protection at Work) Regula-

age-based employment discrimination. For example, employers are allowed to use the age bands of the national minimum wage legislation (which have lower rates than the adult rate for 16–17 year olds and 18–21 year olds respectively, than for those aged 22 and over).[28] Similarly, an employer that bases its pay structure on the national minimum wage legislation is entitled to pay an apprentice who is under the age of 19 or in their first year of apprenticeship at a lower rate than an apprentice who is 19 or over and not in the first year of apprenticeship.[29] Moreover, an employer can offer employees childcare facilities based on the age of a child without being open to a challenge of direct discrimination from other employees.[30]

Overall, the government lost an opportunity to mainstream children's rights in equality legislation by refusing to modify what the JCHR called the 'unnecessarily sweeping and extensive' exclusions outside the field of work and employment.[31]

DISABILITY

From Paternalism to Rights

It is estimated that around 14 per cent of the adult population in Britain are disabled persons. This is set to rise due to greater longevity and the survival of more babies with disabilities as a result of medical advances. Despite progress made in recent years in reducing discrimination and disadvantage, the National Equality Panel reported in January 2010 that nearly one-third of disabled persons of working age have no qualifications at all, compared with 12 per cent of persons who are not disabled. Only 21 per cent of disabled men are employed full-time, compared with two-thirds of men who are not disabled. Children with special educational needs (additional support needs in Scotland) achieve much lower educational attainment levels than others.[32] The *Equalities Review*, in 2007, found that disabled people are 29 per cent less likely to be in work than non-disabled people with otherwise similar characteristics.[33]

---

tions 1998, SI 1998/276 concerning the employment of children; Management of Health and Safety at Work regulations 1999, SI 1999/3242 on the obligations of employers with regard to the health and safety of young persons and the prohibition of certain types of employment of young persons, implementing the Young Persons at Work Directive, 94/33/EC.

[28] EA, sched 9 para 11.
[29] EA, sched 9 para 12.
[30] EA, sched 9 para 15.
[31] JCHR (2008–09) para 45.
[32] National Equality Panel (2010) para 9.4.
[33] *Equalities Review* (2007) 63.

Before 1995, there was no legal protection against discrimination and harassment because of disability. Post-war employment policy focused on voluntary measures to promote rehabilitation, retraining, sheltered employment, and job placement services. There was a register of disabled persons and—an early example of affirmative action—a statutory quota scheme under which employers of 20 or more employees had to allocate vacancies to registered disabled persons and could not dismiss them without reasonable cause if that would bring their number below the specified quota. The standard quota was 3 per cent of the total number of employees, but this was rarely enforced.[34] These measures failed to reduce the common experience of disabled people, as described by Brian Doyle: 'segregated in education, trapped by the benefits system, marginalised by the built environment, immobilised by the transport system, denied full participation in leisure and social activities, and disenfranchised by the political process'.[35] As we have seen,[36] it was only in 1995 that the Disability Discrimination Act was passed, making it unlawful for employers and the providers of services to discriminate on grounds of disability and requiring them to make reasonable adjustments for disabled people. This was later extended to schools and education authorities and institutions of further and higher education. The Disability Discrimination Act 2005 prohibited disability discrimination by public authorities and imposed a public sector equality duty related to disability. Meanwhile, the EU Framework Employment Directive 2000/78 required some changes to British law.

The main change made by the Equality Act in respect of disability is the replacement of disability-related discrimination in previous legislation by two new causes of action: discrimination arising from disability[37] and indirect disability discrimination.[38] A number of other improvements were made in the law on matters such as the provision of auxiliary aids for school pupils,[39] making it clear that the costs of reasonable adjustments cannot generally be passed on to a disabled person,[40] making it unlawful to ask job applicants disability and health questions before job offers except in prescribed circumstances,[41] making it clear that account must be taken of disabilities in the public sector equality duty,[42] and increasing the potential number of

---

[34] Disabled Persons (Employment) Act 1944.
[35] Doyle (1995) 1.
[36] See p 13 above.
[37] See p 91 below.
[38] See p 97 below.
[39] EA, s 20(5), sched 3 para 2.
[40] EA, s 20(7).
[41] EA, s 60.
[42] EA, s 149(4).

wheelchair-accessible taxis.[43] There was also a change in the definition of 'disability', but this change did not go as far as some campaigners would have liked.

Definition of 'Disability'

The question of how the protected class is identified arises more acutely in relation to disability than it does for any of the other strands. Medical and social notions of disability have expanded as conditions that were previously unrecognised have been identified, such as Asperger's syndrome, autism, dyslexia and dyspraxia. The law has struggled to keep pace with such developments. This is reflected in the relatively high proportion of cases in which defendants in disability cases challenge the status of the claimant. This can have a psychological effect in deterring claims, and may be a reason for the higher than average settlement and withdrawal rate of disability complaints.[44]

The Equality Act states that

A person (P) has a disability if—

(a) P has a physical or mental impairment, and
(b) the impairment has a substantial and long-term adverse effect on P's ability to carry out normal day-to-day activities.[45]

An amendment to the Bill clarified that 'substantial' means something that is not minor or trivial.[46]

The effect of impairment is long-term if—

(a) it has lasted for at least 12 months,
(b) it is likely to last for at least 12 months, or
(c) it is likely to last for the rest of the life of the person affected.[47]

Unsuccessful attempts were made in both Houses to modify the 12-month requirement in the case of illnesses that do not last that long but which do recur, in particular severe depression.[48] The organisation Mind gave evidence that they regularly have to advise employees who have been dismissed because of 'mental breakdowns' but who are well enough to return to work

---

[43] EA, s 165.
[44] Doyle (1999) 1.
[45] EA, s 6.
[46] EA, s 212.
[47] EA, sched 1 para 2.
[48] PBC (EB) 7th sitting col 191 (16 June 2009); Hansard HL vol 716 col 375 (13 January 2010) (Baroness Warsi).

after a few months.[49] The government took the view that in the case of fluctuating or recurring conditions, medical opinion that the impairment is 'likely to recur' would be sufficient to afford protection.[50] For example, a person who has experienced a number of separate periods of severe depression over a period of two years, which have been diagnosed as part of an underlying mental health condition, would be able to show that the impairment is long-term.[51] One important change made by the Act is to remove a requirement to consider a list of eight capacities, such as mobility or speech, hearing or eyesight, when determining whether a person is disabled. This had been treated by some tribunals as a comprehensive definition of 'normal day-to-day activities'. This change should make it easier for people whose impairments do not readily match any of the eight capacities to show that they meet the definition of a disabled person. The main criticism of the definition of disability is that it replicates the 'medical model' of disability, found in earlier legislation, rather than a 'social model'.[52] This is reflected in the requirement to show a physical or mental impairment which has a long-term and substantial adverse effect. The focus is on the individual's medical diagnosis rather than on the handicaps or obstacles placed on disabled persons by society and the built environment. Regulations may make provision for a condition of a prescribed description to be or not to be an 'impairment', or as having or not having a 'substantial adverse effect'.[53] The Act does specify that cancer, HIV infection and multiple sclerosis are all disabilities,[54] but the regulations exclude addictions to alcohol, nicotine and other substances and certain other conditions.[55] Instead of this blanket exclusionary approach to certain conditions, it would have been more appropriate to adopt an inclusionary approach covering all impairments, but to allow the defendant to show that the discrimination arising from disability, or indirect disability discrimination,[56] was a proportionate means of achieving a legitimate aim, for example that there was a substantial risk of injury by a person with a history of addiction to alcohol or drugs.[57]

An alternative 'social model' can be found in the UN Convention on the Rights of Persons with Disabilities, adopted in 2006, which the UK govern-

[49] JCHR (2008–09) paras 50–55.
[50] EA, sched 1 para 2(2); Hansard HL vol 716 col 577 (25 January 2010) (Baroness Thornton).
[51] EN, para 675.
[52] Alldridge (2006) 294–302.
[53] EA, sched 1 paras 1, 4, 5, 7.
[54] EA, sched 1 para 7.
[55] The Equality Act 2010 (Disability) Regulations SI 2010 No 2128, regs 3, 4 and 5. Reg 7 deems persons certified as blind, severely sight impaired, sight impaired or partially sighted to be disabled.
[56] See p 9 above.
[57] cf EA, sched 1 para 9 on past disabilities.

ment ratified on 8 June 2009. This recognises that 'disability is an evolving concept and that disability results from the interaction between persons with impairments and attitudinal and environmental barriers that hinder their full and effective participation in society'.[58] It provides that 'Persons with diabilities include those who have long-term physical, mental, intellectual or sensory impairments which in interaction with various barriers may hinder their full and effective participation in society on an equal basis with others.' The Framewok Employment Directive and the Equality Act must be interpreted consistently with the UN Convention on the Rights of Persons with Disabilities.[59] The implication of the social approach is that everyone with an impairment should be protected, without requiring the effects of that impairment to be substantial and long-term. The JCHR concluded that the defence of justification of discrimination arising from disability and indirect disability discrimination, as well as the 'substantial disadvantage' threshold that had to be satisfied before a claim for reasonable adjustments could be made, and the 'reasonableness' test itself, were sufficient to provide protection for employers and service providers against the potential for abuse.[60] These arguments were not accepted. In the British context the categorisation is perhaps more ideological than practical, because the duty to make reasonable adjustments and the public sector equality duty provide means by which barriers to full participation by disabled persons may be overcome, but there is always a danger that the social problems faced by disabled people will be over-medicalised.

RACE AND RELATED CHARACTERISTICS

The Changing Context of Race

Race was the first ground on which discrimination was outlawed in Britain, in 1965.[61] It is a social and not a scientific concept. The Equality Act continues the definition in the RRA 1976 by defining race as including (i) colour, (ii) nationality and (iii) ethnic or national origins.[62] An amendment to the Act in 2013 requires ministers to add 'caste' to this list; this is expected to be implemented in 2015 (see below).[63]

In 1965 a significant element in the treatment of so-called 'inferior' races

---

[58] Preamble, para (e).

[59] Case C-335/11 *HK Danmark, acting on behalf of Ring v Dansk almennyttigh Boligselskab* [2013] EqLR 528.

[60] JCHR (2008–09) para 55.

[61] See p 11 above.

[62] EA, s 9(1).

[63] See p 50 below.

was a persistent belief or prejudice that race is a biological or genetic fact that can be used to explain differences between people. Discrimination based on colour or physical characteristics was widespread. With the growth of settled ethnic minority communities and inter-racial marriage in Britain, biological racism is of declining importance, although it does still occur. Discrimination and harassment are more often based on perceived differences in culture, religion and language. This has made it difficult to disentangle race from other related reasons for hostility and unfair treatment—hence the importance of procedures which enable multiple discrimination to be dealt with more effectively.[64] Religion and ethnicity may have separate effects, but often the adverse treatment is because of perceived membership of an ethno-religious group, for example Muslim Pakistanis or Muslim Bangladeshis.[65] The new kinds of racism share with older forms the features of '(a) stereotypes about difference and inferiority, and (b) the use of power to exclude, discriminate and subjugate'.[66] There is also growing recognition of what the inquiry into the death of Stephen Lawrence called 'institutional racism', defined as

> [t]he collective failure of an organisation to provide an appropriate and professional service to people because of their colour, culture or ethnic origin. It can be seen or detected in processes, attitudes and behaviour which amounts to discrimination through unwitting prejudice, ignorance, thoughtlessness and racist stereotyping which disadvantages minority ethnic people. It persists because of the failure of the organisation openly and adequately to recognise and address the existence and the causes by policy, example and leadership. Without recognition and action to eliminate such racism it can prevail as part of the ethos or culture of the organisation. It is a corrosive disease.[67]

Racial disadvantage is now usually measured in terms of both ethnicity and religion. The ethnic minority population of Britain grew from about 6 per cent of the total population in 1991 to 14 per cent in 2011. Of these the largest group are of Asian or Asian British origin (7.5 per cent), followed by African/Black Caribbean/Black British (3.3 per cent) The number of mixed-race births now greatly exceeds the number of births within any of the other groups. Britain is becoming a more diverse society.[68] The National Equality Panel found significant differences between ethnic groups. For example, in terms of educational achievement at 16 in England, Indian and Chinese boys have median rankings well above the national median, while the median rankings for Pakistani, Black African and Black Caribbean

---

[64] See p 77 below.
[65] National Equality Panel (2010) 227.
[66] Parekh (2000) 62.
[67] Stephen Lawrence inquiry (1999) para 6.34.
[68] *Equalities Review* (2007) 41.

boys are well below the national median.[69] In employment, 44 per cent of Pakistani women and 49 per cent of Bangladeshi women are economically inactive, looking after family and home, compared to 20 per cent or lower for most other groups. Other recent research indicates that 'unequal treatment on grounds of race or colour is likely to be a major factor underlying the pattern of ethnic penalties' in employment.[70] An 'ethnic penalty' is the measure of disadvantage that members of an ethnic group suffer in the labour market. The *Equalities Review* found that in the early 2000s the ethnic penalty for Pakistani and Bangladeshi women was 30 per cent, for Pakistani and Bangladeshi men 12 per cent, for Indian women 8 per cent, Indian men 3 per cent, and Caribbean men 2 per cent, while it was minus 7 per cent for Caribbean women.[71]

Legal Definition of 'Ethnic Origin'

The Act, like its predecessors and the Race Directive, does not define 'ethnic or national origin'. In *Mandla (Sewa Singh) v Dowell Lee*,[72] the House of Lords adopted a broad and flexible test, so as to embrace Sikhs as an ethnic group. Lord Fraser of Tullybelton said that 'for a group to constitute an ethnic group in the sense of the [RRA], it must, in my opinion, regard itself, and be regarded by others, as a distinct community by virtue of certain characteristics'.[73] Two of these characteristics were considered essential:

- a long-shared history, of which the group is conscious as distinguishing it from other groups, and the memory of which it keeps alive; and
- a cultural tradition of its own, including family and social customs and manners, often but not necessarily associated with religious observance.

In addition to these essential characteristics, the following were regarded as relevant:

- either a common geographical origin, or descent from a small number of common ancestors;
- a common language, not necessarily peculiar to the group;
- a common literature peculiar to the group;
- a common religion different from that of neighbouring groups or from the general community surrounding it;

---

[69] National Equality Panel (2010) 223.
[70] Heath and Cheung (2006) 2; Cheung and Heath (2007) table 12.a2.
[71] *Equalities Review* (2007) 63, figure 3.1.
[72] [1983] AC 548; [1983] IRLR 209.
[73] [1983] AC 562 (Lord Fraser).

- being a minority or being an oppressed or a dominant group within a larger community, for example a conquered people or their conquerors.[74]

This test has been used to find that, in addition to Sikhs, Romany gypsies,[75] European Roma,[76] Irish travellers[77] and Scottish gypsy travellers[78] each constitute a distinct ethnic group, but that Rastafarians do not because of the absence of a long-shared history.[79] Religion on its own (eg adherents of Islam) or language (eg Welsh) is not sufficient to constitute an ethnic group if the essential characteristics are absent.

What about Jews? They may be regarded as members of a religion or of an ethnic group. It has long been recognised that Jews constitute an ethnic group for the purposes of anti-discrimination legislation,[80] and this is consistent with the *Mandla v Lee* criteria. But in the *Jewish Free School* (*JFS*) case, it was argued that there is a distinction between a Jew as a member of a *Mandla v Lee* ethnic group, and a Jew according to orthodox religious principles.[81] JFS was a 'faith-based' school with an orthodox Jewish character. It was the policy of the school to give preference in admission to those whose status as Jews was recognised by the Office of the Chief Rabbi of the United Hebrew congregation of the Commonwealth (OCR). It is a fundamental tenet of Jewish religious law that the child of a Jewish mother is automatically and inalienably Jewish (the matrilineal test). Descent from a mother who has become a Jew by conversion would satisfy the OCR's interpretation of the matrilineal test only if the conversion was in accordance with the strict requirements of Orthodox Judaism. M, a 13-year-old boy whose father was Jewish, was denied admission because his mother, an Italian who was previously Roman Catholic, had converted to Judaism under the auspices of a non-Orthodox synagogue. M sought judicial review of the school's decision on grounds that the application of the matrilineal test discriminated against him on grounds of his ethnic origin, even if the motive behind that discrimination was religious. JFS argued that the matri-

---

[74] Ibid, 562–65 (Lord Fraser).

[75] *Commission for Racial Equality v Dutton* [1989] IRLR 8, CA.

[76] *R (European Roma Rights Centre) v Immigration Officer at Prague Airport* [2004] UKHL 55; [2005] 2 AC 1.

[77] *O'Leary v Allied Domeq Inns Ltd*, Central London County Court, July 2000, cited in Monaghan (2013) para 5.229. The Cambridge Review (2000) para 270, recommended that, for the avoidance of doubt, Roma, gypsy and Irish traveller groups should be expressly included. The latter are protected in the Irish Republic and in Northern Ireland.

[78] *MacLennan v Gypsy Traveller Education and Information Project*, Employment Tribunal (Scotland). In view of this decision, the government said it was unnecessary for the Act to mention this group specifically: Hansard HL vol 716 cols 348–50 (11 January 2010) (Baroness Thornton).

[79] *Dawkins v Department of the Environment* [1995] IRLR 284.

[80] *Seide v Gillette Industries Ltd* [1980] IRLR 427.

[81] *R (on the application of E) v Governing Body of JFS* [2009] UKSC 15; [2010] IRLR 136. See p 76 below for discussion of the issue of motive.

lineal test did not identify members of an ethnic group but was founded on religious dogma and constituted religious discrimination, which the JFS as a faith-based school was entitled to exercise.[82] The Supreme Court, by a majority decision (5–4), held that the matrilineal test amounted to discrimination on grounds of ethnic origin; the minority said that the criterion of conversion according to the orthodox faith was solely religious. The majority's decision is consistent with the CERD, which expressly includes 'descent' in the definition of racial discrimination. Although the motives of the JFS were religious, it was because of his descent from a mother who was not Jewish, either by birth or by orthodox conversion, that M was denied admission to the school.

National Origin and Nationality

There is a distinction between ethnic and national origin: the Scots, Welsh, Irish and English are national groups but not ethnic groups.[83] The original Race Relations Acts 1965 and 1968 made no mention of nationality, and the House of Lords held that discrimination on grounds of not being of British nationality was not covered by the term 'national origin', which indicated a connection by birth with a national group rather than citizenship of a certain state.[84] The narrow interpretation of 'national origin' has been adopted in decisions finding that discrimination because a person was 'born abroad' without reference to any particular place or country of origin is not unlawful,[85] nor is discrimination based solely on place of birth.[86] These decisions run counter to the aims of the legislation by making it possible to discriminate against ill-defined groups such as 'immigrants' or 'asylum-seekers' or 'foreigners'.

Even more serious is the restricted scope of unlawful discrimination because of nationality or citizenship. The omission of nationality was corrected by the RRA 1976. The Equality Act replicates this, but the coverage of the law is greatly limited in the case of nationality discrimination. Under the EU Treaty, the principle of equality applies only to citizens of the EU, that is, citizens of the Member States.[87] The EU Race Directive expressly excludes nationality or citizenship of a particular country from its

---

[82] EA, sched 12, Pt 2, para 5, on which see p 147 below.
[83] *BBC Scotland v Souster* [2001] IRLR 150, CS; *Northern Joint Police Board v Power* [1997] IRLR 610.
[84] *London Borough of Ealing v Race Relations Board* [1972] AC 342, HL.
[85] *Tejani v Superintendent Registrar for the District of Peterborough* [1986] IRLR 502, CA.
[86] *R (on the application of Elias) v Secretary of State for Defence* [2006] IRLR 934, CA.
[87] TFEU, Art 9.

scope.[88] This exclusion illustrates how the fundamental right to equality is undermined by the EU's rules relating to the conditions under which third-country nationals (TCNs) are permitted to work, reside and move within the EU's borders. While the rights of EU citizens to freedom of movement and freedom to establish businesses and to provide services continue to be extended, TCNs who are admitted to the EU are treated as an underclass of sub-citizens. Their inferior legal and social status has serious repercussions for the integration of ethnic minorities and for human rights in general.[89]

Caste

The 1965 International Convention on the Elimination of Racial Discrimination (CERD) included the prohibition of discrimination on grounds of 'descent' but did not mention 'caste'. In 2002, on the basis of mounting evidence that the reference to descent was not clear enough to cover caste discrimination, the CERD Committee adopted General Recommendation 29. This strongly reaffirmed that 'discrimination based on "descent" includes discrimination against members of communities based on forms of social stratification such as caste and analogous systems of inherited status which nullify or impair their equal enjoyment of human rights'. General Recommendation 29 requires states party (including the UK) to take steps to identify those descent-based communities under their jurisdiction who suffer from such discrimination.

> This may be recognised on the basis of various factors including some or all of the following: inability or restricted ability to alter inherited status; socially enforced restrictions on marriage outside the community; private and public segregation, including in housing and education, and access to public spaces, places of worship and public sources of food and water; limitation of freedom to renounce inherited occupation or degrading of hazardous work; subjection to debt bondage; subjection to dehumanising discourses referring to pollution or untouchability; and generalised lack of respect for their human dignity and equality.

UK law did not include any prohibition against discrimination based on 'descent' or 'caste' until 2010 when the Equality Act gave ministers the *power* (but not the *duty*) to add this to the list of prohibited characteristics. Ministers took no action to implement this provision despite pressure from interested organisations and from the UN High Commissioner for Human Rights. During the passage of the Enterprise and Regulatory Reform Bill

---

[88] See p 138 below on immigration functions.
[89] Hepple (2004) 4–7.

in 2013, members of the House of Lords forced the government to accept a compromise amendment replacing the power by a duty to add caste as a prohibited characteristic. At the time of writing, the government is consulting on how 'caste' should be defined. The EHRC has published two reports which conclude that 'caste is a complex and evolving concept in Britain' and propose that caste should be be named as a subset of race in order to place caste firmly within the framework of the Equality Act.[90] It is not expected that regulations will come into force until after the general election in 2015. In a case in 2014, an employment tribunal allowed a claimant to add a claim for caste discrimination in the absence of a ministerial order on the ground that it could be argued that 'caste' was already part of the protected characteristic of 'race',[91] but there have been at least two other tribunal cases alleging caste discrimination which were unsuccessful.[92]

RELIGION OR BELIEF

The protection of religion or belief is one of the most controversial issues in equality law. This is not surprising given the potential for conflict between religious and traditional beliefs formulated in ancient patriarchal cultures and modern notions of gender equality, marriage and sexuality in a predominantly secular society.[93] There had long been pressure to amend the RRA so as to include religion, particularly in light of the rise of Islamophobia.[94] While the RRA protected Jews and Sikhs as members of ethnic groups, Muslims in Britain were protected only if they could show indirect racial discrimination, for example in respect of dress codes, by relying on Pakistani or Bangladeshi national or ethnic origins. They could argue that a considerably smaller proportion of Pakistanis or Bangladeshis than other national groups could comply with a particular requirement or practice, such as not to wear headscarves, by virtue of their Islamic belief. The requirement would be indirectly discriminatory on racial grounds unless it could be justified. This did not help Muslims who came from countries where Muslims are in a minority, such as India. The turning point was the Framework Employment Directive, which required Member States to prohibit direct and indirect discrimination and harassment on grounds of religion or belief in employment and related fields. The Equality Act has ironed out inconsistencies

---

[90] The reports are published in two parts, available at www.equalityhumanrights.com/publications/our-research/research-reoports/research-reporta-91-100.

[91] *Tirkey v Chandok* (2014) 246 **EOR** 21.

[92] Ashtiany (2014)14 at 16.

[93] McColgan (2009) 1. See pp 111 and 139 below.

[94] Parekh (2000) 235–46.

between the regulations implementing the Directive and the Equality Act 2006, under which protection was extended outside the employment field.

The Equality Act, replicating earlier Regulations,[95] defines 'religion' as meaning 'any religion'. In their original form, the Regulations referred to a philosophical belief that was 'similar' to a religious belief, but the Equality Act 2010 removed 'similar' so that a belief is protected if it is 'philosophical' even if it is not similar to a religious belief.. The Act thus follows the advice of the Cambridge Review to leave it to the courts to distinguish genuine religions from cults with harmful beliefs or practices, and to resolve definitional issues on a case-by-case basis, given the wide variety of faiths and beliefs in this country.[96] The case law of the ECtHR is particularly relevant given the overriding obligation to observe the right under Article 9 ECHR to 'freedom of thought, conscience, and religion'. 'There never has been a universal legal definition of religion in English law, given the variety of world religions, changes in society, and the different legal contexts in which the issues arise.'[97] In the context of the Places of Worship Act 1855, which provides for the certification of places of worship at which marriages may be solemnised, the Supreme Court, overruling earlier case law, has held that 'religion' should not be confined to faiths involving a supreme deity, since to do so would exclude Buddhism, Jainism and others. Moreover it would involve the court in difficult theological territory.[98] The Supreme Court held that scientology is a 'religion', even though its adherents do not believe in a supreme deity but one of an abstract and impersonal nature. The Court said that religion could summarily be described as a belief system going beyond sensory perception or scientific data, held by a group of adherents, which claims to explain mankind's place in the universe and relationship with the infinite, and to teach its adherents how they are to live their lives in conformity with the spiritual understanding associated with the belief system.[99] Given the Equality Act's purposes of protecting human dignity and promoting mutual respect between groups and valuing of diversity,[100] a smilarly broad definition of 'religious belief' is appropriate.

For the purposes of Article 9 the religion must have a clear structure and belief system. Denominations or sects within a religion, such as Protestants

---

[95] Employment Equality (Religion or Belief) Regulations, SI 2003/1660, reg 2(1); EA 2006, s 44.

[96] Cambridge Review (2000) paras 2.77–2.82; Choudhury (2000) paras 6.1–6.13; Hepple and Choudhury (2001) paras 4.1–4.11.

[97] Per Lord Toulson in *R (on the application of Hodkin and another) v Registrar General of Births, Deaths and Marriages* [2013] UKSC 77, paras 32–34.

[98] Ibid, para 51.

[99] Ibid, para 57.

[100] See p 17 above.

and Catholics within Christianity or Sunni and Shi'a Muslims within Islam, may each be considered to be a religion.

In the *Begum* case,[101] The House of Lords accepted that, for the purposes of Article 9 ECHR, a person's genuine belief that their religion requires certain forms of dress or conduct qualifies as a religious belief even though there is a proliferation of views on the issue among adherents of the religion. In cases where the claimant seeks to assert her belief in an unreasonable way, it is open to the court either to find that there has been no 'interference' with the right under Article 9(1), or that the interference is justified under Article 9(2). In the context of the Equality Act, it would be dangerous to apply the same recognition to subjective fundamentalist beliefs because of the absence of a defence of justification in respect of direct discrimination. It will be argued later that the Equality Act would have provided a clearer conceptual framework in the case of religious discrimination if it had combined the concepts of direct and indirect discrimination and reasonable accommodation of religious beliefs.[102]

The Explanatory Notes accompanying the Act explain the criteria for determining what is a 'philosophical belief':

> It must be genuinely held; be a belief and not an opinion or viewpoint based on the present state of information available; be a belief as to a weighty and substantial aspect of human life and behaviour; attain a certain level of cogency, seriousness, cohesion and importance; and be worthy of respect in a democratic society, compatible with human dignity and not conflict with the fundamental rights of others. So, for example, any cult involved in illegal activities would not satisfy these criteria.[103]

Humanism and atheism are given as examples of philosophical beliefs, but 'adherence to a particular football team' would not be such a belief.[104] A 'philosphical belief' includes a lack of religion or belief.[105] It is sometimes suggested that political beliefs are not included, but this is misleading. Belief in a political ideology, such as communism or fascism, or free-market capitalism, may be philosophical, as may a belief based in science such as Darwinism or the moral imperatives arising from man-made climate change.[106] What is excluded from protection is belief in particular political

---

[101] *R (Begum) v Head Teacher and Governors of Denbigh School* [2006] UKHL 15; [2007] 1 AC 100 (belief that wearing of full-length jilbab required by religion); See too *R (Williamson) v Secretary of State for Education and Employment* [2005] UKHL 15; [2005] 2 AC 245.

[102] See pp 55 and 218 below.

[103] EN, para 52.

[104] EN, para 53.

[105] EA, s 10(1), (2).

[106] *Grainger plc v Nicholson* [2010] IRLR 4, EAT.

parties or political actions.[107] It has been suggested that homophobia, racism and other beliefs not worthy of respect in a democratic society would also not be protected.[108] While this is the case under Article 9(2) ECHR, the absence of a defence of justification of direct discrimination because of belief makes it difficult to see how a genuine philosophical belief could be excluded. In Northern Ireland, it is unlawful to discriminate 'on the grounds of religious belief or political opinion', and there is a duty on public bodies to promote equality of opportunity 'between persons of different religious belief [or] political opinion'.[109] This is generally taken to refer to community-based discrimination. What is protected is the actual or perceived membership of or association with Protestant or Roman Catholic communities, rather than the personal religious beliefs or political opinions of individuals.

The ECHR makes it incumbent on states to give protection against discrimination because of political opinion or affiliation. These grounds have not been included among the protected characteristics in the Equality Act. In *Redfearn v United Kingdom* [110] a bus driver in Bradford was dismissed when he was elected a BNP councillor. This was before the prohibition against 'religion or belief' discrimination had been enacted in the UK, and he had insufficient qualifying service to bring an unfair dismissal claim.[111] The ECtHR held that his rights under Article 9 of the ECHR had been breached. The government's reponse to the ECtHR's ruling was limited to enacting an exception to the unfair dismissal qualifying period in cases where the reason for dismissal relates to the employee's political opinions or affili- ation.[112] This leaves open the question whether discrimination because of membership of or support for the activities of a party which has a distinct ideology, such as fascism, constitutes direct discrimination. It would be neces- sary to show that adherence to the belief is indissociable from membership or support for the party. People join or support parties for a variety or reasons without necessarily adhering to their philosophy, so in most cases the link with belief will be difficult to establish.

Disputes over religious discrimination tend to arise not from the *holding* of particular beliefs, but from their *manifestation*, such as dress codes, dietary requirements, and taking time off for prayer and religious festivals. Where an individual complains that they have not been allowed to follow a particular practice dictated by their religion, a court or tribunal has to undertake a

---

[107] De Marco (2004) 13–14.
[108] *Grainger* (n 104) per Burton J.
[109] Northern Ireland Act 1998, ss 75, 76.
[110] [2013] IRLR 51.
[111] [2006] IRLR 623, CA
[112] ERRA 2013, amending ERA 1996, s 108.

factual inquiry into whether or not the objection was to the belief itself. In *MacFarlane v Relate Avon plc*[113] Underhill J explained that,

> [I]n the absence of any other context, it may be possible to infer that an employer who dismisses an employee for wearing the item in question does so because of an objection to the belief so manifested. … If, however, it appears that there was some other ground for the objection—such as a general policy about the wearing of jewellery or practical reasons why the wearing of a veil was regarded as inappropriate—the position would be entirely different.[114]

The approach of the British equality legislation is not as nuanced and flexible as the case law of the Strasbourg court under ECHR Articles 9 (religion or belief) and 14 (equality). Article 9(2) provides a justification defence for limitations on the freedom to manifest one's religion or belief if such limitations are 'prescribed by law, and are necessary in a democratic society in the interests of public safety, for the protection of public order, health or morals, or the protection of the rights and freedoms of others'. There is no defence of justification in respect of direct discrimination because of religion or belief under the Equality Act and its predecessor regulations. The absence of such a defence has led tribunals and courts to try to avoid findings of direct discrimination and instead to categorise claims as instances of indirect discrimination which can be justified. For example, in *Azmi v Kirklees Metropolitan Borough Council*[115] a Muslim woman wished to wear a niqab (full-face covering) while acting as a classroom assistant giving language support to students. The school refused her request to wear the niqab while teaching, on the ground that language support could be carried out more effectively where the teacher's face was visible. It was held that there was no direct discrimination, and that any indirect discrimination was justified. These conclusions were obviously right: it was not direct discrimination, because she was not being treated less favourably than other classroom assistants, and although the facially neutral dress rule placed her at a particular disadvantage, this was a proportionate means of achieving a legitimate aim.

Arguably, the Equality Act should have adopted a defence of justification for direct religious discrimination, but this risked conflicting with the Framework Employment Directive. The defence could have been introduced in areas not covered by the Framework Employment Directive, so that for example a school could prescribe a dress code which is a proportionate means of achieving a legitimate aim, such as not allowing full-face covering where this limits effective communication between learners and teachers.

---

[113] [2010] **IRLR** 196, EAT.
[114] Ibid, 200.
[115] [2007] **IRLR** 484.

A recommendation of the Cambridge Review which has, unfortunately, not been adopted is that the definition of discrimination should include a concept of reasonable adjustments to meet religious diversity: However, there are signs that the Supreme Court may be willing to treat reasonable accommodation as part of the proportionality assessment in cases of indirect discrimination.[116] The Court of Appeal applied such a proportionality test when deciding whether a requirement of Sunday working, which put a Sunday-observing Christian at a particular disadvantage, was justified in the circumstances of the case.[117] The issue was said to be whether there was a 'viable and practical' alternative to Sunday working, or, in other words, whether the Christian's beliefs could be reasonably accommodated. On the particular facts it was held that such accommodation was not possible.

In cases of manifestation of religious or other belief falling under Article 9 ECHR, it used to be relatively easy for the employer to prove justification, for example in respect of a requirement not to wear a beard which discriminates against Sikhs, or to work on Sundays, which may discriminate against some Christians. It was said, somewhat unrealistically, that so long as the employee had a choice to change his or her job and work where a beard was permitted or Sunday working was not required, the indirect discrimination could be justified. However, this has been changed by *Eweida*[118] in which the ECtHR held that 'given the importance in a democratic society of freedom of religion in the workplace, rather than holding that the possibility of changing jobs would negate any interference with the right, the better approach would be to weigh that possibility in the overall balance when considering whether or not the restriction was proportionate'. The defence of justification (to protect corporate image) failed in the case of Mrs Eweida because there was no evidence of any real encroachment on the interests of others if she wore a cross discreetly over her uniform. However, the ECtHR found that it was justifiable to ask a Christian nurse to remove her cross for health and safety reasons.[119] In this and other cases of religion or belief the ECtHR has been willing to allow states a wide margin of appreciation in striking a balance between competing convention rights. It was justified to dismiss a counsellor for not being prepared to counsel gay couples because the employer's action was intended to implement its policy of providing a service without discrimination.[120] The Supreme Court has held that the genuine religious beliefs of hotel owners that sexual intercourse outside marriage is sinful cannot justify a policy of letting double

---

[116] In *Bull v Hall* [2014] EqLR 76, per Lady Hale, para 47.
[117] *Mba v London Borough of Merton* [2014] EqLR 51.
[118] [2013] EqLR 264.
[119] *Chaplain v United Kingdom* [2013] EqLR 264.
[120] *Ladele v United Kingdom* [2013] EqLR 264.

rooms only to married couples. This was found to put civil partners (a status limited to homosexuals) as a group at a serious disadvantage.[121] The owners argued that they should not be compelled to run their business in a way which conflicted with their right to manifest their religion, but the Supreme Court unanimously held that there was no general exemption for those who disagree with the law, however sincere their beliefs.[122]

By extending the public sector equality duty to religion or belief, something akin to a duty of reasonable accommodation has now been imposed on public authorities.[123] The judicial trend towards reasonable accommodation is to be welcomed because it promotes the fundamental values of equality of law including respect for the dignity of individuals and freedom of choice.[124] The Equality Act could have come closer to these ideals by 'avoiding hair-splitting distinctions between "direct" and "indirect" discrimination in the context of religion'[125] and by adopting a concept of discrimination arising from religion or belief, which combines direct and indirect discrimination and reasonable accommodation. In the absence of such a concept, one may expect much litigation and divisive debate over symbols of faith, diverting attention from the real problems of disadvantage and exclusion experienced by ethno-religious groups.

SEX AND RELATED CHARACTERISTICS

Sex and Gender

There are four protected characteristics that are closely related: sex, gender reassignment, pregnancy and maternity, and marriage and civil partnership. The Equality Act prohibits discrimination and harassment because of 'sex', and 'sex' is one of the protected characteristics for the public sector equality duty and positive action measures. 'Sex' is defined as 'a reference to a man or to a woman'.[126] This can be a male or female of any age.[127] The Act, like its predecessors, uses the term 'sex' rather than 'gender'. 'Sex' is a category that 'relates to the identification of an individual by biological endowments and

---

[121] The legalisation of same-sex marriages (see p 63 below) since 2014, may lead to a different conclusion.

[122] *Bull v Hall* [2014] EqLR 176; see p 66 below.

[123] See p 20 above.

[124] Another example of reasonable accommodation is *R v D(R)* [2013] EqLR 1134, in which a trial court judge allowed a Muslim defendant to wear a niqab during the trial except while giving evidence because a fair trial made it necessary for the judge and jury to assess her credibility by judging her facial reactions to questions put to her.

[125] McColgan (2009) 29.

[126] EA, s 11.

[127] EA, s 212(1).

functions', while 'gender' is 'concerned with the ascription of social characteristics such as "womanly", "manly", "feminine" and "masculine"'.[128] The terms 'sex' and 'gender' are often used indiscriminately in everyday discourse about men and women. The Act itself contains a provision which describes differences in the pay of male and female employees as the 'gender pay gap',[129] and EU Equal Treatment Directive 2006/54/EC refers to 'gender mainstreaming'.[130]

For most legal purposes, however, it is the biological difference that is critical. So, in *Pearce v Governing Body of Mayfield Secondary School*[131] the House of Lords held that 'sex' does not include sexual orientation, with the result that harassment of a lesbian teacher because she was a lesbian was not sex discrimination. Her complaint of sex discrimination failed because a gay male would have been treated equally badly. Sexual orientation was not a protected characteristic until the Framework Employment Directive was implemented. However, the CJEU was willing to apply the Equal Treatment Directive to a person proposing to undergo gender reassignment, and British law was amended to comply with this.[132] The Equality Act has followed earlier legislation by identifying a range of differences—sex, gender reassignment, marriage and civil partnership, pregnancy and maternity, and sexual orientation—rather than developing a concept of socially constructed gender. This has the virtue of specificity, making it clear which particular characteristics are protected and what specific remedies are required, for example in reducing the gap between the pay of males and females.[133] However, it must be recognised that the law's focus on the biological differences between men and women can be an obstacle to the achievement of full equality in practice. The definition of direct discrimination[134] means that a woman must compare her treatment with that of a man in similar circumstances. This has given rise to problems, for example, in trying to compare a woman who is absent from work due to pregnancy or confinement with a sick man.[135] Another example arises in cases where an employer applies a code relating to dress or hairstyles or the wearing of jewellery. The courts have accorded employers a large measure of discretion in controlling the image of the establishment, for example to require women to wear skirts or

---

[128] Browne (2006) 2.
[129] EA, s 78 heading. See p 132 below.
[130] Art 29.
[131] Heard with *Macondald v Ministry of Defence* [2003] UKHL34; [2003] IRLR 512. The ECJ has similarly held that sex discrimination law does not cover sexual orientation: case C-249/96, *Grant v South-West Trains Ltd* [1998] IRLR 206.
[132] See p 59 below.
[133] See p 115 below.
[134] See p 67 below.
[135] See p 68 below.

men to have short hair, so long as a conventional standard of 'smartness' is applied to both sexes.[136] Cross-dressing, even of a limited kind, or unconventional dress or hairstyles, are generally unprotected. This can encourage gender stereotyping and traditional social prejudices, which it is the goal of the law to remove.

Gender Reassignment

Transsexual or transgender or gender variant (trans) people[137] are those who do not identify fully with the gender assigned to them at birth, or do not conform to cultural or societal expectations of the appearance or behaviour associated with that gender. Estimates of the number of people in the UK who have presented for medical treatment to make their physical characteristics or appearance conform more closely to their acquired gender range between 5,000[138] and 10,000.[139] Trans people are highly vulnerable to discrimination and harassment, particularly when they embark on processes to reassign their gender. There is a high unemployment rate among the trans community, and they tend to have lower incomes than other people.[140]

In 1999, the Sex Discrimination Act was amended so as to outlaw direct discrimination in the field of employment on the ground that a person was undergoing or had undergone gender reassignment.[141] This was as a result of a ruling by the CJEU in *P v S and Cornwall County Council*[142] that the Equal Treatment Directive provided protection to an employee who had been dismissed after informing her employer that she proposed to undergo gender reassignment. The amended British legislation did not apply to indirect discrimination or to discrimination outside the employment field. These limitations were plainly inconsistent with other CJEU decisions,[143] and with the decision of the ECtHR in *Goodwin v UK*[144] that the UK's failure to recognise the chosen gender identity of a gender-reassigned person constituted a breach of Articles 8 and 12 ECHR. The Gender Recognition Act 2004 now provides that a person may apply for a gender recognition certificate on the basis of living in the other gender, or having changed gender under

---

[136] See eg *Smith v Safeway plc* [1996] **IRLR** 456, CA; *Department for Work and Pensions v Thompson* [2004] **IRLR** 348, EAT, and on indirect discrimination p 85 below.

[137] The word 'transsexual' is used in the EA, s 7(2).

[138] *Equalities Review* (2007) 146.

[139] Submission to the Public Bill committee on the Equality Bill (2008–09).

[140] National Equality Panel (2010) 221.

[141] Discrimination (Gender Reassignment) Regulations 1999, SI 1999/1102.

[142] Case C-13/94, [1996] **IRLR** 347.

[143] Case C-117/01 *KB v National Health Service Pensions Agency* [2004] **IRLR** 240.

[144] (2002) 35 EHRR 447.

the law of a country outside the UK. Applications are determined by a Gender Recognition Panel. In order to obtain a certificate, it is not necessary to have completed reassignment by undergoing surgery.

The EU Equal Treatment Amendment Directive required equal treatment between men and women in access to and the supply of goods and services, but did not expressly refer to gender reassignment. When the SDA was amended to implement the Directive, direct discrimination and harassment on grounds of gender reassignment in these fields were outlawed, but the issue of applying this to indirect discrimination was left for consideration under the Equality Bill. The Equality Act now covers both direct[145] and indirect[146] discrimination and harassment[147] because of gender reassignment in services and public functions, premises, employment and related fields. Where trans people who are absent from work for the purposes of gender reassignment are treated less favourably than they would have been treated if they were absent due to illness or injury, this amounts to discrimination.[148]

The definition of 'gender reassignment' has been extended by the Act beyond that set out in the SDA, despite some opposition from religious groups.[149] It is no longer necessary for a person to be undergoing a process of gender reassignment under medical supervision in order to be protected. Notably, the original requirement left unprotected children and young people, whose gender identity is less well developed and who, therefore, are unlikely to seek medical supervision. It is now sufficient 'if the person is proposing to undergo, is undergoing, or has undergone a process (or part of a process) for the purposes of reassigning the person's sex by changing physiological or other attributes of sex'.[150]

An Explanatory Note states that, under the new definition, a person who was born physically female but decides to spend the rest of her life as a man, and manages to 'pass' as a man without the need for any medical intervention, will have the protected characteristic of gender reassignment.[151] However, concern was expressed by the JCHR and pressure groups that the new definition would still leave some trans people unprotected, such as those who do not display any intention of undergoing a process but who choose to adopt a different gender identity, and those for whom a process would be of little or no relevance, such as inter-sex persons.[152] The Liberal Democrats

---

[145] EA, s 13. See p 67 below.

[146] EA, s 19(8). See p 78 below.

[147] EA, s 26(5). See p 97 below.

[148] EA, s 16.

[149] See eg the amendment moved by the Lord Bishop of Chichester to restore the requirement of medical supervision: Hansard HL vol 716 cols 378–85 (13 January 2010).

[150] EA, s 7(1).

[151] EN, para 43.

[152] JCHR (2008–09) paras 56–60.

attempted, without success, to move an amendment to replace 'gender reassignment' with 'gender identity', a term used in UN and Council of Europe documents.[153] The government gave its assurances that the definition of 'gender reassignment' and the implicit inclusion of discrimination because of a perception of reassignment[154] is broad enough to cover acts or behaviour by a trans person that are a precursor to gender reassignment.[155] The universality of the principle that gender reassignment is a protected status is weakened by several exceptions, some more controversial than others.[156]

Pregnancy and Maternity

Pregnant women and those returning to work or education following maternity suffer high levels of discrimination and harassment. The original SDA failed to specify discrimination or harassment because of pregnancy as a specific ground of unlawful discrimination. However, as a result of rulings by the European Court of Justice, such discrimination or harassment is now treated automatically as sex discrimination, since only a woman can become pregnant.[157]

The Equal Treatment Amendment Directive 2002/73/EC specifically outlawed pregnancy discrimination. The Employment Equality (Sex Discrimination) Regulations 2005 purported to implement the amending Directive, but the Administrative Court found that this was not compliant with EU law because it stipulated that within the protected period (from the beginning of pregnancy to the end of maternity leave) there was direct sex discrimination against a pregnant woman only if she was treated less favourably than she would have been had she not become pregnant.[158] The requirement of 'less favourable' treatment was retained when the government implemented Equal Treatment Amendment Directive 2004/113/EC, which extends the equal treatment principle to the supply of goods and services. The Equality Act has now removed this requirement in both work and non-work cases. The words 'less favourably' were used in the original Equality Bill, and 'less favourable' was defined as 'less favourable than is reasonable'. This appeared to weaken existing protection against discrimination because of pregnancy. Following representations by an all-party women's group and others, the government amended the Bill at the committee stage by substi-

---

[153] PBC (EB) 6th sitting col 164 (11 June 2009) (Lynne Featherstone).
[154] EA, s 13. See p 75 below.
[155] PBC (EB) 6th sitting cols 168–69 (11 June 2009) (Solicitor-General).
[156] See p 142 below.
[157] See p 68 below.
[158] *Equal Opportunities Commission v Secretary of State for Trade and Industry* [2007] EWHC 483; [2007] IRLR 327.

tuting the word 'unfavourably' for 'less favourably'.[159] It is well established that a mere deprivation of choice, in the sense of depriving a person of something they value, is sufficient to constitute unfavourable treatment.[160] In non-work cases (the Act extends protection to cover discrimination in relation to public functions, education and associations), the woman only has to show 'unfavourable' treatment because of her pregnancy.[161] In work cases the unfavourable treatment may also be because of an illness suffered as a result of pregnancy, or because she is on compulsory maternity leave or exercising rights related to statutory maternity leave.[162] Where there is pregnancy or maternity discrimination as defined in these provisions, there cannot also be sex discrimination.[163] But where these provisions do not apply, outside the protected periods (see below), the general prohibition on sex discrimination can be relied upon. This is an area where the biological differences between women and men are recognised; a man cannot complain that he is being discriminated against because of the special treatment afforded to a woman because of pregnancy or childbirth.[164]

The special protection for pregnant women applies only to defined periods. In non-work cases, the woman is protected from unfavourable treatment based on the fact that she has given birth (including, in particular, the fact that she is breastfeeding) for a period of 26 weeks, beginning on the day on which she gives birth.[165] The reason for the limitation to 26 weeks (the period recommended by the World Health Organization) is that this covers the important first months, when exclusive breastfeeding brings health benefits to mother and child.[166] Outside the 26-week period, a woman who is still breastfeeding might rely on the general prohibition against sex discrimination, since the Act says that 'less favourable treatment of a woman includes less favourable treatment because she is breastfeeding'.[167] Since only a woman can breastfeed, this would automatically amount to sex discrimination, without the need for a comparator.

In work cases, there are two relevant periods in which she receives protection. The first is the period of compulsory maternity leave, during which

---

[159] PBC(EB) 8th sitting col 277 (16 June 2009).

[160] For example, being allowed to drink at the bar in a wine bar (*Gill v El Vinos Co Ltd* [1983] QB 425; [1983] IRLR 206, CA), or a chance to have a selective education (*R v Birmingham City council, ex parte EOC* [1989] AC 155; [1989] IRLR 173, HL).

[161] EA, s 17(2).

[162] EA, s 18(2)–(6).

[163] EA, ss 13(8), 17(6), 18(7).

[164] EA, s 13(6)(b).

[165] EA, s 17(3)–(4). The day on which she gives birth is the day on which (a) she gives birth to a living child, or (b) she gives birth to a dead child (more than 24 weeks of the pregnancy having passed): EA, s 17(5).

[166] PBC (EB) 8th sitting cols 279–80 (16 June 2009) (Solicitor-General).

[167] EA, s 13(6)(a).

she is not allowed to work, a concept defined in employment legislation as being not less than two weeks.[168] The second is the period starting when the pregnancy begins and ending with the end of the statutory maternity leave for which she is qualified. This will be 26 weeks if she is entitled only to ordinary maternity leave,[169] and 52 weeks if she is also entitled to additional maternity leave.[170] If she has no right to statutory maternity leave, the protection lasts for only two weeks, beginning at the end of the pregnancy.[171]

Marriage and Civil Partnership

The original SDA prohibited discrimination against 'married persons' because of their marital status, and this was extended by the Civil Partnership Act 2004 to civil partners.[172] The Marriage (Same Sex Couples) Act 2013 has made marriages of same-sex couples in England and Wales lawful, and such marriages have the same effect as those of heterosexual couples.[173] This does not protect those who are in a cohabiting relationship, however permanent, if they are not married (man and woman) or in a partnership (same sex) not recognised by law. Nor does it protect people against discrimination or harassment because they are single, widowed or divorced. The Equality Act continued these restrictions.[174] The Liberal Democrats unsuccessfully moved an amendment to cover single and cohabiting persons.[175] The government's justification for retaining the old law was that it would be difficult to define when couples were cohabiting, and that responses to the consultation did not provide any evidence that unmarried people and those in other forms of relationship are discriminated against.[176] The exclusion of single and cohabiting persons may, sooner or later, be challenged as being incompatible with ECHR Articles 8 (private and family life) and 14 (equality).[177]

Also questionable under the ECHR is the very limited scope of the

---

[168] EA, s 18(3) and s 213(3); Employment Rights Act 1996 (as amended), s 72(1).

[169] EA, s 18(6). Employment Rights Act 1996, s 71.

[170] Employment Rights Act, s 72.

[171] EA, s 18(6).

[172] SDA, s 3, as substituted by the Civil Partnership act 2004, s 251(1)–(2), which defines civil partnerships (same-sex couples only).

[173] Similar legislation has been enacted in Scotland, but not in Northern Ireland. Civil partnerships may be converted into marriages by following a specified procedure.

[174] EA, s 8.

[175] PBC (EB) 7th sitting col 207 (16 June 2009) (Lynne Featherstone).

[176] JCHR (2008–09) para 64.

[177] See *Re P: Unmarried Couple* [2008] UKHL 38, where it was held that a provision referring to a 'married couple' should include an unmarried couple so as to comply with human rights law.

protection conferred by the Act on married couples and civil partners. The protection is generally limited to direct and indirect discrimination in employment and related fields. There is no protection in respect of harassment[178] or discrimination in a number of fields: in the provision of goods and services,[179] in the disposal, management and occupation of premises,[180] in education,[181] and with regard to membership of associations.[182] Once again the government's justification for these extensive exclusions was the absence of evidence of discrimination in these fields.[183] There may, of course, be circumstances in which a married person or civil partner can claim that the ostensible reason for discrimination (marital status) amounts to direct or indirect discrimination because of sex or sexual orientation, for example the exclusion of a married woman because she may become pregnant or has childcare responsibilities, or refusal of double-bed accommodation to (same-sex) civil partners where this would be offered to a (heterosexual) married couple.[184] But this possibility does not justify the exclusion of marital discrimination from most of the fields covered by the Act. The exclusion undermines the principle of comprehensive equality, and also risks challenge as being incompatible with the ECHR.

One area in which the Act has made English law compatible with European human rights law is in respect of equality between spouses. Article 5 of Protocol no 7 to the ECHR provides that 'spouses shall enjoy equality of rights and responsibilities of a private law character between them'. The Equality Act achieves this by abolishing two common law rules: the duty of a husband to maintain his wife,[185] and the presumption of advancement.[186] The wife was under no similar common law duty to maintain her husband, and the common law rule had little if any application due to the statutory provisions that allow either party to a marriage to apply for financial provision. The presumption that a man who transferred property to his wife, child or fiancée was making a gift of that property unless there was evidence to the contrary did not apply to a woman who transferred property to her husband, child or fiancé. The abolition of the presumption means that the normal rules will apply: where one person transfers property to another without gaining anything in return, the recipient is presumed to

---

[178] See p 97 below.
[179] EA, s 28(1)(b). See p 135 below.
[180] EA, s 32(1). See p 144 below.
[181] EA, s 84(b) (schools); s 90 (further and higher education); s 95 (qualification bodies). See p 145 below.
[182] EA, s 100(1). See p 149 below.
[183] JCHR (2008–09) para 67.
[184] *Bull v Hall* [2014] EqLR 76 (see further p 68 below).
[185] EA, s 198.
[186] EA, s 199.

be holding the property on trust for the transferor unless there is evidence to the contrary. The Married Women's Property Act 1964 is amended so that any money and property derived from a housekeeping allowance will, in the absence of agreement to the contrary, be owned by the husband and wife in equal shares regardless of who paid or received the allowance.[187] A similar rule is applied to civil partners.[188] These changes should allow the UK to ratify Protocol 7 ECHR.

SEXUAL ORIENTATION

It has been estimated that lesbian, gay and bisexual people (LGB) make up about 6 per cent of the UK population.[189] The Framework Employment Directive included sexual orientation amongst the grounds of unlawful discrimination, and this was implemented in the UK. The Employment Equality (Sexual Orientation) Regulations 2007, made under the Equality Act 2006, extended this to non-work areas. The Equality Act replicates the provisions in these regulations.

'Sexual orientation' is defined as a person's sexual orientation towards (a) persons of the same sex, (b) persons of the opposite sex, or (c) persons of either sex.[190] In other words, the protected classes are homosexuals, heterosexuals and bisexuals. Since there must be an orientation 'towards' one sex or both, it appears that asexuals are not protected.[191] Transsexuals receive separate protection.[192] It was held in the *Amicus* case,[193] in which the compliance of the regulations with EU law was unsuccessfully challenged, that 'sexual orientation' is not limited to sexuality but also includes the manifestation of that orientation in sexual behaviour or sexual expression. Some fears were expressed, when the regulations were first introduced, that this might protect paedophilia or sadomasochism, but the Act must be interpreted consistently with the ECHR, under which harmful or dangerous sexual behaviour will not be tolerated.[194]

In cases of alleged direct discrimination because of sexual orientation, the main difficulty for LGB people is finding an appropriate comparator. There

---

[187] EA, s 200.

[188] EA, s 201 amending the Civil Partnership Act 2004.

[189] National Equality Panel (2010) 241, citing an estimate by Stonewall.

[190] EA, s 12(1).

[191] Monaghan (2013) para 5.310.

[192] See p 59 above.

[193] *R (on the application of Amicus—MSF section) v Secretary of State for Trade and Industry* [2004] IRLR 430, HC. The government refused to accept a Liberal Democrat amendment which would have made this explicit in the Act: PBC (EB) 8th sitting col 235 (16 June 2009).

[194] Monaghan (2007) 262, citing *Laskey, Jaggard and Brown v UK* (1997) 24 EHRR 39.

must be no material difference between the circumstances relating to each case.[195] The Civil Partnership Act 2004 removed many of the disadvantages suffered by single-sex partners, and the Marriage (Single Sex Couples) Act 2013 has made it possible for such couples to marry.[196] The link between civil partnership and sexual orientation was considered by the Supreme Court in *Bull v Hall*.[197] The issue was whether a hotel which allowed only married couples to use a room with a double bed discriminated on grounds of sexual orientation against a same-sex couple who were in a civil partnership. By a majority of 3–2 the Supreme Court held that there was direct discrimination on grounds of sexual orientation (for reasons discussed in chapter 3 below).[198] This decision, important as it is, leaves open the question whether the same conclusion could be reached on direct discrimination if the same-sex couple were neither civil partners nor married.[199] The fact that the claimants in *Bull v Hall* were civil partners was crucial to the majority decision. Marriage is now open to same-sex couples, and so a marriage requirement can adversely affect heterosexual couples as well as same-sex couples who are unmarried. The correct approach is to ask whether *but for* their sexual orientation, the couple would be treated in the same way as married persons or civil partners.[200]

As already noted, the most contentious issues arise where the rights to religious freedom and to private life, in respect of sexual orientation, clash.[201] In *Bull v Hall* the Supreme Court made it clear that one protected characteristic (eg sexual orientation) is not more highly valued than another (eg religion or belief). In Lady Hale's words, 'each of these parties has the same right to be protected against discrimination by the other'.[202]

---

[195] EA, s 23(1).

[196] See p 63 above.

[197] [2014] EqLR 76, para 27.

[198] See p 74 below.

[199] This was the situation in *Black v Wilkinson* [2013] EqLR 894, in which the CA held that a marriage requirement amounted to direct discrimination: an appeal was not pursued.

[200] See below, p 72.

[201] See p 51 above.

[202] Para 4.

3

Prohibited Conduct

INTRODUCTION

F OUR CIVIL WRONGS provide the foundations of equality law:
direct discrimination, indirect discrimination, harassment and victimisation. There are now standardised and clear definitions of these
key concepts. Previously, different definitions of prohibited conduct applied
in various circumstances, leading to complexity and arbitrary distinctions.
Now there are special provisions only for age discrimination[1] and discrimination arising from disability.[2] The new definitions have generally levelled
up protection against indirect discrimination[3] and harassment[4] across the
board, and have extended protection against victimisation by removing the
need for the victim to prove that he or she has been treated less favourably
than another person would have been treated in a comparable situation.[5]
Amendments made during the committee and report stages removed several
defects in the original text of the Bill—for example, there is no longer a need
to prove less favourable treatment in the case of pregnancy and maternity.[6]
However, some features of the definitions remain problematical.

DIRECT DISCRIMINATION

Less Favourable Treatment

Section 13(1) EA provides that

> A person (A) discriminates against another (B) if, because of a protected characteristic, A treats B less favourably than A treats or would treat others.

---

[1] See p 78 below.
[2] See p 91 below.
[3] See p 78 below.
[4] See p 97 below.
[5] See p 103 below.
[6] See p 68 below.

This formal or symmetrical model, that likes must be treated alike, has been at the core of anti-discrimination law in Britain since 1965.[7] The model had to be adjusted to deal with disability discrimination, and section 15 of the equality Act sets out a separate definition of direct discrimination arising from disability. Apart from age and discrimination arising from disability, there is no general defence of justification of direct discrimination.

The requirement of 'less favourable treatment' is based on the principle of consistency.[8] Any deprivation of a choice that a person values is regarded as 'less favourable' treatment. So, women denied the choice to drink at the bar in a wine bar when men could do so,[9] and men denied permission to leave work five minutes early so as to avoid the rush hour when women could do so, were less favourably treated.[10] This requires the treatment of the claimant to be compared with that of an actual or hypothetical comparator who does not share the same protected characteristic as the claimant but who is (or is assumed to be) in not materially different circumstances from the claimant.[11] Like must be compared with like. For example, the treatment of a woman with children must be compared with the treatment of a man with children.[12] This requirement can lead to difficulties where there is no appropriate comparator. For example, how can one compare a pregnant woman with a man, who by nature cannot become pregnant? Early case law rejected a claim by a woman alleged to have been dismissed because of pregnancy on the ground that 'when she is pregnant a woman is no longer just a woman'.[13] Later cases attempted comparison with an ill man, but this was unsatisfactory.[14] Pregnancy is a characteristic unique to women, and should not be stigmatised as an illness. If such a comparison is made, the effect is to give the pregnant woman the same rights as an ill man, but if the man is not protected for an absence from work due to illness, neither is the woman protected in respect of an absence for pregnancy. The CJEU recognised this flaw in the comparative approach. In the leading case of

[7] See p 11 above.

[8] See p 24 above.

[9] *Gill v El Vino Co Ltd* [1983] 1 QB 425.

[10] *Ministry of Defence v Jeremiah* [1980] 1 QB 87; see too *Moyhing v Barts & London NHS Trust* [2006] IRLR 860, EAT (male student nurse not allowed to carry out ECG on female patient without a chaperone, while female student allowed to do so without chaperone, was a discriminatory 'detriment', even if done for good reasons).

[11] EA, s 23(1).

[12] Eg *Hurley v Mustoe* [1981] IRLR 208, EAT (waitress dismissed on ground that women with children are 'unreliable', no evidence that this would have been applied to a man with children).

[13] *Turley v Allders Department Stores Ltd* [1980] ICR 66, EAT.

[14] Fredman (1997a) 182–93.

Dekker,[15] the court held that since only women could be dismissed because of pregnancy, such a dismissal constituted direct discrimination on grounds of sex. In later cases, the European Court of Justice held that the equal treatment principle applied throughout the period of pregnancy and maternity leave, and also applied to illness arising from pregnancy.[16] The Equality Act has removed the need to show less favourable treatment in both work and non-work cases of unfavourable treatment because of pregnancy and maternity within certain protected periods.[17]

Levelling Down

Another consequence of the comparative approach has not been remedied by the Equality Act. The principle of equal treatment is satisfied irrespective of whether the individual benefits as a result. More specifically, it is a defence to show that the comparator would have been treated equally badly. For example, an employer who denies a fair procedure to a Black employee may escape a claim for racial discrimination if it is shown that a White employee would have been treated the same way (the so-called 'bastard to everyone' defence). The flaws in the comparative approach have led to the development of separate wrongs of harassment and victimisation, in which the requirement of a comparator has been removed. However, the Act does not follow the recommendation of the Cambridge Review,[18] as reflected in the Lester Bill (2003), that the application of the principle of equal treatment should not result in a reduction in the level of opportunities or benefits enjoyed by any person.[19] This reflects a general principle against regressive interpretation.[20] Although levelling down can still be a consequence of 'equal' treatment in Britain, there are minimum provisions in EU law below which the reduction in protection cannot be allowed to fall. Moreover, implementation of EU equality directives can in no circumstances be sufficient grounds for a reduction in the level of protection of workers in the areas

---

[15] Case C-177/88 *Dekker v Stichting Vormingscentrum Voor Jonge Volwassen (VJV Centrum) Plus* [1990] ECR I-3941.

[16] Case C-109/00 *Tele Danmark A/S v Handels- og Kontorfunktionernes Forbund i Danmark* [2001] IRLR 853; Case C-32/93 *Webb v EMO Air Cargo (UK) Ltd* [1994] IRLR 482, ECJ, and *(No 2)* [1995] IRLR 645, HL.

[17] See p 62 above.

[18] Cambridge Review (2000) recommendation 8, p 35.

[19] Lester Bill, cl 2(2)(a), (4).

[20] Equal Rights Trust, *Declaration of Principles of Equality*, para 26: 'Prohibition of regressive interpretation: In adopting and implementing laws and policies to promote equality there shall be no regression from the level of protection against discrimination that has already been achieved.'

to which it applies.[21] An example, discussed later,[22] is that the UK cannot reduce protection against harassment when implementing EU law.

Knowledge, Intention and Motivation

One of the main purposes of anti-discrimination law is to overcome stereotyping or assumptions about the characteristics of a group, or of their behavioural norms.[23]

Stereotyping may lead to conscious or unconscious discrimination, for example assuming that men are the breadwinners in a family, or that women cannot cope with unsocial hours and working under pressure;[24] assuming that Roma people are more likely than others to put forward false claims for asylum because of the disadvantages they suffer in their home country;[25] or targeting persons of a particular ethnic group in the exercise of police stop and search powers because it is believed that members of their group are more likely than others to be committing an offence.[26] Such stereotypes fall foul of anti-discrimination legislation, which, in Baroness Hale's words, aims 'to ensure that each person is treated as an individual and not assumed to be like other members of the group'.[27]

Conscious discrimination may be the result of personal prejudice, antipathy or deeply held beliefs, or it may be the result of social pressures, such as a threat of industrial action or a consumer boycott.[28] It may even have apparently benign motives, for example to advance the interests of a disadvantaged group.[29] Unconscious discrimination occurs where one treats another less favourably because of a protected characteristic without meaning to do so or realising that one is doing so. This can sometimes be seen by looking at the language used by a person.

---

[21] Directive 2006/54/EC, Art 27(2); directive 2000/43/EC, Art 14; directive 2000/78/EC, Art 16; and see Case C-200/91 *Coloroll Pension Trustees v Russell* [1993] ECR I-4389, paras 31 and 32.

[22] See p 98 below.

[23] These have been stated aims since the inception of anti-discrimination law: see *Report of the Race Relations Board for 1966–67*, para 65; see p 22 above.

[24] Browne (2006) 114–15. In a study of the BBC it was found that widespread discrimination against female employees by managers derived from the common view that women are more likely to be detrimental to overall workplace productivity due to their childbearing and childrearing responsibilities.

[25] *R (European Roma Rights Centre) v Immigration Officer at Prague Airport* [2004] UKHL 55; [2005] 2 AC 1, HL (e), para 97 (Baroness Hale).

[26] *R (Gillan) v Commr of Police of Metropolis* [2006] UKHL 12; [2006] 2 AC 307, para 45 (Lord Hope of Craighead).

[27] *Prague Airport* (n 25) para 82.

[28] For a detailed analysis, see Hepple (1970) 17–31, 175–76.

[29] *R v Commission for Racial Equality, ex parte Westminster City Council* [1985] ICR 627, CA.

'If there is a tendency for ethnic minorities and women to be described in terms of their appearance and manner, rather than their achievements, knowledge and skills, in comparison with white men, this is a sign that the decision-maker's attitudes have affected their decision.'[30] If the law is to be effective, it needs to be able to deal with both conscious and unconscious discrimination.

The phrase 'on grounds of' a particular protected characteristic is used in EU legislation and was used in British legislation before the Equality Act 2010.[31] It is a settled principle that a person can directly discriminate on particular grounds whether they do so consciously or unconsciously, and that the motive of the discriminator is irrelevant. However, the judges in the highest court have found it difficult to formulate an agreed test. In the *Birmingham Schools* case,[32] there were more grammar school places for boys than girls in Birmingham, with the result that girls had to do better than boys in the entrance examination in order to secure a place. The council did not mean to discriminate against girls, and was not hostile to women; it had simply failed to take adequate steps to redress an historical disadvantage. It was nonetheless held to be liable for direct discrimination. Lord Goff, in the leading judgment, following a long line of cases in the lower courts, said:

> The intention or motive of the defendant to discriminate, although it may be relevant so far as remedies are concerned ... is not a necessary condition of liability. ... [I]f [it were] it would be a good defence for an employer to show that he discriminated against women not because he intended to do so but (for example) because of customer preference, or to save money, or even to avoid controversy.[33]

A year later, in *James v Eastleigh Borough Council*,[34] a husband and wife, both aged 61, went to their local municipal swimming pool. The husband was charged 75 pence but his wife was let in free because of a council policy to grant free admittance to those who had reached state pensionable age, which at the time was 60 for women and 65 for men. The Council's motives were 'to give benefits to those whose resources were likely to have been reduced by retirement' and 'to aid the needy, whether male or female'. By a majority, the House of Lords decided that the Council's subjective motive

---

[30] Coussey and Jackson (1991) 9, who give examples from personnel practice, such as a woman described as 'having a bubbly personality' or 'attractive', a Black man as 'having a chip on his shoulder' or 'not our type', while a White man is described as having 'a clear idea of his career'. Modood (1992) 134 gives examples of cultural assumptions in the employment selection process.

[31] See p 75 below regarding the words 'because of' used in the EA.

[32] *R v Birmingham City Council, ex parte EOC* [1989] AC 1155; [1989] IRLR 173, HL.

[33] [1989] IRLR 175.

[34] [1990] 2 AC 751; [1990] IRLR 288, HL.

(to benefit pensioners), however benign, was irrelevant. Lord Goff, with whom Lord Bridge and Lord Ackner agreed, applied a test of causation: 'would the complainant have received the same reason but for his or her sex?'[35] Since the criterion for free admission was gender-based, the court concluded that but for being a man the complainant would have received the same treatment as his wife.

In *Bull v Hall*[36] a hotel allowed only married persons and not civil partners to share a double-bedded room because of the owners' religious beliefs. At the time, same-sex marriages were not lawful and only same-sex couples could enter into civil partnerships. All the Supreme Court Justices were agreed that if this was a case of indirect discrimination, this could not be justified. There was a difference of opinion, however, as to whether there was direct discrimination. A majority (3–2) held that there was direct discrimination on grounds of sexual orientation because the marriage criterion was 'necessarily linked to a characteristic indissociable' from sexual orientation.[37] Lady Hale did not see how discriminating between married persons and civil partners, at a time when only heterosexual couples could be lawfully married , could be anything other than direct discrimination on the grounds of sexual orientation.[38] Lord Kerr[39] relied on a statutory provision that that there is no material difference between civil partners and married persons. Lord Toulson[40] said that it was not possible to separate the fact that the couple were civil partners from their sexual orientation. Lord Neuberger,[41] dissenting on this point, held that for the discrimination to be direct there 'must be an exact correspondence between the criterion and the protected characteristic', and that here the discrimination was against the unmarried, since a double-bedded room would equally have been denied to an unmarried heterosexual couple.[42] Lord Hughes, also dissenting on this point,[43] said that it was wrong to concentrate on the characteristics of the claimants rather than on the defendants' reasons for treating them as they did.

It is true, as Lady Hale acknowledged,[44] that there was not an 'exact correspondence' between those being denied a double bed and those being

---

[35] [1990] IRLR 295. Lord Griffiths and Lord Lowry dissented.

[36] [2014] EqLR 76, see p 56 above.

[37] This is the language used by the Advocate General's in Case C-79/99 *Schnorbus v Land Hessen* [2000] ECR 1-10997, para 33; see too Case C-73/08 *Bressol v Gouvernement de law Commaunté Française* [2010] 3 CMLR 559, para 56.

[38] Paras 17–32.

[39] Paras 56–63. Citing reg 3(4) of the Sexual Orientation regulations, now EA s 23(3).

[40] Paras 66–71.

[41] Paras 72–77.

[42] Para 74.

[43] Paras 89–91.

[44] Para 21.

allowed one, with the protected characteristic of sexual orientation. In *James* only men (between 60 and 65) were disadvantaged, not women; in *Bull*, on the other hand, opposite-sex couples who were unmarried as well as unmarried same-sex couples were disadvantaged..

The differences between the Justices in *Bull* could have been avoided by applying the simple 'but for' test. This has a 'double virtue', as Lord Goff pointed out. [45] First, it embraces the case where the treatment derives from a criterion necessarily linked to a prohibited characteristic, and, secondly, it avoids in most cases complicated questions such as intention, motive, reason or purpose. Some confusion arises from later remarks in *Nagarajan v London Regional Transport*,[46] a victimisation case, by Lord Nicholls and Lord Steyn, who said that 'in every case', the crucial question is 'why the complainant received unfavourable treatment'.[47] These dicta led some to argue that the House of Lords had added the 'reason why' test to the 'but for' test. But in *Amnesty International v Ahmed*[48] Underhill J correctly rejected this argument. He drew a distinction between *James*, where the ground for the treatment was inherent in the act itself (the rule that pensioners were entitled to free entry necessarily discriminated against men because of the difference in pension ages), and cases such as *Nagarajan*, where the act was not in itself discriminatory but was rendered so by discriminatory motivation, that is, by 'the mental processes (whether conscious or unconscious) which led the putative discriminator to do the act'. Even in such a case 'it is important to bear in mind that the subject of the inquiry is the ground of, or reason for, the putative discriminator's action, not his motive'. In both kinds of case the benign motives behind the discriminator's action are not relevant. In the *Amnesty* case, a woman was not appointed to the post of 'Sudan researcher' by a human rights organisation because of her Northern Sudanese ethnic origin, the reason for this being that it was genuinely believed that her ethnic or national origin would result in a conflict of interest which would increase the safety risk for herself and others. The EAT upheld a finding that there was direct discrimination on the ground of her ethnic origin although the motive behind it was a concern about safety.

The vexed question of the defendant's mental state received consideration in the *Jewish Free School* (*JFS*) case,[49] the facts of which were related above.[50] The majority judgments[51] are renewed authority for the distinction between

---

[45] [1990] IRLR 295.
[46] [2000] 1 AC 501, HL (E).
[47] Ibid, 576 per Lord Nicholls.
[48] [2009] IRLR 884, EAT.
[49] [2009] UKSC 15; [2010] IRLR 136.
[50] See p 48 above.
[51] Lord Phillips PSC, Lady Hale, and Lords Mance, Kerr and Clarke.

the subjective reason for and the subjective motive underlying discrimination: the reason for not selecting the applicant for a place was that he was not Jewish by descent from a Jewish mother, but the motive behind this decision was that this was a requirement of orthodox Jewish religious law. The former is relevant, the latter is not.

The important refinement made in the majority judgments, developing the *Nagarajan* and *Amnesty* approach, is between cases where the treatment is 'inherently' based on a prohibited characteristic (such as *Birmingham Schools*, *James* and *Bull*), and those cases where the treatment is not clearly for a prohibited reason—for example, the ostensible reason for rejecting a job applicant might be that he or she lacked 'merit' or appropriate qualifications, and the employer might genuinely believe that the reason for rejecting the applicant had nothing to do with race or sex or some other protected characteristic. In the first class of case it is not necessary to investigate the discriminator's state of mind. In the second category,

> [A]fter careful and thorough investigation of a claim members of an employment tribunal may decide that the proper inference to be drawn from the evidence is that, whether the employer realised it at the time or not, race was the reason why he acted as he did. ... Conduct of this nature by an employer, when the inference is legitimately drawn falls squarely within the language of [direct discrimination].[52]

In *JFS* Lord Phillips did not find the 'but for' test useful. He said that 'it is better simply to ask what were the facts that the discriminator considered to be determinative when making the relevant decision'.[53] The undisputed factual criterion in *JFS* was a matrilineal connection to Orthodox Judaism, and this was ethnically based. In other words, there were not two grounds of discrimination, one ethnic, the other religious: the religious criterion was clearly based on ethnicity. The motive behind the discrimination, namely the Office of the Chief Rabbi's genuine belief ('subjective state of mind') that this discrimination was mandated by religious law, was not relevant. Similarly in *Bull v Hall*, the hotel owners' genuine religious motivation was not relevant.

In the light of these judgments, it appears that the proper approach for a court or tribunal is always to ascertain the factual criteria that constituted the substantial reason for the treatment. If these criteria are found to be 'inherently' based on a protected characteristic (as in *JFS*, *Birmingham Schools*, *James* and *Bull*), then the discrimination is unlawful, and there is no need to examine the defendant's state of mind. However, if the criteria are not 'inherently' based on a protected characteristic (eg allegedly based on merit

---

[52] Per Lord Nicholls [2001] 1 AC, 576.
[53] *JFS* case, para 16.

or lack of qualifications) then it is necessary for the court or tribunal to examine the subjective state of mind of the defendant in order to ascertain whether the reason was in fact a protected characteristic.[54] This will rarely be based on direct evidence (eg 'this job is not suitable for a woman'); rather it will depend on inferences being drawn from circumstantial evidence, so making the burden of proof all-important.[55]

'Because of' a Protected Characteristic

The decisions just discussed were made under earlier British legislation and the EU Directives, which used the words 'on grounds of' a particular characteristic. The Equality Act, however, now uses the words 'because of' a prohibited characteristic.[56] The explanation given for this change was that it was intended not to alter the legal definition but to make it more accessible to the ordinary reader of the Act. It was said that the formulation 'because of' is much more natural than 'on grounds of' when one looks for a reason for something.[57] Some experts suggested that the change might cause confusion and undermine the existing well-established case law, a view with which the JCHR agreed.[58] There were fears that the courts might interpret 'because of' as requiring a conscious intention to treat a person less favourably, and as requiring the protected characteristic to be the whole or main reason for the treatment. However, the government resisted all attempts to amend the Bill so as to revert to the 'on grounds of' formulation.[59] Government spokeswomen claimed that the words 'because of' and 'on grounds of' are 'absolutely synonymous'.[60] Of course, the courts must interpret 'because of' consistently with the phrase 'on grounds of' used in the EU Directives. There is no reason to suppose that the words 'because of' justify a different test from that used in the *JFS* case.

One issue that has been clarified is that it is not a defence to a claim of direct discrimination that the alleged discriminator shared the same protected characteristic as the victim. Previous legislation only expressly provided for this in the case of religion or belief. The Equality Act has extended this to

---

[54] Baroness Hale at paras 64–65, with whom Lord Walker (para 236) and Lord Hope (paras 196–71) agreed, and Lord Mance (para 90) is to similar effect.

[55] See p 203 below.

[56] The DDA 1995, s 3A(1) used the words 'for a reason which relates to the disabled person's disability' (see p 92 below).

[57] EN, para 61; PBC (EB) 8th sitting col 244 (16 June 2009) (Solicitor-General).

[58] JCHR (2008–09) para 77; Rubenstein (2009) 23.

[59] PBC (EB) 8th sitting cols 240–42 (16 June 2009); Hansard HL vol 716 cols 522–27 (19 January 2010).

[60] PBC (EB) 8th sitting col 244 (16 June 2009) (Solicitor-General); Hansard HL vol 716 col 526 (19 January 2010) (Baroness Thornton).

all protected characteristics. For example, a gay employer who rejects an applicant because the applicant is gay cannot escape liability for unlawful discrimination by virtue of the fact that he himself is gay.[61]

Perception and Association

UK legislation prohibiting direct discrimination on grounds of race[62] has long been interpreted as also prohibiting discrimination based on perception or association linked to such a characteristic. For example, if an employer rejects a job application from a White man, whom he wrongly thinks is Black because the applicant has an African-sounding name, this will constitute direct race discrimination based on the employer's perception.[63] Similar wording has been used in legislation on discrimination on grounds of sex, religion or belief, and sexual orientation. But discrimination based on a perception that someone is disabled was not prohibited, nor was discrimination based on an association with someone of a particular age or having a disability. The CJEU in *Coleman v Attridge Law*[64] interpreted the prohibition 'on grounds of' disability in the Framework Employment Directive as not limited to persons who are themselves disabled. It also covers less favourable treatment based on the disability of a person for whom the claimant cares. The Equality Act has levelled up protection by using the words 'because of a protected characteristic'. Section 13 of the Act puts direct discrimination based on perception of or association with disability and age on the same level as other protected characteristics. The new definition of direct discrimination is broad enough to cover cases where the discrimination is based on a mistaken perception that a person has any of the protected characteristics (eg that he or she is thought to be HIV positive), and also cases where the discrimination is because of a person's association with someone who has a protected characteristic (eg A treats B less favourably because B has caring responsibilities for a disabled or elderly person).

The JCHR,[65] agreeing with the EHRC and various campaign groups, wanted an express prohibition on direct discrimination based on association and perception. A Liberal Democrat amendment aimed at achieving this was rejected by the government on the ground that it could result in

---

[61] EA, s 24(1); EN, para 95.
[62] *Race Relations Board v Applin* [1975] AC 259, 289 (Lord Simon); *Mandla v Dowell Lee* [1983] 2 AC 548, 563 (Lord Fraser).
[63] This example is given in EN, para 63.
[64] Case C-303/06 *Coleman v Attridge Law* [2008] ECR I-5603; [2008] IRLR 722.
[65] JCHR (2008–09) paras 81–87.

a narrower interpretation being given to the general prohibition on direct discrimination.[66] Nor was the government persuaded of the need to provide additional protection for those with parenting or caring responsibilities, arguing that, unlike other protected characteristics, 'carer' is not a status, and that measures such as the right of an employee to request flexible working are better suited to supporting carers than the provision of an additional protected characteristic under discrimination law.[67] This does seem to leave carers exposed to discriminatory treatment based on their position as carers as distinct from discrimination based on the characteristics (eg disability or age) of those for whom they care. Those were the assumed facts in *Coleman*, where the parent of a disabled child was said to have been treated less favourably than the parents of non-disabled children by being subjected to harassment and unfair treatment. The case was settled out of court without an opportunity to resolve this issue.

Intersectional or Multiple Discrimination

A Black woman who is unfavourably treated may not know if the reason for such treatment is her race or her gender, or both race and gender. An older disabled worker may not know if the reason for unfavourable treatment is his age or his disability, or a combination of these. This is generally referred to as intersectional discrimination: two or more grounds operate inextricably as the reason for discrimination.[68] In *Bahl v Law Society*[69] the Vice-President of the Law Society claimed that she had been discriminated against both on the ground that she was Asian and on the ground that she was a woman. The employment tribunal held that she could compare herself to a White man, allowing the combined effect of her race and her sex to be considered. The Court of Appeal held that the tribunal should have considered each ground separately and made a judgment in respect of each, even if they were linked. If the tribunal is not satisfied that there is discrimination on grounds of race or of sex, considered independently, it cannot decide that there is nonetheless discrimination on grounds of race and sex when both

---

[66] PBC (EB) 8th sitting col 254 (16 June 2009); Solicitor-General evidence to JCHR, EV 67 at Q 15.

[67] Solicitor-General evidence to JCHR.

[68] 'Multiple discrimination' has been used interchangeably with 'intersectional discrimination' in much of the literature, but this concept is wide enough to cover, as well as intersectional discrimination, cases where there is less favourable treatment on more than one occasion, each on a separate ground. This does not give rise to the same problems as intersectional discrimination.

[69] [2004] EWCA CIV 1070; [2004] IRLR 799.

are taken together.[70] The result of this decision was that the complainant had to choose the ground on which her claim was strongest, although in reality the discriminator would not have treated her unfavourably had she not had both characteristics. She may have difficulty finding the appropriate comparator: she has to compare herself with a Black man if her claim is for sex discrimination, or with a White woman if her claim is for racial discrimination, while in reality it is her characteristic of being both Black and a woman that was the alleged reason for her treatment.

The *Discrimination Law Review* asked for evidence illustrating any difficulties in obtaining legal redress in cases of what was referred to as 'mutltiple discrimination'. A number of organizations provided such evidence. The Labour Government responded by proposing what became section 14 of the EA 2010. This allowed claims where 'because of a combination of two relevant prohibited characteristics, A treats B less favourably than he treats or would treat a person who does not share those characteristics'. This provision was heavily criticised,[71] and was never brought into force.

This need not result in a serious gap in protection.[72] Case law before and after the 2010 Act has recognised that discriminatory treatment of a person may be on two or more grounds. So long as it is established that one prohibited ground had a significant influence on the decision, the treatment will be unlawful.[73] Tribunals do not appear to have been deterred from making findings of discrimination on multiple (intersectional) grounds. The correct approach is for the tribunal to consider each alleged reason for the discrimination in turn and determine whether it was a significant factor.[74] In the cases of indirect discrimination, the Employment Appeal Tribunal indicated that it is possible to bring an indirect discrimination claim that focuses on the combined effect of two different policies, practices or criteria.[75]

Justification of Direct Age Discrimination[76]

If the protected characteristic is age, 'A does not discriminate against B if A can show A's treatment of B to be a proportionate means of achieving a

---

[70] [2004] IRLR 799, para 137, upholding the EAT [2003] IRLR 640.

[71] See 1st edn of this book, pp 61–66.

[72] Robison (2013) 235 EOR 14.

[73] *Nagarajan v London Regional Transport* [1999] IRLR 572; *O'Donoghue v Redcar and Cleveland Borough Council* [2001] IRLR 615, CA.

[74] eg *O'Reilly v BBC* [2011] EqLR 225.

[75] *Ministry of Defence v De Bique* [2010] IRLR 271, EAT.

[76] In addition to this general defence, there are a number of specific exceptions in respect of age discrimination: see pp 113, 136, 145 below.

legitimate aim'.[77] This is similar to, but distinct from, the defence of justifi-cation in respect of indirect discrimination In the leading cases of *Seldon*[78] and *Homer*[79] decided in 2012, the Supreme Court made it clear that the scope for justification of direct age discrimination is narrower than that for indirect discrimination, and that the evidential standard is higher. Direct age discrimination can be justified only if it aims to achieve social policy objectives of a 'public interest' nature, such as 'intergenerational fairness' or the dignity of the person. Section 13(2) of the Equality Act has left it to employers and others who discriminate on age grounds to choose which objectives to pursue, provided that (i) those objectives are legitimate within the meaning of the Framework Employment Directive, (ii) are consistent with the social policy objectives of the state, and (iii) the means used to achieve the objective are proportionate, ie both appropriate to the aim and reasonably necessary to achieve it, The burden of proof is on the discrimi-nator to prove that the discrimination is justified.

A number of examples of legitimate aims can be found in Article 6(1) of the Directive, which says that these include 'legitimate employment policy, labour market and vocational training objectives'.[80] Examples are given:

(a) the setting of special conditions on access to employment and vocational training, employment and occupation, including dismissal and remuneration conditions for young persons, older workers and persons with caring responsi-bilities in order to promote their vocational integration or ensure their protection, (b) the fixing of minimum conditions of age, professional experience or seniority in service for access to employment or to certain advantages linked to employ-ment, (c) fixing of a maximum age for recruitment which is based on the training requirements of the post in question or the need for a reasonable period of employment before retirement.

The evolving case law of the CJEU has developed these.[81] They include (i) promoting access to employment for younger people,[82] (ii) efficient planning of the departure and recruitment of staff,[83] (iii) sharing out employment opportunities fairly between the generations,[84] (iv) ensuring a mix of genera-

---

[77] EA, s 13(2).
[78] *Seldon v Clarkson, Wright and Jakes* [2012] UKSC 16, [2012] EqLR 579.
[79] *Homer v Chief Constable of West Yorkshire Police* [2012] UKSC 15, [2012] EqLR 594.
[80] Art 6(1).
[81] A useful summary of these cases will be found in the judgment of Lady Hale in *Seldon*, para 50.
[82] Case C-411/05 *Palacios de la Villa v Cortefield Servicios SA* [2009] ICR 111; Case C-555/07 *Kücükdeveci v Swedex GmBH 7 Co KG* [2011] CMLR 703
[83] Joined Cases C-159/10 and C-160/10 *Fuchs and another v Land Hessen* [2011] 3 CMLR 1299.
[84] Case C-341/08 *Petersen v Berufungsausschuss für Hahnärtze etc* [2010] 2 CMLR 830.

tions of staff so as to promote the exchange of experience and new ideas,[85] and (v) rewarding experience.[86] The gravity of the effect upon the employees discriminated against has to be weighed against the importance of the legitimate aims in assessing the necessity.[87]

It was found in *Homer* (discussed p 115 below) that justification of indirect age discrimination is not limited to the tests for justifying direct age discrimination. This can include reasons which are specific to the business needs of the employer, such as the need to reduce costs or improve competitiveness. Such individual reasons are not legitimate aims for the purposes of direct discrimination.

What has to be justified is the treatment of the age group to which the individual belongs. For example, educational experts have argued that lifelong learning should meet the different needs of four main groups: those under 25, 25–50, 50–75 and 75+.[88] 'Bright lines' of this kind might subject an individual just under or above the line (eg 24 or 26, 49 or 51, or 76) to a detriment and be degrading to individual dignity. However, in the context of Article 14 ECHR, the House of Lords has accepted that bright lines discriminating between different age groups are justifiable. In *Reynolds*, the claimant for Jobseeker's Allowance was in the 18–24 age range and so was paid at a lower rate than a person aged 25 or over. Their Lordships accepted that persons under the age of 25 could legitimately be expected to have lower earnings expectations and lower living costs than older persons so as to justify them being treated differently as a group, even though the claimant herself was a single mother who had higher needs. Lord Hoffmann said:

> [A] line must be drawn somewhere. All that is necessary is that it should reflect a difference between the substantial majority of people on either side of the line. …
> The objective justification [is] the need for legal certainty and a workable rule.[89]

Under the Equality Act 'bright line' policies and practices in relation to age can be justified if they are shown to be a proportionate means of achieving a legitimate aim, ie both appropriate and necessary to achieve that aim.

The language of section 13(2) of the Equality Act requires an evidence-

---

[85] Joined Cases C-250/09 and C-268/09 *Gerogiev v Technicheski Universitet Sofia* [2011] 2 CMLR 178.

[86] Joined Cases C-297/10 and C-298/10 *Hennigs v Eisenbahn-Bunmdesamt Land Berlin v Mai* [2011] ECR.

[87] *Fuchs* (above n 83).

[88] Schuller and Watson (2009) ch 5 provide demographic, economic and social evidence to support this categorisation.

[89] *R (Reynolds) v Secretary of State for Work and Pensions* [2005] UKHL 37; [2006] 1 AC 173, para 41; See too Lord Rodger, para 45, and Lord Walker, paras 49–65 for an analysis of the scope of Art 14 ECHR.

based approach—to a high standard of proof—in deciding what is 'legitimate' and 'proportionate' in terms of age discrimination.[90]

INDIRECT DISCRIMINATION

Harmonisation

Direct and indirect discrimination are mutually exclusive. They are two separate statutory wrongs, with different criteria and different remedies. They have to be separately pleaded, proved and ruled upon.[91] Direct discrimination aims to achieve formal equality of treatment; one person must not be less favourably treated than another because of a prohibited characteristic. Apart from age discrimination and discrimination arising from disability, it cannot be justified. Indirect discrimination aims to achieve substantive equality.[92] In the words of Lady Hale, it is 'an attempt to level the playing field by subjecting to scrutiny requirements which look neutral on their face but in reality work to the comparative disadvantage of people with a particular protected characteristic'.[93] It is subject to a defence of justification (see below). The origins of this concept are described in chapter 1.

As defined in section 19 of the Equality Act, indirect discrimination occurs where an apparently neutral provision, criterion or practice is applied by a person (A) against another (B), and puts or would put B and persons with whom B shares a prohibited characteristic at a particular disadvantage when compared with persons who do not share that characteristic. It is concerned not with A's treatment of B because of a prohibited characteristic, but with the adverse impact or effects on the group (eg women or an ethnic minority) to which B belongs. Indirect discrimination can be justified if A shows that the provision, criterion or practice is 'a proportionate means of achieving a legitimate aim'. An example given in the Explanatory Notes[94] is that of a woman forced to leave her job because her employer operates a practice that staff must work in a shift pattern which she is unable to comply with because she needs to look after her children at particular times of the day, and no allowance is made to cater for those needs. This would put women as a group at a disadvantage compared to men, because they

---

[90] *R (Age Concern England) v Secretary of Stae for Business, Enterprise and Regulatory Reform* [2009] IRLR 373.

[91] *R (on the application of Elias) v Secretary of State for Defence* [2006] IRLR 934, CA, per Mummery LJ, paras 117–18; *R (on the application of E) v Governing Body of the JFS* [2009] UKSC 15, per Baroness Hale, para 57.

[92] Barnard and Hepple (2000) 564. See p 12 above on the origins of the concept.

[93] *Homer v Chief Constable of West Yorkshire Police* [2012] EqLR 594, para 17.

[94] Para 81.

are more likely to be responsible for childcare than men. The employer will have indirectly discriminated against her unless it can be shown that the practice is justified.[95]

Prior to the Equality Act, there were no fewer than four definitions of indirect discrimination. First, the SDA (sex discrimination) and RRA (race discrimination) originally stated that there must be a 'requirement or condition' that applies to both sexes or different racial groups, but the proportion of one sex or racial group who 'can comply' with it is 'considerably smaller' than the proportion of the other sex or racial group who can comply. There was a defence that the requirement or condition is justifiable irrespective of the sex or racial group to whom it applies. The reference to a 'requirement or condition' was restrictively interpreted. It had to be mandatory and not discretionary: for example, a candidate for the job of legal assistant in the civil service failed to prove indirect discrimination because he could not show that criteria such as knowledge of the English language, British nationality and age were mandatory.[96]

There also was considerable uncertainty as to how disparate impact was to be established. There were two questions: (i) what is the appropriate pool of comparators who 'can comply' with the requirement (eg is it the whole workforce or a particular section of the workforce)? And (ii) is it a requirement with which a 'considerably smaller' proportion of women than men 'can comply' (the 'disparate impact' question)?[97] The test of 'considerably smaller' was controversial.[98] For example, it was never clear whether, in addition to making a comparison between the proportion of men and women able to satisfy (or 'can comply' with) the provision (the qualifiers), a comparison should also be made of the proportion of men and women who are unable to satisfy the requirement (the non-qualifiers). The latter comparison could produce a very different statistical result from the former. The first definition of indirect discrimination led to the courts placing great weight on statistics, which may be difficult to collect, particularly in the absence of a statutory duty to monitor, and the strong opposition in some EU Member States to the collection of ethnic data. Although this was less of a problem in Britain, the courts and tribunals found it difficult to interpret statistics correctly, and controversially resorted to taking judicial notice of social facts without supporting evidence. The emphasis placed on statistical evidence in sex discrimination cases contrasted with the approach taken by the Court of Justice to the concept of indirect discrimination in the

---

[95] See *Edwards v London Underground (No 2)* [1999] ICR 494, CA.

[96] *Perera v Civil Service Commisssion* [1983] ICR 428, CA.

[97] For discussion of the case law see Barnard and Hepple (2000) 570–71; Monaghan (2013) para 6-285.

[98] See Barnard and Hepple (2000) 570–72.

field of free movement of persons, where conditions imposed by national law were regarded as indirectly discriminatory, although applicable irrespective of nationality, if they placed migrant EU workers at a 'particular disadvantage'.[99]

The second definition of indirect discrimination was introduced into the SDA[100] as a result of Burden of Proof Directive 97/80/EC. This largely codified the case law of the Court of Justice on sex discrimination. It differed from the first meaning in two ways. First, it did not require proof of a 'requirement or condition' but instead applied to an apparently neutral 'provision, criterion or practice'. Secondly, it was not necessary to show that the complainant 'cannot comply' with the provision, but the provision, criterion or practice had to be 'to the detriment of a considerably larger proportion of women than of men'. This retained the statistical approach.

The third definition of indirect discrimination was used in the Framework Employment Directive and was applied, in relation to employment, in the Religion or Belief regulations,[101] the Sexual Orientation regulations[102] and the Age regulations.[103] These removed the need to show that a 'larger proportion' of persons of the complainant's group were detrimentally affected, and introduced the test of 'particular disadvantage' adapted from nationality law. This meaning also applied to indirect race discrimination falling under the Race Directive, but the first definition of indirect discrimination continued to apply in areas not covered by the Race Directive. The Directive did not expressly apply to colour discrimination, and so anomalously the first definition under the RRA applied to colour discrimination, while the third definition applied to other forms of race discrimination unless it could be proved that colour was simply a pretext for discrimination on grounds of race or ethnic origin. The third meaning is the one that has now been adopted in section 19 of the Equality Act; it is discussed below.

The fourth definition was introduced by section 45(3) of the Equality Act 2006 in relation to indirect discrimination on grounds of religion or belief in non-employment fields. It was similar to the third meaning, but the comparator group could be some or all others not of the same religion or belief of the complainant; so a Muslim could choose whether to make the comparison with Christians or Jews or atheists, so long as the circumstances as between the complainant's group and the other group were materially the same. The defence of justification was differently worded (and apparently

---

[99] Case C-237/94 *O'Flynn v Adjudication Officer* [1996] ECR I-2617, paras 18–19.
[100] Sex Discrimination (Indirect Discrimination and Burden of Proof) Regulations 2001, SI 2001/2660, reg 2 (this applied to claims from 12 October 2001 to 1 October 2005).
[101] Reg 3(1)(b).
[102] Ibid.
[103] Ibid.

less rigorous) so as to allow indirectly discriminatory measures if these could be reasonably justified by reference to matters other than the complainant's religion or belief.

Section 19 of the Equality Act repeals all the earlier definitions and introduces a single, harmonised definition of indirect discrimination. This applies to all prohibited characteristics. It was not necessary to include pregnancy and maternity because they are already covered by indirect sex discrimination against a woman.[104]

Indirect disability discrimination is now included (below).

Elements of the Tort

The requirements of the newly formulated tort are the following:

(1) A person (A) applies a 'provision, criterion or practice' (shortened here to 'provision') against another (B). A provision does not have to be mandatory. So, British Airways' policy of exercising discretion when making decisions whether to allow a worker to work either 50 per cent or 75 per cent of full-time hours, depending on their personal circumstances, was held by the EAT to be a 'provision'.[105] Other examples are seniority and promotion rules, age rules, word-of-mouth recruiting practices, qualifying periods, different terms for full-time and part-time workers, school uniform requirements, and residence requirements relating to social benefits.

(2) A applies it, or would apply it, to persons with whom B does not share the protected characteristic. In other words, the provision is facially neutral.

(3) It puts, or would put, persons with whom B shares the characteristic at a particular disadvantage when compared with persons with whom he does not share it. This involves a comparison between groups in order to establish disparate impact and, as under earlier legislation, there must be no material difference between the circumstances relating to each case.[106] It is no longer necessary to determine the pool of persons to whom the provision applies and then ascertain whether a 'considerably smaller proportion' of the complainant's group (eg women) than the comparator group (eg men) is able to satisfy the provision, or whether a 'considerably larger' group is detrimentally affected. All that has to

---

[104] This was confirmed by the Solicitor-General: PBC (EB) 8th sitting col 284 (16 June 2009).

[105] *British Airways plc v Starmer* [2005] IRLR 862, EAT.

[106] EA, s 23(1).

be shown is that a provision puts or would put persons belonging to the complainant's protected group at a 'particular disadvantage' when compared with others.[107] This may be supported by statistical evidence, but it is not essential. Hypothetical comparisons may be made without the need to prove the actual state of affairs using statistics. Broader evidence of disadvantage is admissible than the pool in question. For example, if most of the women in a particular job are in fact able to do shift working in unsocial hours, but the complainant is not because of her childcare responsibilities, it can be demonstrated that the provision relating to shift working 'would put' women in general at a disadvantage, and so would amount to indirect discrimination unless justified. This broadening is important in opening up opportunities for women who may have been deterred from applying for a job where it is known that inflexible shift working takes place.

The requirement of group disadvantage' does not always sit easily with the exercise of fundamental human rights such as the right under Article 9 of the ECHR to manifest one's religion or belief. In *Eweida v United Kingdom*[108] a Christian counter clerk was prevented from wearing a cross visible over her uniform because of the employer's general policy of prohibiting the wearing of jewellery. The Court of Appeal upheld a finding that this policy did not put Christians as a group at a 'particular disadvantage' compared to non-Christians. The Court said that solitary disadvantage is not enough, Group disadvantage could not be shown in this case because the visible display of a cross is not a requirement of the Christian faith.[109] However, the ECtHR took a different approach. It held that it was sufficient to amount to a 'manifestation of religion or belief' for the act in question to be 'intimately linked to the religion or belief'. Contrary to the view of the Court of Appeal, it held that there 'is no requirement on the applicant to establish that he or she acted in fulfillment of a duty mandated by the religion in question'. A similar conclusion on this point was reached in three other cases, but in these, unlike *Eweida*, a defence of justification succeeded (below).[110] It follows that it is no longer necessary in a claim of indirect discrimination or belief to prove group disadvantage resulting from a restriction on the right to manifest belief.[111] The degree of group disadvantage

---

[107] *Homer v Chief Constable of West Yorkshire Police*, above, per Lady Hale at para 14.
[108] [2013] EqLR 264.
[109] *Eweida v Britis Airways plc* [2010] IRLR 322, CA, per Sedley LJ at 324.
[110] *Chaplain v United Kingdom* (nurse not permitted to wear crucifx outside her uniform), *Macfarlane v United Kingdom* (Christian counsellor refused to counsel same-sex couples), *Ladele v United Kingdom* (registrar refused to carry out same-sex civil partnerships).
[111] *Mba v London Borough of Merton* [2014] EqLR 51, CA (Christian care officer required to work on Sundays).

in these cases involving fundamental rights goes to the justification of indirect discrimination (below) rather than whether a prima facie case of discrimination was established.

(4) It puts, or would put, B at that disadvantage. This has the effect of limiting the class of complainants to those who are affected by the provision.

(5) A cannot show it to be a proportionate means of achieving a legitimate aim (see below).

Knowledge, Intention and Motive

It is not necessary to prove that there was a discriminatory intention or motive. Intention is, however, relevant to remedies for indirect discrimination. Intentionality may be inferred from evidence that the discriminator wanted to exclude a particular group, or knew that unjustified indirect discrimination would result from the provision.[112] The original legislation prevented any award of compensation in cases of unintentional indirect discrimination. But this was amended, first in relation to sex discrimination, following several tribunal rulings that effective compensation was required under EU law, and later in relation to race discrimination. The Religion or Belief regulations, Sexual Orientation regulations and Age regulations allowed an award of compensation to be made if, having regard to the other orders available, it was just and equitable to do so. The Equality Act has harmonised the law upwards across the board by extending the right to compensation to all protected characteristics. An employment tribunal[113] or court[114] may award compensation or damages in the case of unintentional indirect discrimination, but only after first considering whether to make a declaration as to the rights of the parties, or to make an appropriate recommendation. For example, a recommendation could be made that specific steps be taken by the employer to obviate or reduce the adverse effect of the discriminatory provision on the complainant and on any other person.[115] If considered to be just and equitable, the tribunal or court could then, in addition, award compensation or damages, including for injury to feelings and any actual financial loss suffered by the complainant as a result of the indirect discrimination.

---

[112] *Walker Ltd v Hussain* [1996] IRLR 11, EAT (award of compensation to Muslims who were disciplined for taking time off during Eid, upheld).

[113] EA, s 124(4), (5).

[114] EA, s 119(5), (6).

[115] EA, s 124(3).

Justification

Section 19(2)(d) of the Equality Act places the burden of proof on the discriminator to show, by way of defence, that the indirectly discriminatory provision is 'a proportionate means of achieving a legitimate aim'.[116] This harmonises the test of justification so as to extend this aspect of the third definition of indirect discrimination (above) across all strands.

The significance of the proportionality test can be understood only by considering the development of the defence over time. The proportionality test means that the lax earlier decisions on justification should be considered unreliable. The original British legislation, under the SDA and RRA, simply required the respondent to prove that the provision was 'justifiable' irrespective of the sex or race of the person to whom it was applied. In the early case law this was interpreted in a way that was similar to the American test of 'business necessity'. There was said to be a 'heavy onus' in the sense that the tribunal had to be satisfied that the provision was 'necessary' and not merely convenient. The tribunal had to weigh up all the circumstances, including the discriminatory effect of the provision, and see whether there was some other non-discriminatory method of achieving the object.[117] However, this was later watered down to say that the burden of proof was the normal one in a civil case of a balance of probabilities, and 'necessary' did not mean something without which the employer could not operate. So a 'no beards' rule that had the effect of excluding Sikhs from employment in a chocolate factory was considered justifiable on grounds of hygiene, even though the employer did not bar the wearing of moustaches, whiskers or sideburns, and had not made any attempt to allow for the covering of facial hair.[118] The Court of Appeal went even further, equating 'justifiable' with 'reasonable' and requiring the employer only to adduce 'adequate grounds … which would be acceptable to right-thinking people as sound and tolerable reasons'.[119] So a requirement of 'managerial experience' in order to qualify for student bursaries, which had an adverse impact on West African applicants who lacked managerial experience because of direct discrimination, was upheld.[120] A different result should now be reached on similar facts to those in these cases under the proportionality test (below).

---

[116] EA, s 19(2)(d).
[117] *Steel v Union of Post Office Workers* [1978] ICR 181, EAT, 187–88; and generally Hepple (1983b) 82–83.
[118] *Panesar v Nestle Co Ltd* [1980] ICR 144, CA; *Singh v Rowntree Mackintosh Ltd* [1979] ICR 554. See now the cases on indirect religious discrimination (below).
[119] *Ojutiku v Manpower Services Commission* [1982] ICR 661 at 668.
[120] Ibid.

The Burden of Proof Directive, 'largely declaratory of the case law of the Court of Justice' on sex discrimination,[121] stated that a provision, criterion or practice is indirectly discriminatory unless it is 'appropriate and necessary and can be justified by objective factors unrelated to sex'. The Race Directive and Framework Employment Directive adopted similar definitions. However, the implementing British legislation used an abbreviated formulation—'a proportionate means of achieving a legitimate aim'—which has now been extended to all strands by section 19(2)(d). Despite the difference in wording, the British legislation must be construed consistently with the EU definitions as interpreted by the Court of Justice. During the parliamentary debates the Liberal Democrats, expressing the concerns of various campaign groups, attempted to revert to the wording of the EU directives. However, the Solicitor-General gave her assurances that 'proportionate' has the same meaning as 'appropriate and necessary'. This does not entail that the means used must be the only way of achieving the legitimate aim: 'it is sufficient that the means are not more discriminatory than any other means that could have been chosen to achieve the same end'.[122]

When applying the proportionality test, courts and tribunals would do well to pay close attention to the guidance given by the Court of Appeal in *Elias*.[123] Mrs Elias was a British subject, resident in Hong Kong, who had been held in a Japanese prisoner-of-war camp. She was told that she did not qualify for compensation under a British government scheme because she was not born in the UK, nor did she have a parent or grandparent born in the UK. This criterion was clearly indirectly discriminatory on grounds of national origin. The Court of Appeal held that although the aim of limiting the number of claimants for compensation was legitimate, the criteria were not proportionate to the end to be achieved. Lord Justice Mummery helpfully set out a number of principles, which may be summarised as follows:

(1) The onus is on the discriminator to justify the provision, criterion or practice.
(2) To discharge the burden of proof the discriminator must show that he addressed the issue of indirect discrimination when formulating the provision, particularly in the case of a public authority under a positive duty to promote equality.
(3) The standard of scrutiny should be 'strict' or 'rigorous', particularly when the indirect discrimination is closely related in substance to the direct form of discrimination.

---

[121] Recital 18 of the directive.
[122] PBC (EB) 8th session col 283 (16 June 2009).
[123] *R (on the application of Elias) v Secretary of State for Defence* [2006] IRLR 934, CA.

(4) The objective of the measure must correspond to a real need of the employer or service provider, and the means used must be appropriate and necessary with a view to achieving the objective: the need must be weighed against the seriousness of the detriment to the disadvantaged group.

(5) In determining proportionality, a three-stage test is appropriate: (i) Is the objective sufficiently important to justify limiting the fundamental right to equality? (ii) Is the measure rationally connected to the objective? and (iii) Are the means no more than necessary to accomplish the objective?

In *Elias* the critical facts leading to the failure of the justification defence were that (i) the Ministry was under a positive statutory duty to eliminate discrimination; (ii) the compensation scheme had not been properly thought through; and (iii) the criteria produced anomalous results. In *JFS*[124] it was not necessary for the majority of the Supreme Court to consider indirect discrimination because of their finding of direct discrimination. However, Lord Mance[125] (with whom Baroness Hale and Lords Kerr and Clarke agreed)[126] said that had the matter arisen they would have held that the defence of proportionality failed because there was no evidence relating to the extent to which the criteria enabled the school to succeed in its stated aim of inculcating Orthodox Judaism. Lords Hope and Walker, who dissented on the direct discrimination issue, also held that JFS had not shown that its policy was a proportionate means of achieving the legitimate aim of promoting the religious ethos of the faith school. There was no evidence that the school's governing body had given thought to the question of whether less discriminatory means could be adopted which would not undermine the religious ethos of the school.[127] The two other dissenting judges, however, were satisfied that the criteria for selection were proportionate because to allow applications from anyone who was not Jewish according to Orthodox rules would run counter the central aims of the school and was 'fraught with difficulty'.[128] All the Supreme Court judges approved and purported to follow the *Elias* criteria.[129] It is clear from six of the judgments that there must always be evidence that the decision-maker considered the discriminatory impact of the measure and whether there were other, less discriminatory ways of achieving the objective. This is important in meeting the aim of mainstreaming equality into decision-making. Lords Brown and Rodger

---

[124] See pp 48 and 75 above.
[125] *R (on the application of E) v Governing Body of the JFS* [2009] UKSC 15, paras 93–103. Lord Phillips PSC did not examine this issue (para 51).
[126] Ibid, paras 71, 123–24, 154.
[127] Ibid, paras 212–15, 236.
[128] Ibid, paras 233, 255–56, 258.
[129] See too *Homer v Chief Constable of West Yorkshire*, above, para 20.

(dissenting), who found that there was proportionality, made a generalised assumption as to how a faith school has to operate,[130] and did not apply a strict standard where the justification was closely related to the form of direct discrimination in issue.

The underlying difficulty concerning justification of indirect discrimination, which the Equality Act does not resolve, is that this issue often arises in the context of polycentric disputes, where decisions may have wide and unforeseen repercussions for many persons beyond the immediate parties.[131] An example is *Allen v GMB*,[132] in which an employment tribunal found that a union had indirectly discriminated against female members employed by a local authority when negotiating implementation of the local government single status agreement. The union had agreed to a low back-pay settlement for women with equal pay claims so as to leave as much money as possible for future pay increases for all workers and to give greater priority to pay protection for predominantly male groups whose jobs had been assessed at a lower level under the single status scheme. The 'provision, criterion or practice' identified by the employment tribunal was the 'balance struck' by the union between the interests of the various groups within the membership. The EAT allowed the union's appeal against the finding of indirect discrimination, but the Court of Appeal restored the tribunal decision, in the process giving little guidance to unions as to how they can justifiably balance the interests of various groups. This has had the perverse effect of making unions more reluctant to negotiate collective agreements over equal pay: they now fear crippling claims against them brought by some individuals, imposing on unions greater risks than on employers, who are responsible for taking decisions on pay and grading schemes. The result is more individual litigation but little movement in closing the overall gap between women's and men's pay.[133] Findings of indirect discrimination and justification require an evaluation of social facts and the representation of interest groups beyond the adversarial parties. This makes disputes relating to indirect discrimination more amenable to alternative mechanisms such as collective bargaining and arbitration than to individual litigation.

---

[130] *R v Secretary of State for Employment, ex parte EOC* [1994] IRLR 194, HL; cf *R v Secretary of State for Employment, ex parte Seymour-Smith* [1997] IRLR 315, HL.
[131] See Hepple (1983b) 83–84.
[132] [2008] IRLR 690, CA.
[133] See p 116 below.

DISABILITY DISCRIMINATION

Why Special Provisions?

The definition of discrimination because of disability differs significantly from definitions relating to other protected characteristics. The differences between men and women (pregnancy apart), Black and White people, persons with different sexual orientations, or of different faiths or age groups are generally treated as irrelevant. But the law does not expect disabled people to be treated in exactly the same way as those who are not disabled. The reason for this is that formal equality, comparing a disabled person with others, would not result in genuinely equal treatment or equality of outcomes. The Equality Act recognises that disabled people have special needs. Like the DDA 1995 before it, the Act allows more favourable treatment of disabled people than others, and imposes duties on employers and service providers to make reasonable adjustments to cater for their needs. A new provision in the Equality Act improves protection for disabled people who are treated unfavourably because of something arising in consequence of their disability. The Act also applies the concept of indirect discrimination (above) to disability.

More Favourable Treatment

It is not direct discrimination to treat a disabled person more favourably than a person who is not disabled.[134] This is additional to the duty to make reasonable adjustments (below), and prevents a non-disabled person from challenging positive measures taken by an employer or service provider to help a disabled person. So, if an employer provides special equipment to a disabled person to do their job, a non-disabled employee cannot demand the same equipment.

Discrimination Arising from Disability

A new provision, in section 15(1) of the Equality Act states that:

A person (A) discriminates against a disabled person (B) if—

(a) A treats B unfavourably because of something arising in consequence of A's disability, and

---

[134] EA, s 13(3). The wording, improving on the draft Bill, was the result of a Liberal Democrat amendment: PBC (EB) 8th sitting cols 256–58 (16 June 2009).

(b) A cannot show that the treatment is a proportionate means of achieving a legitimate aim.

This replaces the provisions of the DDA 1995 that aimed to protect disabled people from being discriminated against for a reason related to their disability. It was necessary for the disabled person to show that they had been treated less favourably than other people to whom the disability-related provision did not apply. The person who treated the disabled person less favourably could then seek to justify this treatment.[135] This provision was undermined by the decision of the House of Lords in *London Borough of Lewisham v Malcolm*.[136] Malcolm, who had been diagnosed with schizophrenia, was granted a secure tenancy by Lewisham Council. One of the conditions of the tenancy was that he could not sublet the premises. He did so without the consent of the Council, and thus ceased to be a secure tenant. This happened at a time when he had not been taking his medication; his behaviour had changed, and he had lost his job. Lewisham discovered that he had moved out and had sublet the premises. It served notice to quit, and subsequently issued proceedings for possession. The DDA 1995 precluded a manager of premises from discriminating against a disabled person by evicting them or subjecting them to any other detriment for a reason related to their disability. Malcolm argued that he was a disabled person and that the subletting was a consequence of his disability. The county court judge granted a possession order, holding that Malcolm was not a disabled person and that his actions were not caused by his illness. She suggested, without deciding, that there could be no discrimination unless the Council had knowledge of the disability. The Court of Appeal, by a majority, upheld an appeal on all these issues. However, the House of Lords allowed the Council's appeal and restored the possession order. The key issue was whether the correct comparator was (a) other tenants or (b) other tenants who had sublet their flats. A majority in the Lords held that it was the latter, overruling earlier authority in the Court of Appeal.[137] The effect of this was to require 'like for like' comparisons in disability cases in the same way as in those related to other protected characteristics.

Disability campaigners persuaded the government that this ruling would severely restrict disability discrimination law, and was contrary to the intention of Parliament in the DDA to cater for the special needs of disabled persons. In November 2008, the Office for Disability Issues (ODI) published a consultation paper[138] suggesting the solution of replacing disability-related

---

[135] DDA 1995, s 5(1) (employment), s 20(1) (goods, provisions, services).
[136] [2008] UKHL 45; [2008] IRLR 700.
[137] *Clark v Novacold Ltd* [1999] EWCA civ 1091; [1999] ICR 951.
[138] ODI, *Improving Protection from Disability Discrimination*, November 2009.

discrimination with the model of indirect discrimination. A majority of disability organisations and the EHRC supported the extension of indirect discrimination but believed that it could not be relied upon alone 'to recognise often unique instances of disability discrimination or to achieve the goals of harmonised protection and simplification'.[139] The Employers' Forum on Disability and many other organisations proposed that the need for a comparator should be removed, a view with which the House of Commons' Work and Pensions committee agreed.[140] The government accepted this proposal.

Section 15 of the Act thus does not restate the provisions of the DDA 1995. There is no requirement for a comparator. All that the disabled person has to prove is that he or she has been 'unfavourably' treated.. As in the case of pregnancy and maternity discrimination (above), depriving a person of something they value would constitute 'unfavourable' treatment. A visually impaired person who is not allowed to bring a guide dog into a restaurant passes this threshold simply by showing that this was detrimental to him or her, without having to make a comparison with the treatment of other dog owners. The new provision also simplifies the law by substituting the requirement that the detriment must be 'because of something arising in consequence of [their] disability' in place of the DDA's need to show a reason 'which relates to the disabled person's disability'. In *Malcolm* there was some disagreement between the Law Lords as to how close the connection had to be. The test is now clearly a causal one, which can usually be answered by asking whether 'but for' the disability this would have arisen. On this test, the decision in a case on facts similar to those in *Malcolm* would now depend on whether the court or tribunal is satisfied that the tenant would not have behaved so irresponsibly as to sublet his flat and move elsewhere had it not been for his mental illness.

Another controversial issue that has been settled by the Act is whether knowledge of the disability is required for there to be discrimination. In *Malcolm* all the Law Lords were agreed that knowledge is required, but they differed as to whether knowledge could be imputed and, if so, to what extent. There was disagreement among disability campaigners on this issue. Some argued that a knowledge requirement would be used by employers to create a 'culture of ignorance in which they can be less than proactive in asking questions and finding out details about their employees in order to provide themselves with a defence'.[141] However, the government said that it was necessary to maintain a balance 'between the rights of disabled

[139] EHRC response to *Improving Protection from Disability Discrimination*, January 2009.
[140] HC 158, third report of the session 2008–09, 29 April 2009, paras 31, 34.
[141] Hansard HL vol 716 col 540 (19 January 2010) (Baroness Warsi on a Conservative amendment, later withdrawn, to remove the knowledge requirement).

people and the interests of those with duties'.[142] Section 15(2) of the Act accordingly provides that there is no discrimination if 'A shows that A did not know, and could not reasonably have been expected to know, that B had the disability'. The Court of Appeal has held that in order to have the requisite knowledge of a disability the employer must know the answers to three separate questions: (1) Does the employee have an impairment? (2) Does it have a substantial adverse effect in his or her ability to carry out normal day to day activities? (3) Is that effect long term?[143]

There is a defence of justification in respect of this kind of discrimination, now defined in the same way as in respect of direct age discrimination (above): the discriminator must show that 'the treatment is a proportionate means of achieving a legitimate aim'.[144] For example, the licensee of a public house who ejects a person because of that person's violent behaviour arising from a disability may be able to show that this was a proportionate means of achieving the legitimate aim of protecting other patrons.[145]

Duty to Make Reasonable Adjustments for Disabled People

This has been described as the 'cornerstone of protection' for disabled people.[146] The duty arises where a disabled person is put at a 'substantial disadvantage. … in comparison with persons who are not disabled' by a provision, criterion or practice.[147] There are three situations in which reasonable steps must be taken to avoid the disadvantage. The first covers changes in the way things are done, for example providing sign language interpreters, a palantypist or an induction loop to ensure that hearing-impaired delegates at a public conference are not substantially disadvantaged.[148] The second covers changes in the built environment, for example providing a ramp for wheelchair users, or special furniture which will enable them to work alongside colleagues.[149] The third is the provision of auxiliary aids, such as computer software, or auxiliary services.[150] Where the first or third requirement relates to the provision of information, reasonable steps include

---

[142] Hansard HL vol 716 col 541 (19 January 2010) (Baroness Royall).
[143] *Gallop v Newport City Council* [2013] EWCA Vic 1583.
[144] EA, s 15(1)(b).
[145] EN, para 70.
[146] Hansard HL vol 716 col 561 (19 January 2010) (Baroness Thornton).
[147] EA, s 20.
[148] EA, s 20(3); EN, para 86.
[149] EA, s 20(4), (9), (10).
[150] EA, s 20(5), (11).

ensuring that the information is provided in an accessible format, such as large print or Braille.[151]

Failure to comply with any one of the reasonable adjustment requirements amounts to discrimination against the disabled person to whom the duty is owed.[152] An example given in the Explanatory Notes is the refusal of an employer to provide a modified keyboard or voice-activated software to an employee who develops carpal tunnel syndrome, which makes it difficult to use a standard keyboard. This could constitute actionable discrimination.[153] But no other action can be taken for failure to comply with the duty.[154]

These provisions replicate similar ones in the DDA 1995, but also make some changes to provide consistency, for example extending the third requirement to employment, and referring throughout to 'provision, criterion or practice' consistently with the Framework Employment Directive. The DDA provided for different thresholds: 'substantial disadvantage' in relation to employment,[155] but 'impossible or unreasonably difficult' in relation to use of a service.[156] The Equality Act now provides for the single threshold of 'substantial disadvantage' in all fields. Regulations[157] have been made relating to the matters to be taken into account in deciding whether it is reasonable for a step to be taken, and on a number of other related issues.[158]

It is necessary to consult six different schedules to the Act[159] to ascertain the precise circumstances in which the duty to make reasonable adjustments applies. For example, the duty applies in different ways to public transportation in different types of vehicle.[160] Broadly speaking, the specific duties fall into two categories. First there are specific duties that are reactive, that is, they are only triggered where a provision, criterion or practice substantially disadvantages a particular disabled person. For example, the duty to make alterations to the physical features of the common parts (eg the entrance hall) of let residential premises owned on a commonhold basis applies only if a

---

[151] EA, s 20(6). this was introduced following amendments proposed by Lord Low of Dalston, who produced evidence of widespread non-compliance with the guidance on these matters in the DRC Code of Practice: Hansard HL vol 716 col 555 (19 January 2010).

[152] EA, s 21(1), (2).

[153] EN, para 88.

[154] EA, s 21(3).

[155] DDA 1995, s 6(1).

[156] DDA 1995, s 21(1).

[157] The Equality Act 2010 (Disability) Regulations , SI 2010 No 2128.

[158] EA, s 22.

[159] EA, s 31 and sched 2 (services and public functions); s 38 and sched 4 (premises); s 83 and sched 8 (work); s 98 and sched 13 (education); s 107 and sched 15 (associations); s189 and sched 21 (supplementary).

[160] EA, sched 2.

request is made by or on behalf of a disabled person.[161] Another example is that an employer is not required to anticipate the needs of potential disabled employees or job applicants.[162] The employer must have actual or imputed knowledge that an 'interested disabled person'[163] is or may be an applicant for the work in question, or in other aspects of employment has a disability or is likely to be placed at a substantial disadvantage.[164] A new provision states that an employer must not ask about a job applicant's health before offering work.[165] The reason for this provision is that pre-employment questionnaires can be a powerful deterrent for potential applicants who are disabled, often leading them to hide their disability or not to apply.[166] The new provision is subject to a number of exceptions, such as finding out whether a job applicant can participate in a pre-offer assessment. The duty can be enforced by the EHRC, and can also be used in evidence in a direct disability discrimination claim where the applicant is rejected.[167]

Secondly, there are anticipatory duties, such as requiring service providers and persons exercising public functions to take proactive steps to make their services accessible. For example, the manager of a large shop might be expected to install a ramp, automatic doors, hearing induction loops, and to allow guide dogs.[168] Another example is that a police officer might have to arrange for a sign language interpreter or other aid when interviewing a deaf person.[169] The purpose is to provide access to a service as close as is reasonably possible to achieve the standard normally offered to the public at large. Associations must anticipate the needs of members and guests and make appropriate reasonable adjustments, for example arranging meetings in accessible rooms.[170] The duties to make adjustments in the field of education, although limited, are also anticipatory, requiring schools to ensure that disabled pupils are not at a substantial disadvantage compared to non-disabled pupils. For example, a school could negotiate special arrangements for disabled pupils taking examinations or provide Braille texts for

---

[161] EA, sched 4. This is a new requirement for disability-related alterations.

[162] EA, sched 8.

[163] Tables set out who is an 'interested disabled person' in relation to different categories of 'relevant matters': EA, sched 8, Pt 2.

[164] EA, sched 8, Pt 3, para 20.

[165] EA, s 60, subject to a number of exceptions such as finding out whether the applicant would be able to participate in a pre-offer assessment of their suitability for the work, or to make reasonable adjustments to enable the applicant to participate in the recruitment process.

[166] JCHR (2008–09) para 136.

[167] EA, s 60(2), (4), (5).

[168] EN, para 678.

[169] Ibid.

[170] EA, sched 7.

visually disabled pupils, or replace a revolving door which causes problems for wheelchair users with an automatic one.[171]

Indirect Discrimination

The DDA included a failure to comply with the duty to make reasonable adjustments for a disabled person as a form of discrimination, but did not cover indirect discrimination. The Framework Employment Directive, however, applied to indirect discrimination on all the specified grounds, including disability. This, and the decision in *Malcolm* (above), persuaded the government to extend the coverage of the Act to indirect disability discrimination. This had been proposed by the Cambridge Review.[172] Disability organisations argued that this, coupled with the public sector equality duty, would 'promote better practice amongst employers and service providers making them identify and remove barriers in advance, rather than providing individual solutions to individual problems which the current duty to make reasonable adjustments under the DDA ensures'.

HARASSMENT

There are many forms of unlawful harassment. These include public order offences, and the criminal offence of harassment, which is also a civil wrong, under the Protection from Harassment Act 1997. The latter can be used against harassers who target others on racial, religious, sexual, homophobic or other grounds.[173] The most important provisions are, however, those that form part of equality legislation.

The Equality Act provides a single, uniform definition of harassment. There are three types of harassment under the Act. The first covers unwanted conduct which is related to a relevant protected characteristic and has the purpose or effect of (i) violating the complainant's dignity, or (ii) creating an intimidating, hostile, degrading, humiliating or offensive environment for the complainant.[174] This applies to all the protected characteristics except pregnancy and maternity and marriage and civil partnership. The second type is conduct of a sexual nature or related to gender reassignment

---

[171] EA, sched 13; EN, para 898.

[172] Para 2.32.

[173] See Hepple (2000) 178–83 for a discussion of these and other wrongs; see too Barrett (2010) 194 on recent case law. These must be distinguished from 'hate-speech' crimes (group defamation) such as incitement to racial or religious hatred, which fall outside the scope of this book.

[174] EA, s 26(1).

or sex which has the same purpose or effect as the first type of harassment.[175] The third type is less favourable treatment of someone because they have either rejected or submitted to conduct of a sexual nature or related to gender reassignment or sex.[176] The early law in the UK on this subject was a patchwork, with many inconsistencies between protected grounds.[177] The main defect was that the harassment had to be shown to be discriminatory, ie less favourable, treatment. This led to absurd results: for example, a woman could not complain about pornographic displays at the workplace because a hypothetical man might also have complained, so making the displays gender neutral.[178] Another consequence of the reliance on discrimination law was that there had to be shown to be a 'detriment'. Although this was broadly interpreted as going beyond so-called quid pro quo harassment (eg denying promotion to a woman who refused sexual favours), racial or sexual abuse or insults were usually not regarded as a 'detriment'. Some vulnerable groups (eg those subject to homophobic bullying) were unprotected.

The Race Directive, Framework Employment Directive and Recast Equal Treatment directive necessitated changes in UK law on harassment so as to create a free-standing right. One significant difference between the wording of the EU Directives and the implementing UK legislation was that under the former the definition was conjunctive. The unwanted conduct had to have the purpose or effect both of violating the complainant's dignity and of creating an intimidating, hostile, degrading, humiliating or offensive environment for the complainant. Under the UK legislation, however, the definition was disjunctive, requiring either a violation of dignity or the creation of an intimidating, hostile etc environment. The reason for the wider British definition was that the judicial interpretation of the direct discrimination provisions, influenced by a European Commission Code of Practice[179] in this respect, had been wider than the wording of the EU Directives. The UK Government believed that it could not adopt the narrower definition set out in the directives without violating the non-regression provisions of the directives. For the same reason of non-regression, the Equality Act continues the disjunctive definition. This, as we shall see below, has had some unfortunate consequences in respect of harassment relating to religion or belief and sexual orientation outside the employment field.

The Equality Act requires that the unwanted conduct is 'related to' a

---

[175] EA, s 26(2).

[176] EA, s 26(3).

[177] Cambridge Review (2000) paras 2.50–2.56; Hepple (2000) 177; Monaghan (2013) para 6.507.

[178] *Stewart v Cleveland Guest (Engineering) Ltd* [1994] IRLR 440, EAT.

[179] Attached to Commission recommendation on the protection of dignity of women and men at work 91/131/EEC.

relevant protected characteristic. Earlier UK legislation had required that it be 'on grounds of' the characteristic, and the new wording was introduced in 2008 in order to be consistent with the Recast Equal Treatment Directive.[180] In other words, the unwanted conduct need not be because of the complainant's race, sex, disability, etc; it must simply be related to one of those characteristics. Some harassment not directly of a sexual nature may be related to the complainant's sex.[181] For example, if male colleagues deliberately put office equipment on a high shelf out of a woman's reach, this could be 'related to' her sex because women are on average shorter than men. Moreover, it is not necessary to show less favourable treatment under the first two types of harassment. So the unwanted display of pornographic material at a workplace could now be unlawful even though only women object.[182] The unwanted conduct may relate to the protected characteristic of a person other than the claimant. For example, the harassment of a female colleague may create a hostile working environment for others.

The Equality Act states that in deciding whether the conduct has the purpose or effect of creating an intimidating, hostile etc environment for the complainant, three matters must be taken into account: (i) the perception of the complainant; (ii) the other circumstances of the case; and (iii) whether it is reasonable for the conduct to have that effect.[183] This makes it clear that harassment must be assessed both subjectively (from the complainant's viewpoint) and objectively in all the circumstances (reasonableness). The sensitivity of the complainant is not conclusive. The subjective perception of the complainant has to be weighed against the objective circumstances. The definition under the previous legislation was more ambiguous and possibly violated the non-regression provisions of the directives.[184]

The new provisions do not apply to all the protected characteristics. Harassment because of pregnancy or maternity is excluded, the government's explanation being that this form of harassment would be covered by discrimination against a woman because of sex. Marriage and civil partnership status are also not covered, the government's reason being that there is no evidence of a problem of harassment on these grounds and that, in any event, a civil partner harassed because of their sexual orientation is protected.[185] The JCHR found these arguments unconvincing. The Committee pointed out that the exclusions undermine the clarity and

---

[180] Sex Discrimination Act (Amendment) Regulations 2008, SI 2008/656.
[181] Illustrations are given in *Pearce v Governing Body of Mayfield Secondary School* [2003] UKHL 34; [2003] IRLR 512, such as 'lesbian shit', 'dyke', 'dumb blonde', 'dollybird' and 'floozy'.
[182] EN, para 99.
[183] EA, s 26(4).
[184] Monaghan (2013) para 6.513.
[185] JCHR (2008–09) paras 106–07.

comprehensiveness of the Act, and compel those who suffer these forms of harassment to follow a roundabout route to prove their case.[186] The Cambridge Review argued that there should be a statutory tort of harassment and bullying at work, in which it would not be necessary to prove that the conduct was because of one of the prohibited characteristics. This would avoid the need to establish the motivation of the harasser, although aggravated damages might be made available if the reason was a protected characteristic. This would be an inclusive approach protecting all employees against bullying, but this proposal has not been acted upon.[187]

A more serious exclusion is that the Act, re-enacting earlier legislation, exempts harassment related to religion or belief and sexual orientation from its application to the provision of services, the exercise of public functions,[188] and the disposal, management and occupation of premises.[189] The 'responsible body' of a school (local education authority, governing body, proprietor or managers) cannot be liable for harassment of a pupil because of gender reassignment, religion or belief, or sexual orientation.[190] In effect, these exemptions limit the prohibition on harassment because of religion or belief and sexual orientation to the field of work. This reflects concerns that were expressed during the parliamentary debates on the Equality Act 2006, when the law was being extended beyond the Framework Employment Directive to services, housing and education, relating to the impact on the protection of freedom of religion under Article 9 and freedom of expression under Article 10 ECHR.

The basic problem is that when implementing the Framework Employment Directive, the government went further than required by using a disjunctive definition of harassment.[191] If the same definition were applied outside the field of work, then, using an example given in the debates by Lord Lester,[192] it would be enough for a Jewish tenant of a Christian landlord who displayed a poster on the premises reading 'Belong to Jews for Jesus' to allege simply that his 'dignity' was violated, or that the poster created an 'offensive' environment. Moreover, there were fears that there could be legal challenges to religious practices or symbols such as grace before school meals, or preaching of religious doctrine on issues such as homosexual behaviour. The JCHR was satisfied that harassment on grounds of religion or belief should not be prohibited outside the field of work,

---

[186] JCHR (2008–09) para 108.
[187] Cambridge Review (2000) para 2.56.
[188] EA, s 29(3), (8).
[189] EA, s 34(4).
[190] EA, s 85(3), (10).
[191] See p 98 above.
[192] Hansard HL vol 716 col 577 (25 January 2010).

but considered that harassment on grounds of sexual orientation should be outlawed in all fields.[193] During the debates a number of attempts were made to achieve this objective, but they were rejected by the government on the grounds that a narrower definition of harassment outside the field of work would introduce a two-tier approach involving unnecessary legal complexity, and that there was insufficient evidence of harassment to warrant any extension into those fields.[194] The government maintained, in relation to situations where a teacher harasses a pupil because of gender reassignment or sexual orientation, that this would be 'less favourable' treatment involving a 'detriment', and hence unlawful direct discrimination.[195] In general, a 'detriment' does not include unlawful harassment, so it is not possible to bring a claim for direct discrimination by way of detriment on the same facts.[196] But a convoluted exception to this means that where harassment is not prohibited, for example sexual orientation or gender reassignment harassment in schools, this can amount to a 'detriment'.[197] The government also claimed that the public sector equality duty would ensure that schools take proactive steps to prevent all forms of bullying and harassment of pupils, including homophobic and transphobic harassment by pupil on pupil.[198] However, the duty to advance equality is not directly enforceable by individuals who have suffered harassment. Arguably the Human Rights Act could provide a remedy where the harassment amounts to a breach by a public authority of the right to education under the first protocol to the ECHR together with Article 14 (equality).

It is regrettable that the government did not decide to cover harassment because of sexual orientation in the provision of services, the exercise of public functions, housing and education by way of an express provision, as has been done in the case of work. Such a provision could be interpreted in a manner which respects ECHR Articles 9 (freedom of religion) and 10 (freedom of expression). Indeed, the Northern Ireland High Court has given guidance as to how this can be done under Northern Ireland legislation, which is in broadly similar terms to the British Equality Act.[199] A more precise and narrower definition of harassment in these fields would give clear protection to Article 9 and 10 rights and help to avoid the potentially

---

[193] JCHR (2009–09) para 114; JCHR (2006–07) para 56.

[194] JCHR (2008–09) para 113; Hansard HL vol 716 cols 581–84 (25 January 2010).

[195] Hansard HL vol 716 cols 581–82 (25 January 2010) (Baroness Thornton).

[196] EA, s 212(1).

[197] EA, s 212(5), EN, para 661. 'It is hilarious to think that anyone should come to the conclusion that this is the right way of dealing with an important problem': Lord Lester, Hansard HL vol 716 col 584 (25 January 2010).

[198] Hansard HL vol 716 col 582 (25 January 2010) (Baroness Thornton).

[199] *Application for Judicial Review by the Christian Institute and others* [2007] NIQB 66; [2008] IRLR 36.

chilling effect on free expression of such vague concepts as 'dignity'[200]and 'offensive' conduct.[201]

Another area in which the protection against harassment is inadequate is in respect of obligations on employers to prevent harassment by third parties (ie persons other than the employer or fellow employees of the victim). In *Burton*[202] an employment tribunal found that a hotel manager had failed to protect waitresses from racist and sexist abuse by a comedian, who was not an employee of the hotel, during his performance on behalf of one of the hotel's customers. The EAT held that the situation was sufficiently under the control of the hotel manager to render the hotel responsible. The manager could, by the application of good employment practice, have prevented the harassment or reduced its effect. This appeared to place a positive duty on a private sector employer to prevent harassment. The decision was overruled in a later case by the House of Lords on the ground that there was no direct discrimination in *Burton* because White or male waitresses would have been treated in the same way.[203] The Recast Equal Treatment Directive, requires Member States to encourage employers to take preventive measures against harassment in the workplace.[204] The Equality Act makes it unlawful for an employer to harass employees and persons applying for employment.[205] The 2010 Act also made the employer liable for harassment of employees by third parties, such as customers or clients, where the employer fails to take such steps as would have been reasonably practicable to prevent the third party from doing so.[206] Liability arose only if the employee had been harassed on at least two other occasions by the same or a different third person.[207] In the only reported case, a care worker employed by a care home claimed that she was sexually harassed by a client at the home and her employer took no action to prevent or minimise the harassment. An employment tribunal upheld the claim.[208] Despite the fact that this provision had been used, the liability for third party harassment was repealed in 2013[209] on the ground that that it had 'no practical purpose' and was

---

[200] See p 20 above.

[201] JCHR (2008–09) para 118.

[202] *Burton v De Vere Hotels Ltd* [1996] IRLR 596.

[203] *Macdonald v Advocate General for Scotland; Pearce v Governing Body of Mayfield Secondary School* [2003] IRLR 512.

[204] Art 26.

[205] EA, s 40(1). This follows amendments made by the sex discrimination Act (Amendment) regulations 2008, SI 2008/656.

[206] EA, s 40(2).

[207] EA, s 40(3).

[208] *Blake v Pashun Care Homes Ltd* [2011] EqLR 1293.

[209] ERRA 2013, s 65.

'an unnecessary burden on business', especially small employers.[210] In the absence of such a provision, employees subjected to third party harassment are left to rely on the inadequate common law duty of care, or on the law of constructive unfair dismissal, or the provisions of the Protection from Harassment Act.

VICTIMISATION

One of the most welcome changes in the law effected by the Equality Act is that victimisation is no longer defined as a species of discrimination. Under previous legislation a person who complained of victimisation was required to establish that there was a comparator who would not have been unfavourably treated in comparable circumstances for doing a 'protected act' (eg instituting proceedings).[211] At first, a narrow interpretation was given. For example, an employee dismissed for giving evidence in a race discrimination case against her employer had to be compared to a person who had given evidence against her employer in non-discrimination proceedings.[212] The House of Lords later broadened the protection by deciding that the proper comparator is a person who has not done the act which gave rise to the less favourable treatment; so a police officer who was refused a reference by the chief constable after bringing proceedings under the RRA had to be compared with a person who had not brought proceedings rather than with a person who had brought proceedings under non-discrimination legislation.[213]

As proposed by the Cambridge Review, the new Act provides that victimisation takes place where one person subjects another to a detriment because he or she in good faith does a 'protected act'.[214] There is no need to show less favourable treatment. It is also sufficient if the respondent believes that the person had done, or may do, a protected act.[215] The previous legislation required that the victimisation be 'by reason of' doing a protected act, and this was interpreted as not requiring any conscious motivation.[216] This continues to be the case: the change of wording to 'because of' is one of

---

[210] Government Equalities Office, 'Equality Act 2010 – Employer Liability for Harassment of Employees by Third Parties: A Consultation' (2012).

[211] Cambridge Review (2000) para 2.24.

[212] Monaghan (2007) 437; *Kirby v Manpower Services Commission* [1980] IRLR 229.

[213] *Chief Constable of West Yorkshire Police v Khan* [2001] UKHL 48; [2001] ICR 1065.

[214] EA, s 27(1)(a).

[215] EA, s 27(1)(b).

[216] *Nagarajan v London Regional Transport* [2000] 1 AC 501.

style rather than substance. Doing the protected act need not be the sole cause, but it must be a significant influence or an important cause.[217]

'Protected acts' are defined as bringing proceedings under the Act, giving evidence or information in connection with such proceedings, doing any other thing for the purpose or in connection with proceedings, and making allegations that another person has contravened the Act.[218] But giving false evidence or information, or making a false allegation in bad faith, is not protected.[219] The protection applies only to individuals, not to corporations or legal persons.[220] An issue on which the 2010 Act is ambiguous is whether a claim for victimisation can be brought after the employment relationship has ended. Section 108 provides that post-employment discrimination or harassment is covered, codifying the pre-existing law on this point,[221] but does not explicitly cover victimisation. Section 108(7) provides that '[post-employment] conduct is not a contravention of this section insofar as it also amounts to victimisation'. This led the EAT to find that post-employment discrimination (giving a poor reference to an ex-employee because he had made a complaint of age discrimination) was not covered. However, the Court of Appeal overruled this. It was held that since the 2010 Act had to be construed so as to give effect to the UK's obligations under EU law, which outlaws post-employment victimisation, the opaque section 108(7) had to be interpreted so as to be compatible with the EU legislation. There had been an error by the Parliamentary drafter which the Court could correct.[222]

---

[217] Ibid, per Lord Nicholls, para 19, Lord Steyn, para 34.
[218] EA, s 27(2).
[219] EA, s 27(3).
[220] EA, s 27(4).
[221] *Relaxion Group Ltd v Rhys-Harper* [2003] IRLR 484 (HL).
[222] *Jessemey v Rowstock Ltd* [2014] EqLR 230.

4

Work and Equal Pay

INTRODUCTION

THE PROHIBITED CONDUCT discussed in chapter 3 gives rise to a statutory tort only if it falls within one of the areas described in this and the next chapter. If it does, it may be subject either to a general exception or to a specific restriction, qualification or exclusion. These chapters do not aim to give a detailed or comprehensive account of these areas or the exceptions; rather they will focus on some of the more controversial issues of coverage. Those exclusions that are embedded in the definitions of the protected characteristics and of discrimination and harassment were discussed in chapters 2 and 3 above.

Over time the scope of protection has expanded and the Equality Act can now be said to create a comprehensive equality scheme,[1] covering services (including the provision of goods and facilities) and public functions, premises, work, education, and associations (including political parties). The coverage of the earlier single-strand legislation was inconsistent. For example, discrimination by public authorities in the exercise of their public functions was at first outlawed only by race legislation (from 2000), then by disability and sex legislation. The regulations on religion or belief, sexual orientation and age, implementing the Framework Employment Directive, covered only employment and related fields. The Equality Act 2006 extended the coverage in non-work situations in relation to religion and belief, and regulations did so in 2007 in respect of sexual orientation, but it was only in the Act of 2010 that discrimination in non-work areas was extended to age. In principle, the Equality Act now provides uniform coverage for prohibited conduct relating to any of the protected characteristics, and aims to exclude, restrict or qualify coverage only where there is a need to treat people differently for legitimate reasons. That treatment must be propor-

---

[1] Cf *Rhys-Harper v Relaxion Group plc* [2003] UKHL 33; [2003] IRLR 484, para 133, in which it was said that earlier enactments did not create 'a comprehensive anti-discrimination regime'.

tionate to the aim in question.[2] The Act does not provide a general defence of justification for direct discrimination, apart from age[3] and discrimination arising from disability.[4] Instead it provides a number of specific exceptions. Unlike the Lester Bill (2003), the Act does not contain a statement of the general principle that any 'restriction, qualification, or exclusion is not given a wider effect than is strictly necessary in all the circumstances',[5] but one may argue that such a principle is implicit in the Act.[6]

WORK

General Scope

Part 5 of the Equality Act, replicating earlier legislation, makes it unlawful for an employer to discriminate against or victimise[7] employees and those seeking work because of any of the protected characteristics. This applies to selection arrangements, terms of employment, access to opportunities for promotion or training or other benefit, dismissal and any other 'detriment'. 'Detriment' has been interpreted broadly in a way similar to 'less favourable treatment' in the definition of direct discrimination.[8] There are special provisions dealing with equality of terms between women and men (sex equality clause)[9] and relating to pregnancy and maternity (maternity equality clause). It is also unlawful for an employer to harass an employee or job applicant.[10] 'Employment' to which the Act applies is defined as employment under a contract of employment, a contract of apprenticeship or a contract personally to do work.[11] This is much wider than some other employment legislation, such as that relating to unfair dismissal, which applies only to those under contracts of employment.[12] In relation to EU equality law, which underpins much of the Equality Act, the Court of Justice has held that the rights to equal pay and equal treatment 'cannot be defined by reference to the legislation of the Member States but has a Commu-

---

[2] *Discrimination Law Review* (2007) 31, 171.
[3] See p 78 above.
[4] See p 91 above.
[5] Lester Bill, cl 2(2)(a).
[6] *Johnston v Chief Constable of the Royal Ulster Constabulary* [1987] 1 QB 129 (implicit that justification required under SDA for discrimination purporting to have been done for purposes of national security).
[7] EA, s 39.
[8] See p 67 above.
[9] See p 121 below.
[10] EA, s 40. See p 97 above.
[11] EA, s 83(2)(a).
[12] For detailed discussion of the definitions see Deakin and Morris (2012)) paras 3.16 *et seq.*

nity meaning'.[13] Because these rights 'form part of the foundations of the Community', the concept of 'worker' 'cannot be interpreted restrictively'.[14] The Court of Justice said that a 'worker' is 'a person who, for a certain period of time, performs services for and under the direction of another person in return for which he receives remuneration'.[15] Applying this definition, the Court of Justice has held that an agency worker employed by the agency under a contract for services, and who had no contract of any kind with the user to whom the agency supplied her services, was covered by the principle of equal treatment.[16] The Court of Justice has also decided that a part-time worker under a 'framework' contract that did not set any working hours was covered by the Equal Treatment Directive.[17] Since the Equality Act aims to achieve consistency across all the protected characteristics, the definition of 'employment', although still couched in the language of British employment statutes, should be interpreted so as to comply with the Court of Justice test. The Supreme Court has held that this does not cover a volunteer who is unpaid and has no binding contract, but that an intern hoping to learn and impress might fall within the scope of the Directive (and UK legislation) which applies to access to vocational training.[18] The Equality Act also applies to Crown employment, employment as a member of House of Commons or House of Lords staff,[19] and service in the armed forces.[20] EU equality law contains no reservation where the purpose of the contract is illegal under domestic legislation. However, the Court of Appeal has held that an illegal migrant who has no right to be employed in the UK cannot claim that she has been unlawfully discriminated against because her claim is clearly connected with her own illegal conduct.[21] This ruling fails to treat the right to equal treatment as a fundamental human right, and leaves undocumented workers, who are particularly vulnerable to abusive treatment, without protection. A decision by the Supreme Court in this case is pending at the time of writing.

'Contract workers' are protected from discrimination by their employer, for example the employment agency or business for whom they work. There is also a duty on a person who makes work available to contract workers (referred to as a principal) not to discriminate against, harass or victimise

---

[13] Case C-256/01 *Allonby v Accrington and Rossendale College* [2004] IRLR 224, para 66.

[14] Ibid, paras 65, 66.

[15] Ibid, para 67.

[16] Ibid.

[17] Case C-313/02 *Wippel v Peek & Coppenburg GmbH & Co KG* [2005] IRLR 211.

[18] *X v Mid-Sussex Citizens' Advicew Bureau* [2013] EqLR 154.

[19] EA, s 83(2)(b), (c), (d).

[20] EA, s 83(3) but see p 137 below for exceptions in respect of 'combat effectiveness'.

[21] *Hounga v Allen* [2012] EqLR 679, CA.

them.[22] This provision is based on earlier legislation, but now codifies the case law to make it clear that there does not need to be a direct contractual relationship between the employer and the principal for this protection to apply. This is a significant provision in light of the growth of franchising, concessions, licensing and similar agreements. In *Harrods Ltd v Remick*[23] an employee of a company which was a concessionaire selling goods belonging to Harrods, in Harrods' department store, alleged that because she had not complied with a dress code imposed by Harrods her 'store approval' by Harrods had been withdrawn, as a result of which she was dismissed by her employer. She claimed that the dress code had been applied to her by Harrods in a way that constituted direct race discrimination. The Court of Appeal did not accept an argument for Harrods that this was not 'contract work' as defined because the object of the contract was for the concessionaire to promote the sale of the goods, and not to supply labour as such, and Harrods had no direct powers of direction or control over the concessionaire's staff. Deakin and Morris suggest that 'the Court can be seen as having identified the true source of the economic power to which the complainants were subject',[24] and this was Harrods because they had the power to withdraw 'store approval' in relation to the worker. The revised definition contained in the Act certainly reinforces an approach that focuses on the economic reality of the relationship.

The Act sets out detailed provisions and exceptions relating to discrimination, harassment and victimisation by the police,[25] partnerships,[26] limited liability partnerships,[27] barristers,[28] advocates,[29] office holders,[30] qualifications bodies,[31] employment service providers,[32] trade organisations[33] and local authority members.[34] These provisions replicate those in earlier legislation but the Act makes them more consistent and extends them, with a

---

[22] EA, s 41.
[23] [1997] IRLR 583, CA; and *Abbey Life Assurance v Tansell* [2000] IRLR 387 (end user of services under duty even though under no direct contractual relationship).
[24] Deakin and Morris (2012) para 3.65.
[25] EA, s 42.
[26] EA, s 44.
[27] EA, s 45.
[28] EA, s 47.
[29] EA, s 48.
[30] EA, s 49 (personal offices), s 50 (public offices), s 51 (recommendations for appointment to public offices).
[31] EA, s 53.
[32] EA, s 55.
[33] EA, s 57.
[34] EA, s 58.

few qualifications, to all prohibited characteristics. There are also special provisions regarding work on ships and hovercraft[35] and offshore work.[36]

Every occupational pension scheme must be taken to include a non-discrimination rule.[37] This prohibits a 'responsible person' from discriminating against, harassing or victimising a member or a person who could become a member of the scheme.[38]

'responsible persons' comprise trustees or managers of the scheme, employers whose employees are or may be members of the scheme, and, where office holders may become scheme members, persons responsible for appointing those persons to office.[39]

A breach of a non-discrimination rule can give rise to proceedings under the Act and as well as an investigation by the pensions ombudsman. These provisions have been taken over from earlier legislation in respect of age, disability, religion or belief and sexual orientation. They have been extended to gender reassignment, marriage and civil partnership, and sex. The new rule, introduced by the Act, does not apply to pension rights built up or benefits payable for periods of service before the commencement date of the new provision. Periods of service prior to that date are subject to previous anti-discrimination legislation.

Schedule 9 to the Act re-enacts and clarifies existing legislation which sets out exceptions to the work provisions. The main exceptions are summarised in Box 4.1. Those that raise significant issues are discussed below.

Box 4.1
Work: Main Exceptions (Equality Act schedule 9)

1. Occupational requirements (para 1, see p 110 below).
2. Religious requirements relating to sex, marriage etc, sexual orientation (para 2, see p 111 below).
3. Other requirements relating to religion or belief (para 3, see p 112 below).
4. Armed forces (para 4, see p 137 below).
5. Employment services (para 5).
6. Benefits based on length of service (para 10, see p 115 below).

---

[35] EA, s 81.

[36] EA, s 82.

[37] EA, s 61. Where there is a sex equality rule in a scheme (see p 121), then that rule and not the non- discrimination rule applies: EA, s 61(10).

[38] EA, s 61(2).

[39] EA, s 61(4). Powers to make non-discrimination alterations in schemes are set out in EA, s 62.

7. National minimum wage: young workers and apprentices (paras 11–12).
8. Redundancy payments (para 13).
9. Life assurance: early retirement for ill-health (para 14).
10. Child care for children of particular age group (para 15).
11. Contributions to personal pension schemes (para 16).
12. Non-contractual payments to women on maternity leave (para 17).
13. Benefits dependent on marital status (para 18).
14. Employer who provides services to public not liable to employee in relation to those services under part 5 of Act (para 19).
15. Differences in treatment on sex and related grounds for insurance or risk-related matters where this is done by reference to reliable actuarial or other data and is reasonable in all the circumstances (para 20).

Genuine Occupational Requirements

The SDA and RRA contained specific lists of 'genuine occupational requirements' which granted exemptions in respect of sex and race discrimination in recruitment, promotion, training, transfer, and in some cases dismissal. These lists were inflexible and outdated. There was no similar provision in the DDA for disability. The Race Directive and the Framework Employment Directive contained broad but somewhat problematic wording exempting legitimate and proportionate 'genuine and determining occupational requirements', without going into detail. The implementing regulations and amendments in respect of age, religion or belief, and sexual orientation broadly followed the Directives, but there were anomalies between, for example, discrimination because of racial or ethnic origin, which was covered by the Directives, and discrimination because of colour or nationality, which continued to be covered by the old legislation. The Equality Act now provides a single, clearly worded exception in relation to all protected characteristics, including disability, or not being a transsexual person or a married person or a civil partner. The burden is on the person seeking to rely on the exception to show that:

(1) it is an occupational requirement;
(2) the application of the requirement is a proportionate means of achieving a legitimate aim (implicit in this is that it is genuine and not a sham); and
(3) the person to whom the requirement is applied does not meet it or, except

in the case of sex, there are reasonable grounds for not being satisfied that the person meets it.[40]

The exception can be used by employers, principals of contract workers, partners, members of limited liability partnerships and those with the power to appoint or remove office holders or to recommend an appointment to a public office. Examples given in the Explanatory Notes include the need for authenticity in an acting role, employing a person who uses British Sign Language as a counsellor to deaf people whose preferred language is BSL, and a woman counsellor working with victims of rape.[41] Another example given is this: '[A]n unemployed Muslim woman might not take advantage of the services of an outreach worker to help them find employment if they were provided by a man.'[42] This is a dubious example because the requirement must be a 'determining' or essential one, and not simply a preference or an important consideration.

Religious Requirements

There are two circumstances in which religion or belief may constitute an occupational requirement: employment for purposes of an organised religion, and employment by an organisation with an ethos based on religion or belief. Both again raise issues, discussed earlier in relation to the manifestation of religion or belief,[43] and later in the provision of services,[44] regarding the proper balance between the right to equality and religious freedom.

Where employment (including appointment to a personal or public office) is 'for the purpose of an organised religion', an employer is permitted to require that a person be of a particular sex, require that they not be a transsexual person, and impose requirements relating to the employee's marriage, civil partnership or sexual orientation.[45] Three conditions must be satisfied: (1) the employer must apply the requirement so as to comply with the doctrines of the religion (the 'compliance principle');[46] (2) the employer must show that, 'because of the nature or context of the employment, the requirement [was] applied so as to avoid conflicting with the strongly held religious convictions of a significant number of the religion's followers (the

---

[40] EA, sched 9 para 1.
[41] EN, para 798.
[42] EN, para 798.
[43] See p 51 above.
[44] See p 139 below.
[45] EA, sched 9 para 2(1).
[46] EA, sched 9 para 2(5).

'non-conflict principle')',[47] and (3) the employer must show that the person to whom the requirement is applied does not meet it or, except in the case of sex, that there are reasonable grounds for not being satisfied that the person meets it.[48] This makes it possible, for example, for the Catholic Church to require that its priests be men.

The wording of this exception is similar to that in previous legislation, which was held by the High Court in *R (on the application of Amicus–MSF section) v Secretary of State for Trade and Industry*[49] to be compliant with the Framework Employment Directive. In that case Mr Justice Richards said this was a 'very narrow exception', and that it was subject to a test of proportionality. In the original version of the Equality Bill, the government sought to reflect this judgment by providing that the application of the requirement must be a proportionate method of achieving a legitimate aim. The government also, for the first time, inserted a definition of when employment is 'for the purposes of an organised religion', namely when employment wholly or mainly involves (a) leading or assisting in the observation of liturgical or ritualistic practices of the religion, or (b) promoting or explaining the doctrine of the religion (whether to followers of the religion or otherwise). These changes of wording were strongly opposed by the Catholic Bishops' Conference amongst others, and in the House of Lords the government suffered a defeat. In order to ensure that the Bill was passed before the then pending general election, the government did not seek to reverse this when the Bill returned to the Commons.[50]

The government's defeat on this issue will make no difference to the judicial interpretation of the exception in the *Amicus* case. The Act must be read so as to be compliant with the Directive, which clearly applies a proportionality test. All that has been lost is a more precise definition of the relevant employments. A tribunal case cited during the debates involved a refusal to appoint as a diocesan youth worker a person who had just ended a homosexual relationship and had indicated that he might enter into another such relationship. The question of fact for the tribunal to determine is whether the person making the appointment has shown that the compliance and non-conflict principles are satisfied, and whether the application of the requirement of heterosexuality (or celibacy) was proportionate to a legitimate aim.

The second exception is potentially wider. This permits an employer with an ethos based on religion or belief to discriminate in relation to work by applying a requirement that a person be of a particular religion

---

[47] EA, sched 9 para 2(6).
[48] EA, sched 9 para 2(1)(c).
[49] [2004] IRLR 430.
[50] Hansard HC vol 508 col 931 (6 March 2010) (Solicitor-General).

or belief. The employer or appointing authority must show that (a) it is an occupational requirement, (b) the application of the requirement is a proportionate means of achieving a legitimate aim, and (c) the person to whom the requirement is applied does not meet it, or there are reasonable grounds for not being satisfied that the person meets it.[51] This exception replicates the effect of earlier legislation, and purports to be derived from an ambiguously worded provision of the Framework Employment Directive. However, it does not accurately reflect the Directive, which provides that discrimination on grounds of religion or belief is justified only where 'by reason of the nature of those activities or of the context in which they are carried out, a person's religion or belief constitute a genuine, legitimate and justified occupational requirement, having regard to the organisation's ethos'.[52] The purpose is said to be to allow religious organisations to preserve their ethos. The exception applies only to religion or belief and not to other protected characteristics, such as sexual orientation or being a transsexual. However, it remains uncertain whether a requirement to manifest one's religious belief by avoiding certain forms of behaviour such as homosexual acts comes within the scope of the exception.[53] For example, could a church hospice require its head, who is gay, to remain celibate? This could be justified only if it is an 'occupational' requirement, pursues a legitimate aim and is proportionate. This is ultimately a question of fact in the particular circumstances.

Mandatory Retirement Age

In the field of employment, two important derogations from the Framework Employment Directive were made in the Employment Equality (Age) Regulations 2006 and were continued in the Equality Act, in respect of mandatory retirement and seniority rules respectively. Article 6 of the Directive allows Member States to provide that differences in treatment on grounds of age shall not constitute discrimination if they are 'objectively and reasonably justified by a legitimate aim, including legitimate employment policy, labour market and vocational training objectives, and if the means of achieving that aim are appropriate and necessary'.[54] The retirement derogation in the Equality Act, like the 2006 Regulations, provided that it was not age discrimination to dismiss a worker at or over the age of 65 if the reason for the dismissal is retirement.[55] The 2006 Regulations amended the Employment

---

[51] EA, sched 9 para 3.
[52] Directive 2000/78/EC, Art 4(2).
[53] JCHR (2008–09) para 172.
[54] Art 6(1).
[55] EA, sched 9 para 8.

Rights Act 1996 (ERA) so as to make 'retirement' a potentially fair reason for dismissal and to set out in detail the circumstances in which a dismissal was deemed to be for 'retirement'. The Regulations were challenged in an action brought by Age Concern. The Court of Justice of the EU gave a preliminary ruling that it is not a breach of the Directive to fail to set out in national legislation specific lists of differences in treatment which are legitimate aims under the Directive.[56] However, as already noted, the Court of Justice was at pains to emphasise that the Member State has the burden of establishing to a 'high standard of proof' the legitimacy of the aim relied on as a justification. When the matter came back to the High Court, Blake J held that the Explanatory Notes and the consultation process preceding the Regulations showed that the government had genuine concerns about the confidence and integrity of the labour market, and these concerns were legitimate. He did not regard the choice in 2006 of 65 as the critical age as disproportionate, but indicated that, had it been adopted for the first time in 2009 and had there not been an imminent review planned by the Labour government, the age specified could have been a disproportionate choice.

The Coalition Government published a consultation document in July 2010,[57] announcing that the default retirement age was to be removed beginning in April 2011, with transitional arrangements covering the period until 1 October 2011. This was done by the Employment Equality (Repeal of Retirement Age Provisions) Regulations 2011.[58] Since April 2011, employers who retain a compulsory retirement policy have had to rely on the general defence of justification of direct age discrimination. They have to show that the mandatory retirement age is a proportionate means of achieving a legitimate aim. Employers are also not allowed to discriminate in selection arrangements against those aged 65 or over on grounds of age. The rules affect only employees, those in Crown employment and House of Commons and House of Lords staff. Other important groups, such as office holders in the police and judiciary, partnerships, and professions where there is a statutory age limit, such as commercial pilots, are unaffected.

---

[56] Case C-388/07 *R (Age Concern England) v Secretary of State for Business, Enterprise and Regulatory Reform* [2009] IRLR 173. This follows Case C-411/05 *Palacios de la Villa v Cortefiel Servicios SA* [2007] IRLR 989, where the ECJ held that there is no requirement to set out in national legislation the precise circumstances in which age discrimination is justified, provided this can be gathered from the context.

[57] Department for Business and Department of Work and Pensions, *Phasing Out the Default Retirement Age* (July 2010).

[58] SI 2011 No 1069.

The Supreme Court gave valuable guidance as to the scope of justification in relation to compulsory retirement in *Seldon*[59] and *Homer*.[60]

In the first of these cases, a partner in a firm of solicitors challenged a clause in a partnership deed requiring a partner to retire at the age of 65. An employment tribunal found that the firm had established that they had three legitimate aims in mind: (1) ensuring that associates had the prospect of a partnership and so did not leave the firm, (2) facilitating planning by having a realistic long-term expectation as to when vanacnacies would arise, and (3) limiting the need to expel partners by way of performance management, thus contributing to a congenial and supportive culture in the firm. The tribunal also found that compulsory retirement was an appropriate means of achieving the firm's legitimate aim of staff retention, workforce planning, and allowing an older and less capable partner to leave without the need to justify his departure and damage his or her dignity. The first two objectives could not be achieved in any other way, and there was no other non-discriminatory way to achieve the third objective of collegiality. The Supreme Court found that the first two aims were directed to the legitimate social policy objective of sharing out professional employment opportunities fairly between the generations, and the third aim was directly related to the objective of preserving dignity. However, the case was remitted to the tribunal to find out whether the age chosen of 65 was an appropriate means. At the subsequent tribunal hearing, the tribunal held that the age of 65 was appropriate and reasonably necessary taking into account the consent of all partners when signing the partnership deed and that at the relevant time the default retirement age was 65. The implication is that if the age is unilaterally imposed by the employer or it is prescribed when there is no longer a general default retirement age, a tribunal may reach a different conclusion depending on all the facts.

Alongside the removal of the default retirement age, the procedural requirements relating to retirement (above) have been repealed. Any dismissal of an employee is subject only to the normal requirements of unfair dismissal law to follow a fair procedure.

Seniority Rules

The second derogation in respect of age concerns seniority rules, which are aimed at assisting employment planning in the sense of being able to attract, retain and reward experienced staff through service-related benefits.

---

[59] [2012] UKSC 16, [2012]Eq LR 579; see above p 79.
[60] [2012] UKSC 15, [2012] EqLR 594.

The Equality Act, replacing the earlier regulations,[61] provides that it is not age discrimination 'for a person [A] to put a person [B] at a disadvantage when compared with another person [C], in relation to the provision of a benefit, facility or service, in so far as the disadvantage is because B has a shorter period of service than C'.[62] The longer the period of service, the harder it is to justify different treatment. Accordingly, the absolute exception applies only to length of service up to five years. The government believed that this five-year cap makes the exception proportionate.[63]

This exception cannot be used to justify the level of benefits when an employee is made redundant, because a service-related termination payment is not a reward for experience from which the employer can benefit. Part 11 of the ERA provides for statutory redundancy payments based on the employee's age, length of service and weekly pay. The government considered this to be objectively justified under Article 6(1) of the Framework Employment Directive.[64] The Equality Act allows employers to provide enhanced redundancy payments that mirror the qualifying ages and length of service set out in the statutory scheme, but which are more generous than the statutory scheme requires them to be.[65] There is also an exception relating to employers who provide life assurance cover to workers who have had to retire early on grounds of ill-health.[66]

EQUAL PAY FOR MEN AND WOMEN

The Long Struggle for Equal Pay

In 1888, the Trades Union Congress (TUC) unanimously passed a motion that 'in the opinion of this Congress it is desirable, in the interests of both men and women, that in trades where women do the same work as men, they shall receive the same payment'. This was reiterated by the TUC on more than 40 occasions in the following 75 years. However, voluntary collective bargaining failed to achieve this goal. In the 1960s, most agreements in the private sector still had a men's rate and a women's rate,

---

[61] Employment Equality (Age) Regulations 2006, SI 2006/1031, reg 32, as amended by the employment Equality (Age) Regulations 2006 (Amendment) Regulations 2008, SI 2008/573.

[62] EA, sched 9 para 10.

[63] In *Rolls-Royce plc v Unite Union* [2009] IRLR 576, a collective agreement providing for length of service to be taken into account was upheld, but Wall LJ criticised the failure to address expressly whether the criterion of length of service was a proportionate means of achieving a legitimate aim.

[64] EA, sched 9 paras 9, 13.

[65] EA, sched 9 para 13.

[66] EA, sched 9 para 14 as amended by SI 2011 No 1069.

and the women's rate was significantly lower than the men's. In the civil service, following extensive extra-parliamentary pressure, equality of pay was achieved, under a Whitley council agreement, in 1961. In 1946, the majority of a Royal Commission on equal pay had opposed the introduction of legislation on equal pay because of the possible adverse effect on the demand for female labour and because, in their view, existing differentials reflected real differences in efficiency.[67] The Labour Government, elected in 1964, was committed to legislate on equal pay, but it was only in January 1970 that a Bill was introduced by Barbara Castle MP, Secretary of State for Employment, and this received Royal Assent on 29 May 1970, just before the Wilson government lost office. Employers were given five years to adjust their pay structures before the Equal Pay Act came into force on 29 December 1975, and prior to this it was substantially amended and re-enacted in the Sex Discrimination Act 1975 (SDA).[68]

The 1970 Act required equal terms and conditions of employment for men and women in the same employment when employed on 'like' work or on work rated as equivalent under a job evaluation study, but there was no obligation to undertake such a study. There was no general right to equal pay for work of equal value, the standard adopted by the ILO Convention No 100 on Equal Remuneration of Men and Women on Work of Equal Value (1951). The UK Government had opposed the draft convention on the ground that equal pay could not be afforded at a time of huge national debt occasioned by the war.

Meanwhile, the UK had acceded to the Treaty of Rome, Article 119 of which set forth the principle that 'men and women should receive equal pay for equal work'. This was 'clarified' by equal pay directive 75/117/EEC, which declared that the principle of equal pay 'means for the same work, *or for work to which equal value is attributed*, the elimination of all discrimination on grounds of sex with regard to all aspects and conditions of remuneration' (emphasis added). In the second *Defrenne* case,[69] the Court of Justice held that Article 119 was directly applicable in the Member States as regards 'direct and overt' discrimination. In 1981 the European Commission brought infringement proceedings against the UK, leading the Court of Justice to find that the UK had failed to fulfil its obligations under the treaty and stating that 'Member States must endow an authority with the requisite jurisdiction to decide whether work has the same value as other work, after obtaining such information as may be required'.[70] The Conservative Government responded with the Equal Pay (Amendment) Regulations

---

[67] Creighton (1979) 94.
[68] Ibid, chs 3 and 4.
[69] Case 43/75, *Defrenne v Sabena SA* [1976] ECR 455.
[70] Case 61/81, *Commission of the European Communities v United Kingdom* [1982] ECR 578.

1983.[71] The gist of the Regulations was to add a new residual basis for establishing entitlement to equal pay, where a woman is employed on work which is 'in terms of demands made on her (for instance under such headings as effort, skill and decision) of equal value to that of a man in the same employment'. This equal value claim could be brought only if claims for like work, or work rated as equivalent, were unsuccessful. The 1983 regulations have been amended on several occasions, mainly to give effect to EU law, but the basic concepts and structures of the legislation have remained unchanged. Lord Denning told the House of Lords in 1983 that their 'tortuosity and complexity is beyond compare', that 'no ordinary lawyer would be able to understand them', and that 'the industrial tribunals would have the greatest difficulty and the Court of Appeal would probably be divided in opinion'.[72] The complex and compendious case law under the Act has shown the accuracy of Lord Denning's predictions. One striking fact is that, of 23,000 equal pay claims in employment tribunal proceedings in the year ending 31 March 2012, only 32 (less than 1 per cent) were successful at a hearing, and 76 were unsuccessful at a hearing. The remainder resulted in ACAS-conciliated settlements (37 per cent) or were withdrawn.[73] Research on the implementation of the 1997 Local Authority Single Status Agreement, which aimed to give effect to equal pay principles, resulted in lengthy and complex litigation in which individual rights and collective interests clashed.[74]

The main objective of the Equal Pay Act was to equalise *rates* of pay, not earnings as such, given that women generally have fewer opportunities for overtime or seniority or long-service payments. The SDA was supposed to complement the Equal Pay Act by opening up chances for promotion, training, continuity of employment, and other opportunities that affect the level of earnings. Initially, the Equal Pay Act had a significant impact. In 1970, women's average gross hourly earnings (excluding the effects of overtime) were 63.1 per cent of men's. They reached 75.5 per cent in 1977 and in the following years settled in the range 73–75 per cent, before reaching 80 per cent in 1994. Between 1997 and 2013 the gap has narrowed, but was still 19.7 per cent measured by hourly earnings for all employees in 2013. The gap remains consistently high for those in skilled trades (plumbers, electricians, etc) and for managers and directors.[75] The National Equality

---

[71] SI 1983/1794.
[72] Hansard HL vol 445 cols 901–02 (5 December 1983).
[73] See p 194 below..
[74] McClauglin (2014).
[75] DCMS, *Secondary Analysis of the Gender Pay Gap* (March 2014).

Panel found that women from nearly all ethno-religious groups are paid less than the least well-paid group of men.[76]

Equal pay legislation is only one of the many complex factors that contribute to determining women's pay relative to that of men. In addition to the Equal Pay legislation, the National Minimum Wage has been a factor in raising the pay of women, who are concentrated in low-paid jobs. The reasons for the persistence of unequal pay include the level of educational achievements, but the National Equality Panel pointed out that, despite the fact that younger women now have qualifications equal to or higher than men, they continue to be disadvantaged in the labour market.[77] The most important reason is continuing occupational segregation of women in low-paid jobs where their work is undervalued. The causes of this include stereotypical assumptions about the social role of women, pervasive bias against women with children, and the practical difficulties of reconciling work and family life.[78] The failure of the legislation to bring about significant change over a period of 40 years must, therefore, be understood in the context of social stereotypes and socio-economic structure. The Act has produced some modest and welcome improvements for groups of women who have won their cases or used the Act as a basis for negotiating better pay and conditions, but, on the whole, it has proved to be ineffective and unworkable.

In 2004, the then Prime Minister appointed a Women and Work Commission to make recommendations on how to reduce the gender pay gap, but the Commission was precluded by its terms of reference from proposing changes in legislation. In reports in 2006 and 2009,[79] the Commission produced a raft of recommendations designed to change the stereotyping and low aspirations of women and to make it easier for parents to combine work and family life. The Commission pointed out that discrimination in the workplace is often unintended and arises through the way in which pay systems operate. They favoured an 'equality check' by employers, pay reviews by public sector employers, and the involvement of trade union equality representatives.

The Cambridge Review undertook a detailed analysis of the failings of the Equal Pay Act, and proposed three main strategies: placing positive legal duties on employers to review their pay structures and take active steps towards pay equity; extending the basis of comparison and improving the methods of assessing the relative value of jobs; and establishing new and

---

[76] National Equality Panel (2010) 220.
[77] Ibid.
[78] Browne (2006) chs 3 and 4.
[79] Women and Work Commission (2006), (2009).

improved tribunal procedures.[80] Similar proposals were later made by the EOC and by many of the organisations that responded to the government's Discrimination Law Review. Apart from some relatively minor changes in tribunal procedures for determining equal value introduced in 2004,[81] none of these proposals was accepted. The Labour Government gave three reasons for rejecting mandatory pay reviews.

The first was that they 'address only one of the causes of the gender pay gap—that of gender pay discrimination'.[82] It is true that discrimination is only one of the causes of disadvantage, but this is no reason to fail to address it. As already noted, the Women and Work Commission suggested that unintentional and often indirect discrimination is a significant factor contributing to the gender pay gap and arises from the way in which pay systems operate. It must follow that it is only through the provision of a mechanism for reviewing those structures that the less favourable treatment of women can be significantly reduced. The second reason given was that pay reviews 'have had a relatively minor impact in the private sector in those countries and provinces where they are mandatory'.[83] No countries are specifically mentioned, nor are any studies of the impact in those countries. Evidence of the success of positive duties in the USA, Canada and Northern Ireland produced in the Cambridge Review is totally ignored. Thirdly, it is argued that 'enforced equal pay reviews may also contravene better regula-tion principles as the costs to employers may be out of proportion to the scale of the problem they address'.[84] This voices the objections raised by the Confederation of British Industry, but some other employers' groups saw positive benefits to business in ending the undervaluation of women's work. The Cambridge Review proposals were carefully designed so as to ensure that mandatory pay reviews would be a proportionate response to the legitimate aim of gender pay equality. For example, it was recommended that the duty to conduct a review should arise only once every three years and be confined to employers with more than 10 full-time employees; that it should be possible to contract out of the individual's right to equal pay by collective agreement or workforce agreement in respect of a defined period to allow the employer time to absorb the costs of implementation of an agreed pay equity plan; and that provision be made for arbitration in cases of dispute.[85] Instead, government policy continues to rely on methods,

---

[80] Cambridge Review (2000) paras 3.41–3.60.
[81] See p 199 below.
[82] *Discrimination Law Review* (2007) para 3.7.
[83] Ibid.
[84] Ibid.
[85] Cambridge Review (2000) paras 3.45–3.52. The *Discrimination Law Review*, para 3.24, suggested that an equal pay moratorium might be incompatible with EU law, but the

which have been largely ineffective over a 40-year period, of 'promoting the spread of good practice' and 'developing a light-touch diagnostic tool—the gender equality check tool' on a voluntary basis.[86] One may safely predict that this failure to bring about significant changes in the gender pay gap will continue, particularly in a time of recession and pay freezes.

Relationship between Equality Clause and Sex Discrimination Claims

The equal pay provisions have now been brought within the scope of the single Equality Act. The Discrimination Law Review promised to simplify and clarify the law in this area, but very few substantial changes were made by the Equality Act and the legislation remains unnecessarily complex and to some extent unintelligible. One of the reasons for these failings is the retention of the distinction between the contractual sex equality clause and claims for the tort of discrimination. A person who claims that they are being paid less than a comparator because of their race, religion or belief, disability or sexual orientation can bring an ordinary claim for direct or indirect discrimination without having to prove that their work is equal to that of their comparator, and they are not subject to any special defence that the difference in pay is due to a 'material factor' other than the prohibited characteristic.

However, a woman who claims that her pay or some other term of employment is not the same as that of a male comparator must rely on a sex equality clause which is implied by law into every contract of employment.[87] A similar provision (a sex equality rule) is implied into the terms of occupational pension schemes.[88] The effect of the clause and rule is that any term of the contract or pension scheme that is less favourable to the employee than a corresponding term of the contract or pension provision of a comparator of the opposite sex is modified so as not to be less favourable. If the comparator benefits from a term that is not included in the employee's contract, the effect of the sex equality clause is to include that term in the employee's contract. For example, if a male employee's contract enables him to use his employer's car for private purposes, his female comparator

---

Cambridge Review proposal was designed to ensure that the individual's rights were properly safeguarded during and after the moratorium.

[86] *Discrimination Law Review* (2007) para 3.8.

[87] EA, s 66.

[88] EA, ss 67, 68. the provision applies in relation to pensionable service before 17 May 1990 (the date of the Court of Justice's decision under Art 119 EEC in Case C-262/88 *Barber v Guardian Royal Exchange Assurance Group* [1990] ECR I-1899): EA, s 67(10).

doing equal work is entitled to the same benefit.[89] Similarly, if a term in
a pension scheme confers a discretion capable of being exercised in a way
that would be less favourable to a member of one sex than to a member
of the opposite sex, then the term is modified so as to prevent the exercise
of the discretion in that way.[90]

The tort of discrimination does not apply where a sex equality clause
or sex equality rule operates. The sex discrimination tort does, however,
apply to non-contractual pay and benefits (such as an ex gratia Christmas
bonus) and matters such as recruitment, promotion, transfer, training and
dismissal.[91] In principle, there can be no overlap between sex equality clause
or rule claims and other sex discrimination claims. If the matter is regulated by the contract of employment or pension scheme, only the equality
clause or rule can operate.

Hypothetical Comparators

The main problem that the distinction between contract and tort claims has
created in the past is that a person can bring a claim for breach of a sex
equality clause or rule only if there is a real comparator of the opposite
sex.[92] She cannot bring a claim for breach of an equality clause because
the comparator is hypothetical. Nor, under the law before the Equality Act,
could she bring a claim for the tort of sex discrimination. This meant that
the law was ineffective in gender-segregated workforces, where it might not
be possible to identify actual comparators of the opposite sex. The government had two options when it came to closing this obvious gap in protection.
The first, favoured by the EHRC and the Women and Work Commission,
would have been to allow a hypothetical comparison in equality clause or
rule claims. This was rejected for two reasons: it would be impractical to
make a comparison with the value of a job or the contractual terms of a
person who does not exist,[93] and it would create 'intolerable uncertainty' as
to whether an employer's pay arrangements were lawful or not because it
would be impossible to envisage every scenario from which a comparator
might be drawn.[94]

The second option, which was adopted as an important new provision in

---

[89] EN, para 230.
[90] EA, s 67(2)(b).
[91] EA, s 70.
[92] EN, para 219.
[93] Hansard HL vol 716 col 943 (27 January 2010) (Baroness Royall). This accords with EU
law: Case 129/79, *Maccarthys Ltd v Smith* [1980] ICR 672, 691.
[94] *Discrimination Law Review* (2007) para 3.27.

the Equality Act,[95] was to allow a claim for the tort of direct sex discrimination to be brought where a term relates to pay but a sex equality clause
or rule has no effect. This means that where there are no comparators in
the employer's establishment doing the work, the employee can now bring
a claim for the tort of direct sex discrimination, which allows a comparison with a hypothetical comparator. For example, where work has been
contracted out to another undertaking which pays women less than they
were receiving from their former employer, there could be a tort of direct
sex discrimination but not a breach of the sex equality clause. The same
applies to dual discrimination where one of the protected characteristics is
sex, for example where a Black woman is paid less than would be paid to
a White man.

However, indirect sex discrimination in contractual pay can be challenged
only by means of an equality clause.[96] For example, part-time workers, most
of whom are women, may be put at a particular disadvantage compared
to male full-time workers by a policy, practice or criterion whose effect is
to require that they work full-time to get certain benefits.[97] The responsible
person then has to show that this policy, practice or criterion is a proportionate means of achieving a legitimate aim.[98] This is the same defence as in
an indirect sex discrimination claim. The government did not believe that an
indirect sex discrimination claim could in practice succeed in circumstances
where an equality clause claim is not possible.[99] This issue is, however, not
free from doubt and may have to be resolved by litigation. In theory, a
hypothetical comparator is possible in an indirect sex discrimination claim,
although in practice where there is an attack on systemic indirect discrimination in a pay structure the need for a comparator does not usually arise.[100]
However, there is always a possibility that, in order to show a 'particular
disadvantage', reliance would need to be placed on a hypothetical comparison, and this would not be possible under the equality clause.

Choice of Comparator

The Act replicates the substance of earlier provisions by providing that a
sex equality clause or rule applies when a person (A) is employed in work

---

[95] EA, s 71.
[96] EA, s 71(2).
[97] EA, s 69(2). See p 84 above.
[98] EA, s 69(1)(b).
[99] Hansard HL vol 716 col 943 (27 January 2010) (Baroness Royall).
[100] See the examples given by Lord Lester of Herne hill, Hansard HL vol 716 col 944
(27 January 2010).

that is equal to the work of a comparator of the opposite sex (B).[101] A's work is equal to that of B if it is (1) like B's work, or (2) rated as equivalent to B's work, or (3) of equal value to B's work.[102] There are two situations where such comparisons can be made. The first is where A and B share the same employer, and work at the same establishment.[103] The second, is where they work at different establishments but share the same employer. In the second case case they can make a comparison only if common terms and conditions apply at the establishments (either generally or as between A and B).[104] These common terms need not be identical so long as they are 'substantially comparable'.[105] The paradigm is where a collective agreement prescribes common terms.[106] A person can also be a comparator in either of these circumstances if employed by an 'associated employer'.[107]

At one time, it seemed that Article 119 of the EC treaty (now Article 157 TFEU) would allow wider comparisons. Indeed Ellis has argued, on the basis of *Defrenne v Sabena*,[108] which referred to comparisons between men and women 'in the same establishment or service', that comparison should not be confined to single establishments or even single employers.[109] Later the Court of Justice was more restrictive, requiring the identification of a 'single source' which was responsible for the unequal pay and could put this right.[110] The result was that dinner ladies whose employment had been transferred from a local authority to a private contractor could not claim equal pay with the employees of their former employer, whose work had been rated as of equal value to theirs. Similarly, civil servants employed by one government department could not compare their pay with civil servants in another department. Although they were all Crown employees, the Court of Appeal said that the Crown was not a 'single source'.[111]

An issue that has been controversial in the context of cross-establishment comparisons is what has to be shown by the woman about the prospect of the man employed by the same employer in a different establishment coming

---

[101] EA, s 64(1).

[102] EA, s 65, which gives definitions of these concepts.

[103] EA, s 79(3).

[104] EA, s 79(4).

[105] *British Coal Corp v Smith* [1996] IRLR 404, HL, 410 per Lord Slynn.

[106] *Leverton v Clwyd County Council* [1980] AC 706; [1989] IRLR 28, HL, 31 per Lord Bridge.

[107] EA, s 79(9) provides that employers are associated if one is a company of which the other (directly or indirectly) has control, or both are companies of which a third person has control.

[108] Case 43/75, [1976] ECR 455, para 22.

[109] Ellis (1991) 62.

[110] Case C-320/00 *Lawrence v Regent Office Care Ltd* [2002] IRLR 822; Case C-256/01 *Allonby v Accrington and Rossendale College* [2004] IRLR 224.

[111] *Robertson v DEFRA* [2005] IRLR 363. But the correctness of this decision is now open to doubt in the light of *North v Dumfries and Galloway Council* (below): see Naper (2014) 246 EOR 8 at 9.

to work at the woman's establishment. Is it necessary to show that there is at least a possibility that the man could ever carry out his duties at the same establishment? In *North v Dumfries and Galloway Council*[112] the Supreme Court answered this question in the negative. Lady Hale, delivering the sole judgment, said that there was no requirement in the legislation that it had to 'feasible' that the male comparators could come to work alongside the female workers. Such an interpretation would be incompatible with the principle of 'single source' in EU case law. The function of the 'same employment' test is not to establish comparability between the jobs done— that is the purpose of the 'like work', 'work rated as equivalent' and 'equal value' criteria. 'Its function is to establish terms and conditions with which the comparison is to be made, and to weed out those cases where geography plays a significant role in determining what those conditions are.'[113] The Supreme Court in this case was interpreting section 1(6) of the Equal Pay Act 1970 which referred to common terms for the 'relevant classes of employees'. Those words are omitted in section 79 (4) of the 2010 Act which replaces section 1(6) of the 1970 Act. There is an argument that this change may have narrowed the scope of valid comparisons, but this was never the aim of the consolidation of the equal pay provisions and would have been incompatible with EU law with which the UK law was being harmonised.[114] The *North* decision should be regarded as authoritative under the 2010 Act.

The virtual disappearance of centralised collective bargaining, the outsourcing of services by public authorities, and the growth of budgetary devolution within the public sector, means that in practice the permitted pay comparisons are increasingly incapable of breaking through the barriers of gender segregation. The Cambridge Review anticipated this by making a number of proposals for extending the scope of comparison. For example, it was suggested that an employer should be obliged to achieve pay equity at the level of the whole undertaking rather than within a particular establishment or establishments, subject to the general defence of objective justification of pay differences.[115] The Review also proposed that comparisons should be possible with any other employer that forms part of the same public service.[116] A further recommendation was the introduction of a principle of proportionality. The legislation does not provide a right to proportionate pay; a woman's claim can succeed only if her work is of equal value or more than equal value to that of her male comparator, so if she receives 80 per cent of the man's pay but her work is worth 90 per cent,

---

[112] [2013] EqLR 817.
[113] Para 13 per Lady Hale.
[114] Napier (2014) 246 EOR 8 at 9.
[115] Cambridge Review (2000) para 3.56.
[116] Ibid, para 3.55.

she has no redress. The Review argued that the principle of proportionate value would overcome some of the difficulties connected with the absence of a male comparator doing equal work. None of these proposals has been adopted. The only concession has been a codification of the Court of Justice case law to provide that the comparator's work need not be done contemporaneously with that of the person seeking equal pay.[117] A predecessor or successor's work can be compared. However, the defence of genuine material factor (GMF) (below) is more likely to succeed the longer the time gap between the two employments. In addition, in order to make a meaningful comparison using statistical evidence, as large a group of comparators as possible, not confined to a single successor or predecessor, will be needed.[118] The unreformed definition of 'equal work' remains complex and unsatisfactory. The following are the primary questions in equal pay claims:

(1) Is the employee in *like* work to a person of the opposite sex (the comparator)? This is work that is the same or broadly similar, and such differences as there are not of practical importance to the terms of their work.[119] It is necessary to have regard to the frequency with which differences between their work occur and the nature and extent of the differences. For example, men and women who do similar wok as shelf-fillers in a supermarket will be in 'like work' even though from time to time in practice men carry heavier objects or fill higher shelves. Few cases arise nowadays under this category, which is largely of historical interest.

(2) If there is not like work, then is the employee on *work rated as equivalent* to that of the comparator under an analytical job evaluation study? This presupposes that the employer has voluntarily carried out a job evaluation study, which has been accepted by the employer and any other parties that commissioned it, such as a trade union.[120] The work is rated as equivalent if the study gives an equal value to the two jobs in terms of the demands made on the worker.[121] If a woman's job is rated higher than that of a male comparator under a study, this will not prevent her

---

[117] EA, s 64(2); Case 129/79 *Macarthys Ltd v Smith* [1980] IRLR 210, ECJ. The government accepted an amendment at the committee stage in the House of Lords moved by Lord Lester, and also changed the original Bill's reference to comparison with a 'colleague' in order to make it clear that the comparator need not be contemporaneously employed: Hansard HL vol 716 col 939 (27 January 2010).

[118] *Cheshire & Wirral NHS Trust v Abbott* [2006] IRLR 546, CA.

[119] EA, s 65(2).

[120] *Arnold v Beecham Group Ltd* [1982] IRLR 307.

[121] The Equal Pay Act gave instances of demands such as effort, skill and decision. These are not mentioned in the EA, s 65, but are elaborated in the EHRC's statutory code of practice, para 12.

from claiming equal terms.[122] There is a risk that employers will resort to bogus job evaluation studies in order to thwart claims based on equal value (below). One potential safeguard against this is that sex-specific systems, setting different values for men to those for women, have to be disregarded. For example, if a study gives undue weight to the physical demands on male physical education teachers when comparing them to female classroom assistants, this should be disregarded.[123]

(3) If there is no work rated as equivalent under a job evaluation study, the claimant has to prove that the work is of *equal value* to the job of a comparator of the opposite sex. This is the residual category, introduced in 1983. It requires an analysis in terms of the demands made on the worker by reference to factors such as effort, skill and decision-making.[124] There is a complex and slow procedure for the determination of 'equal value' by an employment tribunal, which can involve the appointment of an independent expert.[125] In practice, despite reforms in 2004, the procedural obstacles have been yet another nail in the coffin of equal pay legislation.

Genuine Material Factor (GMF) Defence

The Equal Pay Act 1970 and the Pensions Act 1990 permitted employers and trustees to objectively justify differences in pay to which an equality clause or rule would otherwise apply. For example, an individual may be paid more than another because of greater seniority. This was called the 'genuine material factor' (GMF) defence. It pre-dated the UK's accession to the Treaty of Rome but was amended when the equal value principle was introduced. The British case law on the scope of this defence has not always been compatible with EU law. For example, EU law does not allow a defence of justification of direct sex discrimination in pay, but there have been suggestions that the British defence would permit this.[126] In practice, most equal pay cases involve unintentional indirect discrimination. The Court of Justice has held that once a prima facie finding is made that a pay system has an adverse impact on female employees, the burden of proof shifts to the employer to show that the pay practice is a proportionate means of

---

[122] In *Redcar and Cleveland Borough Council v Bainbridge (No 1)* [2007] **IRLR** 984, this was read into the SDA, s 1(5) (now replaced by the EA, s 65(4)), so as to allow a comparison with someone who had been put in a lower band but received more pay.

[123] EHRC, Code of Practice on Equal Pay, para 14.

[124] EA, s 65(6).

[125] See p 199 below.

[126] *Strathclyde Regional Council v Wallace* [1998] **IRLR** 164, HL, para 18; *Armstrong v Newcastle upon Tyne NHS Hospital Trust* [2006] **IRLR** 124.

achieving a legitimate aim.[127] For example, the Court of Justice has held that although in principle differential pay and benefits for part-time workers might be justified, it is insufficient for an employer to make generalised assumptions that this would reduce overheads and training costs.[128] Unfortunately, the interpretations of the Court of Justice have not always been clear, for example in relation to incremental pay scales based on seniority.[129] The Court of Appeal in England complicated matters even further in *Armstrong v Newcastle upon Tyne NHS Hospital Trust*[130] by holding that once a disparate adverse impact is established the burden passes to the employer in relation to two issues: first, that the difference in treatment is not due to a difference in sex, and second, if the employer cannot show that the difference in treatment is not attributable to a difference of sex, the employer must then demonstrate an objective justification for the difference in pay. This finding was at odds with the Court of Justice rulings.[131] Rubenstein points out that *Armstrong* is also illogical because essentially it holds that a finding of indirect discrimination can be disregarded by proving that there was no direct discrimination.[132] The problem was explained by Mr Justice Elias in *Coventry City Council v Nicholls*:

> There is a debate as to whether … [t]here is an irrebuttable presumption of prima facie indirect discrimination requiring justification where the statistics demonstrating discrimination are sufficiently striking—or whether it is in principle open to an employer to show that notwithstanding apparently stark statistics, in fact there is an explanation for the difference in pay which is wholly unrelated to sex so that the issue of justification does not arise.[133]

The government promised to 'clarify and simplify' equal pay law,[134] but the original Equality Bill was far from clear on the material factor defence and, on one interpretation, appeared to codify the *Armstrong* principle.[135] However, a government amendment at the committee stage in the House of Lords appears to have reversed the effect of *Armstrong*. The employer must now prove that the difference in pay is because of a material factor reliance on which

---

[127] Case 109/89 *Danfoss* [1989] IRLR 532.
[128] Case C-170/84 *Bilka-Kaufhaus v Weber von Hartz* [1986] IRLR 317.
[129] Compare *Danfoss* with Case C-184/89 *Nimz v Freie und Hansestadt Hamburg* [1991] IRLR 222, and the attempt to reconcile these cases in *Cadman v HSE* [2004] IRLR 971 and *Wilson v HSE* [2009] IRLR 282.
[130] [2006] IRLR 124.
[131] Case C-127/92 *Enderby v Frenchay Health Authority* [1993] IRLR 591.
[132] Rubenstein (2009b) 33.
[133] [2009] IRLR 345, EAT, at 347.
[134] *Discrimination Law Review* (2007) para 321.
[135] Rubenstein (2009) 33; JCHR (2008–09) paras 196–99.

(a) does not involve treating the claimant less favourably because of the claimant's sex than the employer treats the comparator, *and*
(b) if the factor is indirectly discriminatory, is a proportionate means of achieving
a legitimate aim.[136]

The effect was summed up by the Minister as follows:

> The material factor defence to an equal pay claim should be able to succeed
> where the employer shows that the factor on which he relies to explain the
> difference in pay is real and not a sham; that it is not directly discriminatory,
> and if the complainant brings forward evidence that is indirectly discriminatory,
> the employer can show that reliance on the factor is nevertheless justified and
> proportionate … [t]hat has always been our intention for this clause.[137]

Collective Bargaining and Transitional Arrangements

The implementation of the legal principle of equality 'has frequently
encountered collective bargaining', but 'collective bargaining as a concept is
not particularly focused on equal opportunities'.[138] The problem, according
to the late Brian Bercusson, who made a careful analysis of the interaction
between collective bargaining and equal opportunities, is that 'the sophisticated concepts of equal opportunities policy contrast with the relatively
restricted agendas of trade unions' bargaining platforms and employers'
personnel policies'.[139] As we have seen,[140] before 1975, many collective
agreements were directly discriminatory. There continued to be indirect
discrimination after the 1970s. One issue is whether separate collective
bargaining agreements for different groups can be a defence to equal pay
claims. In the leading case, *Enderby v Frenchay Health Authority*,[141] the Court of
Justice held that the existence of separate collective bargaining agreements,
one for a group of predominantly men and the other at lower pay rates for
a group of predominantly women, did not, without more, provide a justification for unequal pay. More recently, however, in the *Redcar* and *Middlesbrough*
cases,[142] the Court of Appeal has said that 'the fact that different jobs have
been the subject of separate collective bargaining can be a defence to an
equal pay claim in that the reason for the difference in pay for those jobs
has been separate collective bargaining not the difference of sex of the

---

[136] EA, s 69(1)(a), (b).
[137] Hansard HL vol 716 col 939 (27 January 2010) (Baroness Royall).
[138] Bercusson (1996) 182–83.
[139] Ibid, 183.
[140] See p 116 above.
[141] Case C-127/92, [1993] IRLR 439.
[142] *Redcar & Cleveland Borough Council v Bainbridge (No 1), Surtees v Middlesbrough Borough Council,
Redcar & Cleveland Borough Council v Bainbridge (No 2)* [2008] IRLR 776, CA.

employees'.[143] In other words, 'a difference in pay which is explained by the process of non-discriminatory collective bargaining could therefore provide a complete answer to an equal pay claim'.[144] A different conclusion might be reached under the new material factor defence (above). This makes it clear that not only must the separate agreements be untainted by sex; if the separate agreements are indirectly discriminatory, this must be a proportionate means of achieving a legitimate aim.

A second issue is whether transitional arrangements which continue past indirect discrimination will be lawful if they can be justified. This is important when pay protection is negotiated for previously advantaged groups as part of an agreement to harmonise the terms of manual and white-collar workers. In the *Redcar* and *Middlesbrough* cases, the Court of Appeal held that pay protection schemes could not constitute a material factor defence if they were tainted by indirect sex discrimination. Those covered by the schemes were predominantly men who had benefited from discrimination against female employees in the past. The Court left open whether the employer could justify the indirectly discriminatory practices. In the *Redcar* case it was said that if the employer was aware of the sex-tainted nature of the practice and had not considered what to do about the discriminatory element, it could not rely on the material factor defence. In the *Middlesbrough* case, the Court of Appeal said that instituting a pay protection scheme aimed at mitigating the effects of a pay reduction did not necessarily amount to justification without more.

The new GMF defence provides that 'the long-term objective of reducing inequality between men's and women's terms of work is always to be regarded as a legitimate aim'.[145] This would not have changed the outcome in the *Redcar* and *Middlesbrough* cases. Even if the aim is legitimate, the means used must be proportionate to that aim. Simply to provide a 'soft landing' for those who will suffer a drop in pay is not proportionate if the group who were discriminated against in the past are not consulted, equal pay is delayed for some years to accommodate the advantaged group, and the disadvantages to the discriminated group are not minimised.

It is significant that the new GMF test is cumulative. In a case of indirect discrimination it is therefore necessary to prove both that the provision, policy or practice is not sex-tainted, and that it is proportionate. In the Irish case of *Kenny v Minister for Justice, Equality and Law Reform*[146] the Court of Justice said that 'the interests of good industrial relations' could be taken as one factor among others in deciding whether objective justification was made

---

[143] Ibid, at 800.
[144] Ibid, at 800.
[145] EA, s 69(3).
[146] [2013] EqLR 380

out. Napier points out that 'good industrial relations' may have discriminatory connotations. The wording of the GMF provision in the Equality Act[147] makes it clear that the employer cannot rely on a collective agreement that is itself sex-discriminatory nor can it rely on a union's resistance to the removal of discriminatory pay.[148]

Discussions about Pay

Instead of mandatory pay reviews, the Labour government placed its faith in facilitating greater transparency and dialogue in relation to pay in the belief that this would enable employees to challenge discriminatory pay differences. A new provision is intended to make contractual clauses that seek to prevent employees disclosing details of their pay to one another unenforceable, and to outlaw victimisation for seeking or making or receiving a relevant pay disclosure.[149] This is confined to a disclosure made for the purpose of enabling the person who makes it, or the person to whom it is made, to find out whether any differences in pay are connected to any protected characteristic, not limited to sex.[150]

As originally drafted, this provision applied only to discussions between colleagues and former colleagues in the same employment. It did not cover disclosure to trade union officials or journalists who are not work colleagues. The JCHR and the Liberal Democrats, in the interests of freedom of expression, urged an extension to all discussions about pay that are directed towards finding out whether the differences are connected to a protected characteristic.[151] This was accepted by the government, and the Bill was amended during the committee stage in the House of Lords. According to the government spokeswoman: 'It applies to any disclosure of information about pay which the employee can show had the necessary purpose— that of finding out whether or to what extent there is a connection between pay and the possession of a protected characteristic.'[152]

It is not clear, however, that the wording of the revised provisions fully meets the government's intentions. Although disclosure for the relevant purpose by an employee of their own terms to any person is protected, a term in an employee's contract to prevent them from *seeking* disclosure of another employee's terms is unenforceable only if this other employee is a

---

[147] EA, s 69 (1)(a)(b).
[148] Napier (2014) at 10; *Coventry City Council v Nicholls* [2009] IRLR 345, EAT.
[149] EA, s 77(1), (4).
[150] EA, s 77(3), defining a 'relevant disclosure'.
[151] JCHR (2008–09) para 192.
[152] Hansard HL vol 716 col 947 (27 January 2010) (Baroness Thornton).

'colleague' or former 'colleague'. As Baroness Butler-Sloss pointed out, the word 'colleague' 'would assume somebody working alongside, or at least in the same employment'.[153] This would not include an external trade union official or a representative of the EHRC, or a lawyer or a journalist. In the old case of *Bent's Brewery Co Ltd v Hogan*[154] it was held that a trade union official who sent out a questionnaire to some of the union's members, who were managers of licensed premises owned by brewery companies, to find out about their wages bill, takings and expenses, could be liable for inducing a breach of the managers' duty, implied by law as a term of their contracts, not to disclose confidential information. This was a tort not protected in the circumstances of the case as being 'in contemplation or furtherance of a trade dispute'. The Act does not appear to protect a *request* for information unless it is made by a colleague. If a union wants to avoid this legal obstacle it should ensure that the request is made by a trade union equality representative who is a colleague of the employee, and not by an external official.

A further potential obstacle to obtaining pay information is the Data Protection Act 1998, which allows for the disclosure of personal data only where it is 'necessary for the purposes of legitimate interests pursued by the data controller or by the third party or parties to whom the data are disclosed'. The Supreme Court has held that a campaigner, who had suspicions about whether employees of a local authority were receiving equal pay, had a 'legitimate interest' in obtaining information about their pay and was entitled to make a Freedom of Information Act request for such information. The word 'necessary' was interpreted as 'reasonably necessary' and the data was sought only in a form that did not identify individuals.[155]

Gender Pay Gap Information

Section 78 of the Equality Act enables a minister to make regulations requiring private and voluntary sector employers with at least 250 employees in Great Britain to publish information relating to differences in pay between their male and female employees. Employers who do not comply with the requirements could face civil enforcement procedures or be held liable for a criminal offence punishable by a fine of up to £5,000. The purpose of this was said to be so that 'their gender pay gap (the size of the difference between men and women's pay expressed as a percentage) is in the public domain'.[156] The Labour Government's aim was for employers to publish this information regularly on a voluntary basis. The Coalition Government,

---

[153] Ibid, col 948.
[154] [1945] 1 All ER 570.
[155] *South Lanarkshire Council v Scottish Information Commissioner* [2013] EqLR 1066.
[156] EN, para 273.

like the Labour Government before it, does not intend to use the power to make regulations unless insufficient progress has been made voluntarily on reporting.

Mandatory Equal Pay Audits

The closest that legislation has come to providing for mandatory equal pay audits was introduced by the Coalition Government in the Enterrpise and Regulatory Reform Act 2013.[157] Regulations are to be made requiring an employment tribunal to order an equal pay audit in any case where it finds that there has been an equal pay breach. An 'equal pay breach' is a breach of an equality clause or a contravention relating to pay in other sex discrimination provisions. The audit is designed to identify action to be taken to avoid equal pay breaches in the future. Regulations will provide for the content of the audit and other details.[158] There are exceptions where an audit has been completed in the last three years, or pay arrangements are already transparent, or there is no reason to believe that the employer's breach is systematic, or where the disadvantages of an audit outweigh the benefits.[159] The first Regulations must specify an exemption period which firms with less than 10 employees and start-up businesses will not be covered.[160] The sanction for failure to comply with an order will be payment of a penalty to the Secretary of State to a maximum of £5,000. Independent auditors can be commissioned by the tribunal to sign off the audit and to advise the employer on how to close the pay gap. The Consultation Document on audits states that best practice is for the audit work to be done by a team comprising managers, staff and any staff representative body.[161] The government has decided not to require publication of audits in company reports or its website. However, there must be disclosure to 'relevant parties' and this presumably includes all company employees and their representatives. There is an understandable fear that the requirement for audits may lead some companies to offer early settlements in order to avoid judgment and any consequential audit. However, an impact assessment has indicated that there is likely to be an increase of only 10–25 per cent in settlements (£149 per case). Such a price may prove to be worth paying for the possibility of a full-scale audit. The exception where an audit has been conducted in the past three years, may encourage employers to conduct independent audits *before* proceedings are brought.

---

[157] ERRA 2013, s 98 inserting new s 139A EA.
[158] Government Equalities Office, *Equal Pay Audits*: consultation (2013).
[159] EA, s 139A(5).
[160] EA, s 139A(10).
[161] Para 32.

5

Services, Premises, Education, Associations, and Other Unlawful Acts

SERVICES AND PUBLIC FUNCTIONS

General Scope

P ART 3 OF the Equality Act prohibits discrimination, harassment and victimisation in the supply of services (including goods and facilities) and the performance of public functions. This harmonises and extends protection against discrimination in these areas in respect of all protected characteristics except marriage and civil partnership and age so far as relating to persons under 18.[1] The harassment provisions do not apply to the provision of services and the exercise of public functions if the relevant characteristic is religion or belief or sexual orientation.[2] The definition of 'public functions' is the same as that in the Human Rights Act 1998.[3] These functions, not involving the provision of a service, include licensing functions, government and local authority consultation exercises, the provision of public highways, planning permission decisions, and core functions of the prison and probation services.[4] Since discrimination is now prohibited in respect of both the performance of public functions and the provision of services by public authorities that do not constitute the performance of public functions, the complex case law under the Human Rights Act on the distinction between these two areas should be of little importance under the Equality Act.[5]

---

[1] EA, s 28(1). See pp 63 and 40 above.
[2] EA, s 29(8). See p 99 above.
[3] EA, s 31(6).
[4] EN, para 125.
[5] JCHR (2008–09) para 141.

135

Age Exceptions

Direct age discrimination in the provision of services can be justified if it is a 'proportionate means of achieving a legitimate aim'.[6] There is no EU Directive on age discrimination in the provision of services, but the British courts are likely to be influenced by the case law of the Court of Justice in respect of justifying age discrimination in employment. Indirect age discrimination may also be justified.[7] In addition to these general defences, the Act and its schedules set out a number of wide-ranging exceptions. These were added by Ministerial Order amending schedule 3 to the Act, with effect from October 2012.[8] The exceptions include:

- use of age criteria in immigration control;
- age-based treatment in financial services, provided that any assessment of risk when providing financial services must be done by reference to relevant information from a source on which it is reasonable to rely;
- general age-based concessions, such as cheaper access to leisure facilities for senior citizens or younger people;
- age-related holidays, such as Club 18–30;
- restrictions where a person needs to be above a minimum age, provided that the service provider displays an age warning, eg for buying alcohol or tobacco;
- minimum age limits for occupants of residential mobile homes;;
- age-based concessions in private clubs and associations;
- age limits in sport, such as competitions for under 18s.

There is no exception for health and social care. Any age-related discrimination in treatment will have to be objectively justified. Nor is there is protection against age discrimination in respect of premises.

Constitutional Functions

There is a group of exemptions that recognise the sovereignty of Parliament and the independence of the courts. The prohibitions do not apply to the exercise of parliamentary functions, but those providing services in Parliament such, as the tea room, are not free to discriminate.[9] Activities related to the preparation and making of primary legislation are not covered, but

---

[6] EA, s 13(2), see p 77 above.
[7] See p 87 above.
[8] The Equality Act 2010 (Age Exceptions) Order 2012 SI 2012 No 2466.
[9] EA, sched 3 para 1; example given by the Solicitor-General PBC (EB) 10th sitting col 344 (18 June 2009).

the making of bye-laws by a local authority is.[10] A decision of a judge on the merits of a case, or of a prosecutor whether or not to commence or continue criminal proceedings cannot give rise to a claim of discrimination or harassment under the Act, but an administrative decision by court staff on the supply of services can do so.[11] Any challenge to a judicial act will have to be brought under the Human Rights Act. For example, the ECtHR has held that racial stereotyping in sentencing violates ECHR Articles 6(1) (fair trial) and 14 (equality).[12]

Armed Forces and Security Services

There are three sets of exclusions in respect of the armed forces. First, in respect of the performance of public functions, they can discriminate because of age, disability, gender reassignment or sex when the reason is to ensure combat effectiveness.[13]

Secondly, women and transsexual people can be excluded from service in the armed forces if it can be shown that this is 'a proportionate means of ensuring the combat effectiveness of the armed forces'.[14] This re-enacts exemptions set out in earlier legislation, but narrows the scope of the combat effectiveness exemption so as to apply only to direct discrimination in respect of recruitment, access to training, promotion and transfer opportunities. At present, only ground close-combat roles requiring Service personnel to deliberately close with and kill the enemy face-to-face are confined to men, and this is under review.[15] Thirdly, the armed forces are exempt from the work provisions of the Act relating to disability and age.[16] The justification offered by the Labour government is that '[p]ersonnel have to meet fitness standards to ensure they have the fitness attributes to cope with the physical demands of service ... [a]nd do not become a liability or danger to others in an operational environment'.[17] The JCHR considered that this exemption of the armed forces 'is unnecessary and incompatible with the UN Convention on the Rights of Persons with Disabilities' and may also be incompatible with ECHR Articles 8 (private life) and 14 (equality).[18] There

[10] EA, sched 3 para 2; EN, para 683.
[11] Ibid.
[12] *Todorova v Bulgaria* (application 37193/07) 25 March 2010 (refusal to suspend sentence because of defendant's Roma ethnic origin).
[13] EA, sched 3 para 4.
[14] EA, sched 9 para 4(1)–(2).
[15] EN, para 799.
[16] EA, sched 9 para 4(3).
[17] JCHR (2008–09) para 181.
[18] Ibid, paras 177–82.

is a blanket exclusion in relation to the security services,[19] in addition to the general exception in respect of any proportionate action taken for the purpose of safeguarding national security.[20]

Immigration Functions

Human rights and immigration controls are uneasy bedfellows.[21] There are three major exemptions in respect of immigration functions in the Equality Act: nationality and ethnic or national origins, religion or belief, and disability. With regard to the first of these, the EU Member States were worried that their immigration controls might be susceptible to challenge under the Race Directive, so they secured changes to the draft Directive in order to limit its application. The preamble makes it clear that the Directive does not apply to provisions governing the entry and residence of third-country nationals (TCNs) and their access to employment and occupation. There is nothing to prevent Member States granting more extensive protection against discrimination, but in many countries there is widespread discrimination against TCNs. Since the amending RRA in 2000, British law on racial discrimination has applied to the exercise of immigration functions. This is continued by the Equality Act and in principle applies to all protected characteristics.[22] In the *Prague Airport* case, selective intensive scrutiny of Roma people from the Czech Republic on the basis of a stereotype that they were more likely to put forward false claims than other groups was held by the House of Lords to be direct racial discrimination.[23] However, the Equality Act,[24] replicating provisions in the RRA, permits discrimination on the basis of nationality and ethnic or national origin if this is authorised by a minister in relation to the examination of a claim, detention, and conditions of temporary admission.[25] Authorisations enable immigration officers to scrutinise people of a specific nationality or ethnic or national group more closely than is the norm, for example where there is statistical or other evidence of high levels of abuse of the controls by people of that nationality. It is doubtful whether ethnic profiling, as distinct from nationality discrimination, would be compatible with the ECHR or CERD, under both of which there is strict scrutiny of race or ethnic-based classifications.[26] The Chief Inspector

---

[19] EA, sched 3 para 5.

[20] EA, s 192.

[21] Hepple (2004) 1. See p 49 above.

[22] s 29 EA.

[23] *R (European Roma Rights Centre) v Immigration Officer at Prague Airport* [2004] UKHL 55; [2005] 2 AC 1, HL (e). See p 70 above.

[24] EA, sched 3 para 17.

[25] EA, sched 3 para 17.

[26] See p 88 above. JCHR (2008–09) para 152.

of the Immgration Service, like the previous independent Race Monitor, is under a duty to monitor and make recommendations regarding the compatibility of immigration decisions with anti-discrimination law. Reports so far published by the Chief Inspector have not featured any information on the operation of nationality or ethnic authorisations in recent years.

The second exemption allows a person to be refused entry to or expelled from the UK on the basis of their religion or belief if to do so is conducive to the public good.[27] This includes barring people who provide services in connection with a religion, such as a clergyman or imam. The government's stated aim was to exclude so-called 'preachers of hate'. Arguably, the exception is not necessary because there are wide powers to exclude persons where this is 'conducive to the public good', such as those likely to stir up racial hatred. The JCHR thought that this provision might fall foul of ECHR Articles 8 (private life), 9 (religion) and 14 (equality).[28]

Most controversial of all is the new exclusion of claims for disability discrimination in respect of certain immigration decisions where the decision is 'necessary for the public good'.[29] In effect this allows the continuation of long-established health screening, for example for TB, of those wishing to remain in the UK for a lengthy stay. A specific exemption was considered necessary when immigration functions were brought within the equality legislation. In the face of concerns that the exercise of this power would not be limited to cases of a serious danger to public health and safety, the government gave its assurances that it was not the intention to use the power to exclude someone because of the potential cost of NHS or other care, provided that the person meets the requirements of the immigration rules.[30] The 'necessary for the public good' test appears to be stricter than a justification or proportionality test.[31] The government has expressed a reservation in this respect from the UN Convention on the Rights of Persons with Disabilities. The JCHR suggested that the exemption might be incompatible with Article 2 (right to life) and Article 3 (inhuman and degrading treatment of disabled persons).[32]

Religion or Belief Exceptions

The conflict between gender equality and religious freedom was reflected in the lengthy parliamentary debates concerning exceptions to the general

---

[27] EA, sched 3 para 18.
[28] JCHR (2008–09) para 156.
[29] EA, sched 3 para 16.
[30] Hansard HL vol 716 col 906 (27 January 2010) (Baroness Thornton).
[31] Ibid, col 905 (Baroness Thornton).
[32] JCHR (2008–09) para 147.

prohibition on discrimination and harassment because of religion or belief, both in the context of services.[33] The conflict between conscientious religious objection and the application of the principle of equality was also debated. This has arisen in several cases, which were discussed in chapter 2.[34] Religious beliefs are respected by means of exceptions to the general prohibition on gender reassignment discrimination in relation to the religious solemnisation of marriages.[35] So a Church of England clergyman or Roman Catholic priest will not be acting unlawfully if he refuses to solemnise a marriage because he believes that one of the couple has acquired his or her gender under the Gender Recognition Act 2004.[36] But a Registrar, whatever their religious beliefs, may not refuse to conduct a civil partnership or same-sex marriage for this reason.[37] There has been some liberalisation in respect of registering civil partnerships. The Civil Partnership Act 2004 prohibited such registrations from taking place in religious premises, but this restriction has been removed. However, a couple seeking to register their civil partnership cannot require those responsible for a church to hold the registration there.[38] The Marriage (Same Sex Couples) Act 2013 permits same-sex marriages but this does not apply to marriages solemnised according to the rites of the Church of England.[39] There are also exceptions that allow ministers of religion to provide separate services for men and women, or services only for persons of one sex,[40] so long as this is done for religious purposes in a place which is occupied or used for those purposes, and it is necessary either to comply with the tenets of the religion or for the purpose of avoiding conflict with the strongly held religious views of a significant number of the religion's followers.[41]

Separate, Single-Sex, and Single-Group Services

There is an express statutory provision that racial segregation always amounts to unlawful direct discrimination.[42] There has been a long line of case law that has established a similar principle in relation to gender segregation, for example service in a wine bar where women could not order at the bar,[43]

---

[33] See p 111 above regarding work exceptions.
[34] See p 51 above.
[35] EA, sched 3 para 24 (England and Wales), para 25 (Scotland).
[36] EN, paras 724 (England and Wales), 727 (Scotland).
[37] *Ladele v United Kingdom* [2013] EqLR 264.
[38] EA, s 202.
[39] Marriages Act 1949, s 26A(5) inserted by Marriage (Same Sex Couples) Act 2013, s 4(1).
[40] Acts of worship are not 'services' and fall outside the Act.
[41] EA, sched 3 para 29.
[42] EA, s 13(5). See p 67 above.
[43] *Gill v El Vinos Ltd* [1983] QB 425, CA.

school selection procedures where there were fewer places for girls than boys,[44] and even women being allowed to leave the factory gates five minutes earlier than men.[45] To deprive women of a choice afforded to men or vice versa, is 'less favourable treatment' and a 'detriment'. As the US Supreme Court famously established in 1954, there is no such thing as 'separate but equal' because imposed separation is inherently discriminatory.[46] It is unfortunate that this principle was not codified in the Equality Act, because there was a public controversy in 2013 as to whether it is legitimate and lawful for universities to accept a demand from an external speaker on religious grounds requiring women in the audience to sit separately from men.[47] The representative body of UK universities issued guidance that such a demand should be accepted. This was based on legal advice that this requirement was necessary in order to comply with duty of universities in England and Wales under section 43 of the Education (No 2) Act 1986 is 'to take such steps as are reasonably practicable to ensure that freedom of speech within the law is secured ... for visiting speakers'. It was suggested this duty coupled with Articles 9 and 10 ECHR, which protect the right to manifest religious beliefs and to freedom of epression, could justify at least what was somehat confusingly described as 'voluntary segregation' (apparently where mixed seating was also available). However, the EHRC then gave clear and, in the author's view, correct guidance that 'in an academic meeting or in a lecture open to the public it is not ... permissible to segregate by gender'.[48] The same would apply, in the author's view, to segregation on the basis of other protected characteristics such as religion or sexual orientation, unless specifically authorised by statute.

One such statutory provision is that it is permissible for a public or private provider to supply separate services for men and women, provided that a joint service would be less effective and the limited provision is a proportionate means of achieving a legitimate aim.[49] An example given in the Explanatory Notes is separate hostels for homeless men and women, where a unisex hostel would be less effective.[50] Single-sex services are permitted provided defined conditions are met and the limited provision is a proportionate means of achieving a legitimate aim.[51] Examples are where only people of one sex require the service (such as a cervical cancer screening service for women); where joint provision is not sufficient or it is not reason-

---

[44] *R v Birmingham City Council , ex parte EOC* [1989] AC 1155, HL.
[45] *Ministry of Defence v Jeremiah* [1980] QB 287, CA.
[46] *Brown v Board of Education* 347 US 483 (1954).
[47] (2014) EOR 2.
[48] EHRC, press statement, 11 December 2013; legal guidance, 18 July 2014.
[49] EA, sched 3 para 26.
[50] EN, para 732.
[51] EA, sched 3 para 27.

ably practicable to provide separate services; services in a hospital or other place where users need special attention; services that may be used by more than one person, such as a changing room, where a woman might object to the presence of a man or vice versa; or where the service may involve physical contact between the user and someone else and the other person might reasonably object if the user is of the opposite sex (such as a female massage therapist providing a service to women only in their own homes because she does not wish to massage men in their homes).[52]

Sensitivities about sharing separate and single-sex services with people whose gender has been reassigned led to an exception in the SDA, now replicated in the Act, which allows such provision to be justified if it is a proportionate means of achieving a legitimate aim.[53] An example given in the Explanatory Notes is the exclusion of a male-to-female transsexual person from a group counselling session provided for female victims of sexual assault.[54]

The prohibition on discrimination could potentially give rise to problems for a person who provides a service in such a way that it is commonly only used by persons who share a protected characteristic, for example an Afro-Caribbean hairdressing service, or a butcher who supplies halal meat. If the supplier reasonably thinks that it is impracticable to provide the service to persons who do not share the characteristic, the supplier can refuse to provide the service. So the halal butcher need not sell kosher meat, but may not refuse to sell halal meat to a non-Muslim customer. The hairdresser does not have to supply European hairdressing as well, but may not refuse to braid the hair of a White person if there is no technical difficulty in doing so.[55]

Health and Care

A series of exceptions are based on public health considerations. It is not unlawful for someone operating a blood service to refuse to accept a person's donation of blood provided they have reliable evidence (eg that people who have been sexually active in a particular country are more likely to be infected with HIV) that accepting it would put the public or the individual donor at risk and that such a refusal would not be unreasonable.[56] Services may be refused to a pregnant woman where it is reasonably believed that to do otherwise would create a risk to her health and safety. However, it

---

[52] EN, paras 733–38.
[53] EA, sched 3 para 28.
[54] EN, para 740.
[55] EA, sched 3 para 30.
[56] EA, sched 3 para 13; EN, paras 696–99.

must be shown that the provider would take similar measures in respect of persons with other physical conditions.[57] For example, air travel may be refused to a woman beyond her 35th week of pregnancy if it is reasonably believed that this would create a risk to her health and safety, but only if air travel would be refused to persons with other physical conditions affecting health and safety.[58]

The right to private and family life is preserved by a provision that people who provide foster care or similar forms of care (paid or unpaid) in their own home are not subject to the prohibitions on discrimination, harassment and victimisation in the provision of services while providing that care.[59] An example given in the Explanatory Notes is a Muslim family who could choose to foster only a Muslim child.[60]

Insurance

Employers quite often enter into group policies and schemes with an insurer to provide health insurance or pensions to their employees. Policies are based not on individual characteristics but on the nature of the employer's business and the profile of the organisation's employees. As health insurance is part of the package of benefits provided by the employer, the employer must ensure that there is no unlawful discrimination under the work provisions of the Act; for example, the employer must justify any differences in the treatment of men and women. The insurer or pension provider is not responsible for ensuring compliance with the services and public functions provisions of the Act.[61] Another provision enables insurance providers to offer different premiums and benefits to disabled people where it is reasonable to do so.[62] For example, life insurance may be refused to a person with cancer based on a medical report, or higher premiums for travel insurance may be charged to people with heart disease where actuarial evidence indicates that such people are at increased risk of a heart attack.[63]

Broadcasting

Freedom of expression and the independence of broadcasters is safeguarded

---

[57] EA, sched 3 para 14.
[58] EN, para 701.
[59] EA, sched 3 para 15.
[60] EN, para 704.
[61] EA, sched 3 para 20; EN, paras 712–13.
[62] EA, sched 3 para 21.
[63] EN, paras 714–15.

by a provision that makes it clear that claims for discrimination, harassment and victimisation cannot be brought in relation to broadcasting and distribution of content.[64] This does not apply to sending signals through an electronic communications network, service or facility.

Sport

The Act[65] allows separate sporting competitions for men and women where physical strength, stamina or physique are major factors in determining success or failure, and in which one sex is generally at a disadvantage in comparison with the other. It is lawful to restrict participation of transsexual people in competitions if this is necessary to uphold fair or safe competition, but not otherwise. National sports teams and regional or local clubs may limit participation to people who meet requirements relating to nationality, place of birth or residence. Age-banded limits (such as under 18s) may be imposed in sport to secure fair competition or safety, to comply with the rules of national or international competition, or to increase participation in a sporting activity.[66] These are defined to include both physical sports such as football and also more mental or intellectual activities such as bridge or chess.

PREMISES

Part 4 of the Act prohibits discrimination, harassment and victimisation in respect of the disposal, management and occupation of premises. This applies to all protected characteristics (see chapter 2 above) other than age or marriage and civil partnership,[67] which were also not covered in earlier legislation. Harassment of someone because of their sexual orientation or religion or belief when disposing of premises, or refusing permission to do so, or when managing premises, is not covered, but such harassment may amount to direct discrimination.[68] The curious reasons for this exclusion were considered earlier.[69]

There are limited exceptions to the prohibition on discrimination and harassment in respect of premises. The first is where a person who lives in a property disposes of all or part of it privately without using an estate agent

---

[64] EA, sched 3 para 31.
[65] EA, s 195; EN, paras 614–16.
[66] EA, s 195(7) inserted by SI 2012 No 2466, para 9.
[67] EA, s 32(1).
[68] EA, ss 33(6), 34(4), 35(4), 212(5).
[69] See p 99 above.

or publishing an advertisement.[70] This exception does not apply to race discrimination. It only applies to permission to dispose of premises where the refusal is based on religion or belief or sexual orientation. So a Christian landlord who is an owner-occupier could refuse permission to a tenant to sub-let to anyone who is not a Christian, but could not refuse permission to sub-let to a person because he is disabled.[71] The second exception applies to the disposal, occupation or management of part of small premises[72] where a person engaging in the conduct in question, or a relative[73] of that person, lives in another part of the premises and the premises include facilities shared with other people who are not part of the household. This exception does not apply to race discrimination. So a religious Jewish homeowner could refuse to let out part of the premises to a non-Jew, who would have to share a kitchen and might not respect religious dietary rules, but could not refuse to let out the premises because the prospective tenant is Black.[74]

There is an exception to the general prohibition on sex and gender reassignment discrimination in respect of communal accommodation, that is, residential accommodation which includes shared sleeping accommodation which should only used by members of one sex for privacy reasons.[75] In restricting use of the accommodation to one sex, account must be taken of various factors, including whether and how far it is reasonable to expect that the accommodation should be altered or extended or that further accommodation should be provided. The frequency of demand or need for the use of the accommodation by one sex compared to the other is also a relevant consideration. Restrictions relating to transsexuals must be a proportionate means of achieving a legitimate aim.

EDUCATION

Exceptions Relating to Marriage etc, and Age

Part 6 of the Equality Act makes it unlawful for education bodies to discriminate against, harass or victimise a school pupil, student or applicant for a place, subject to a number of exceptions. Most of these provisions replicate the effect of earlier legislation. The protection does not apply to those discriminated against, harassed or victimised by schools, further and higher

---

[70] EA, sched 5 para 1; EN, paras 765–72.
[71] EN, para 131.
[72] Defined in EA, sched 3 para 3(3), (4).
[73] Defined in EA, sched 3 para 3(5).
[74] EA, sched 5 para 3; EN, para 770.
[75] EA, sched 23 para 3.

education bodies, and general qualification bodies, because of marriage or civil partnership.[76] Nor does it apply to discrimination, harassment and victimisation against school pupils because of age.[77]

School admissions policies and curricula can be based on the ages of pupils and candidates, and school transport may be provided for children of a particular age group.[78]

The first draft of the Bill excluded protection of school pupils in respect of pregnancy and maternity from education in schools. However, the government was persuaded by pressure groups that it is desirable to ensure support for schoolgirls who become pregnant or return from maternity leave, and that the pregnancy discrimination provisions could be applied to schools without undermining the policy of reducing teenage pregnancies.[79] The effect of the Act is that a girl may not be told to leave the school, or not to take an examination, or not to continue with her education, because she is pregnant.[80]

Exceptions Relating to Harassment

A further serious limitation, as previously noted,[81] is that the responsible body of a school cannot be liable for harassment of a school pupil because of gender reassignment, religion or belief, or sexual orientation.[82] However, where a teacher harasses a pupil because of gender reassignment or sexual orientation this may amount to a 'detriment', in respect of which a claim for direct discrimination can be brought.[83]

Exceptions Relating to Religion or Belief

The Equality Act preserves the status quo in respect of faith schools. The Act makes it unlawful for the responsible body of a school to discriminate against, harass or victimise a person in its admissions arrangements, in the

---

[76] EA, ss 84(b) (schools), 90 (further and higher education), 95 (general qualification bodies).
[77] EA, s 84(a). See p 40 above.
[78] EA, sched 3 para 9. There are also exceptions allowing further and higher education institutions to confine benefits and facilities (eg residential accommodation) to married people and civil partners: EA, sched 12 para 6; and to confine childcare facilities for children of students to children of a particular age group: EA, sched 12 para 7.
[79] Hansard HL vol 716 cols 552–53 (19 January 2010).
[80] EN, para 74; Hansard HL vol 716 col 553 (19 January 2010).
[81] See p 100 above.
[82] EA, s 85(3), (10).
[83] EA, s 212(1).

terms on which it offers to admit a pupil, or by not admitting them.[84] However, there is an important exception relating to discrimination in respect of admissions because of religion or belief by schools that have a religious ethos ('faith schools').[85] This allows a faith school to give preference to members of its own religion when it is oversubscribed. Local authorities and education authorities are also protected from the risk of claims of discrimination when they provide schools for pupils of one faith but not another.[86] A public body is not open to claims of discrimination for anything done in connection with establishing, altering or closing a faith school,[87] its curriculum or acts of worship or other religious observance,[88] and the provision of school transport,[89] and it can select a person of a particular religion or belief to be a governor of a school with a religious ethos.[90]

The decision of the Supreme Court in the *JFS* case[91] on the refusal of admission by a Jewish faith school to a boy who was not considered Jewish by matrilineal descent does not challenge that status quo. The finding of the majority was that the discrimination was unlawful because it was based on ethnicity and not on religion. The unresolved issue is whether the fact that the law allows publicly funded schools to use faith-based admissions criteria is compatible with Article 2 of Protocol 1 (right to education) and Article 14 (equality) ECHR. This is a matter that has troubled the JCHR for some time.[92] Sooner or later, the government is likely to be called upon to provide evidence to support a defence that this discrimination because of religion or belief is 'necessary' and proportionate in a democratic society 'for the protection of the rights and freedoms of others' under Article 9(2) ECHR, particularly in the context of the growth of academy or 'free' schools which are not accountable to local authorities.

In general, schools cannot discriminate in the way they provide education to pupils,[93] but none of the prohibitions apply to anything done in connection with the content of the curriculum.[94] According to the Explanatory Notes, 'this ensures that the Act does not inhibit the ability of schools

---

[84] EA, s 85. The 'responsible body' for a maintained school is the local authority or the governing body, and for an independent or non-maintained special school it is the proprietor.

[85] EA, sched 11 para 5.

[86] EA, sched 3 paras 6 and 7; EN, para 686.

[87] EA, sched 3 para 11(f).

[88] EA, sched 3 para 11(a) and (c).

[89] EA, sched 3 para 11(e). The JCHR (2008–09) paras 234–38 thought that the government had not demonstrated the necessity of the exception relating to school transport.

[90] EA, sched 3 para 11(d); EN, para 695.

[91] *R (on the application of E) v Governing Body of JFS* [2009] UKSC 15; [2010] IRLR 136. See pp 48 and 74 above.

[92] JCHR (2008–09) paras 209–12.

[93] EA, s 85(2)(a).

[94] EA, s 89(2).

to include a full range of issues, ideas and materials in their syllabus and to expose pupils to thoughts and ideas of all kinds'.[95] Previous legislation granted an exemption only in respect of discrimination in the curriculum because of religion or belief. This saves British schools from the kinds of challenge mounted in the United States by Christian fundamentalists against the teaching of evolution without giving equal weight to the teaching of creationism.[96] The Equality Act now extends the curriculum exemption to all protected characteristics. The JCHR was concerned that the exemption relating to sexual orientation discrimination in the curriculum could result in a gay pupil being taught that homosexuals are sinful or of less moral worth because of their sexuality. The government's response was that they wished to ensure the full educational freedom of schools and to prevent them from being distracted by having to justify in legal proceedings the inclusion in the curriculum of particular works of literature or history, for example.[97]

There is an exception to the prohibition on religious discrimination for acts of worship or other religious observance organised by or on behalf of any school, not just faith schools, and whether or not forming part of the curriculum.[98] The purpose of this is to avoid any conflict with the existing legislative framework, which generally requires acts of collective worship to be of a broadly Christian nature.[99] Parents can withdraw their children from acts of collective worship, and sixth-form pupils may withdraw themselves,[100] but schools do not have to provide opportunities for separate worship for rmembers of different religions. The bias in favour of Christianity is hard to justify in modern multi-faith Britain; indeed in non-Christian faith schools it is impossible to do so. There are several ways in which schools can avoid the strict legal obligation; for example, they may apply to the local authority to have the requirement lifted, or they may introduce an act of collective worship relevant to all pupils whatever their background or beliefs. But as the JCHR pointed out, the Equality Act exemption is still vulnerable to challenge under the ECHR. The Committee recommended that instead of exempting collective worship from the duty not to discriminate because of religion or belief, the requirement that faith schools include a daily act of Christian worship should be re-examined.[101]

The Act replicates provisions in previous legislation that allow higher and further education institutions to discriminate in relation to training that

---

[95] EN, para 303.
[96] JCHR (2008–09) para 214.
[97] JCHR (2008–09) paras 216–21.
[98] EA, sched 11 para 6.
[99] EN, para 881.
[100] The JCHR (2008–09) para 232 wanted this right to be given to all pupils aged 16 and over.
[101] JCHR (2008–09) para 228.

would help fit a person for work, if the training is for work which could be refused because of a genuine occupational requirement.[102] For example, a Catholic theological college can refuse to admit a woman for training on a course designed only to prepare candidates for the (all-male) Catholic priesthood.[103] Where an institution (in practice a small number of sixth-form colleges) has a religious ethos, it may be designated by a goverment minister so as to admit students who share the relevant religion or belief in preference to those who do not, but this applies only to courses which do not constitute vocational training.[104]

Exception Relating to Single-Sex Institutions

The Act replicates a number of provisions of the SDA in relation to single-sex schools and institutions of further and higher education. Local authorities may establish single-sex schools but must provide similar numbers of places for boys and girls.[105] A school is single-sex even if it admits a small number of pupils of the opposite sex on an exceptional basis to particular courses or classes of study.[106] There are similar provisions in respect of single-sex institutions of further and higher education, and to make transitional arrangements for single-sex institutions that are turning co-educational.[107]

ASSOCIATIONS

Private Clubs

The Equality Act aims to achieve a balance between the right to freedom of association, which is guaranteed by Article 11 ECHR, and the right to non-discrimination and equality. Part 7 of the Act does so by making it unlawful for an association to discriminate against, harass or victimise an existing or potential member, or an associate, or a guest.[108] This applies to associations with at least 25 members where admission to membership is regulated by the association's rules and involves a process of selection.[109]

---

[102] EA, sched 12 para 4. See p 110 above.
[103] EN, para 882.
[104] EA, sched 12 para 5.
[105] EA, sched 3 para 8.
[106] EA, sched 11 para 1, and para 2 regarding single-sex boarding. Transitional exemptions can be obtained for schools that are going through the process of changing from a single-sex to a coeducational institution: paras 3 and 4.
[107] EA, sched 12 paras 1–3.
[108] EA, ss 101, 102.
[109] EA, s 107(2).

So a private book club run by a group of friends which has no formal rules governing admission could discriminate,[110] as could a small club, not open to the public, with fewer than 25 members. Gyms, nightclubs, casinos and similar facilities that require 'membership' as a condition of admission without operating a genuine selection process are not covered as associations, but instead are subject to the provisions of Part 3 of the Act regarding the provision of services to the public.[111] It does not matter whether the association is incorporated, or whether its activities are carried on for profit.[112]

An anomaly in the previous legislation was that although discrimination was unlawful in respect of race,[113] disability[114] and sexual orientation,[115] this did not apply to sex or other protected characteristics. The Equality Act now extends protection in respect of discrimination and victimisation to sex, age, religion or belief, pregnancy and maternity, and gender reassignment, but excludes marriage and civil partnership.[116] The harassment provisions apply to all protected characteristics except religion or belief and sexual orientation.[117]

An association cannot refuse a member access to a benefit. For example, a private golf club which admits both men and women cannot require women to play only on certain days, while men can play at all times.[118] However, the Act does not prevent associations from restricting their membership to people who share a protected characteristic.[119] If membership is restricted in this way, similar restrictions can be imposed on associates and guests.[120] It is, however, unlawful to restrict membership to people of a particular colour.[121] So 'gentlemen's' or 'ladies-only' clubs are still lawful, as are clubs, for instance, for Muslims, Poles, pensioners, or people with a particular disability such as deafness, but a colour bar is prohibited. Although it is unlawful for an association to discriminate against a pregnant woman, an exception allows her to be differently treated in the terms on which she is admitted, or in access to benefits, if it is reasonably believed that this is necessary for her health and safety and similar conditions would be applied

---

[110] EN, para 348.
[111] EN, para 348, and see *Dockers' Labour Club & Institute Ltd v Race Relations Board* [1976] Ac 285, HL, under the corresponding provisions of the RRA.
[112] EA, s 107(4).
[113] RRA, s 25.
[114] DDA, s 21F.
[115] Equality (Sexual orientation) Regulations 2007, made under the Equality Act 2006, s 81.
[116] EA, s 100(1).
[117] See p 100 above.
[118] EN, para 337.
[119] EA, s 101, sched 16 para 1(1).
[120] EA, sched 16 para 1(2), (3).
[121] EA, sched 16 para 1(4).

to persons with other physical conditions.[122] For example, a private club might restrict access to a squash court at a certain point in the pregnancy if it would similarly restrict a man with a heart condition.[123] The Act does not prevent a club from organising separate sporting competitions for men and women, or children, where physical strength, stamina or physique are major factors determining success or failure;[124] it also allows selection for national, regional or local sporting teams based on nationality or place of birth or residence.[125]

There is a general exception in respect of religious or belief organisations (other than commercial ones) in respect of the provisions of the Act relating to services, public functions, premises and associations.[126] This allows such organisations to restrict membership and participation in their activities, and the use of goods, facilities, services and premises that they provide. These restrictions can only be imposed by reference to a person's religion or belief or sexual orientation. In relation to religion or belief, the exception only applies where this is necessary to comply with the purpose of the organisation or to avoid causing offence to members of the religion or belief whom the organisation represents. In relation to sexual orientation, the exception only applies where it is necessary to comply with the doctrine of the organisation or in order to avoid conflict with the strongly held convictions of members whom the organisation represents. The organisation cannot discriminate because of sexual orientation where it contracts with a public body to carry on an activity on that body's behalf. For example, a religious organisation which has a contract with a local authority to provide meals or accommodation to vulnerable people cannot discriminate against gays and lesbians.[127]

Political Parties

The exception relating to associations whose membership is limited to persons who share a protected characteristic does not apply to registered political parties.[128] This means that a party cannot restrict its membership on racial or religious grounds. An example is the proceedings brought by the EHRC against the British National Party (BNP) because its constitution

---

[122] EA, sched 16 para 2.
[123] EN, para 909.
[124] EA, s 195(1)–(4).
[125] EA, s 195(5), (6).
[126] EA, sched 23 para 2.
[127] EN, para 996.
[128] EA, sched 16 para 1(5). This is a party registered in the Great Britain register under Part 2 of the Political Parties, elections and referendums act 2000.

and membership criteria discriminated against those who were not 'indigenous Caucasians'.[129] The BNP agreed to change this, but the new criteria for membership, requiring support for racist principles, were held to be indirectly discriminatory and unlawful because those who are not indigenous British by descent or origin cannot comply with the requirement consistently with their customs and cultural traditions as a racial group. The Judge said that there is a crucial distinction between holding discriminatory views and employing discriminatory principles as part of the mechanism for admission to membership of a political party.

The main issue debated in Parliament during the passage of the Equality Bill was that of positive action by political parties to increase the number of female and Black representatives in elected bodies.[130]

OTHER UNLAWFUL ACTS

Liability of Employers and Principals

The Equality Act, replacing similar provisions in earlier legislation, makes employers liable for acts of discrimination, harassment and victimisation by their employees in the course of their employment.[131] 'Employee' includes those under a contract of employment or a contract personally to do any work.[132] It does not matter whether the employer knows about or approves of the employee's acts.[133] There is a statutory defence for an employer to show in respect of anything alleged to have been done by the employee in the course of employment that the employer took all reasonable steps to prevent the employee from doing that thing or from doing anything of that description.[134]

The leading case of *Jones v Tower Boot Co Ltd*[135] gave a wide interpretation to the concept of 'course of employment'. A 16-year-old was subjected to severe physical and verbal racial harassment by some fellow employees. The EAT applied what was at the time the standard tort law test of whether an act is in the course of employment. This was whether the act was authorised, or, if not authorised, whether it was so connected with acts which the

---

[129] *Equality and Human Rights Commission v Griffin* [2010] EQLR 42 (Central London County Court).

[130] See p 161 below.

[131] EA, s 109(1).

[132] EA, s 83(2), (4), s 212(1). Chief Officers of police or the responsible police authority are responsible for acts by constables and police cadets: EA, s 42.

[133] EA, s 109(3).

[134] EA, s 109(4).

[135] [1997] IRLR 168, CA.

employer had authorised that they may rightly be regarded as modes—although improper modes—of doing them. The EAT, by a majority, held that the assaults were so severe that they could not be described as an unauthorised mode of performing authorised tasks. However, the court of appeal examined the purpose of the vicarious liability provisions in the RRA and held that they were intended

> to deter racial and sexual harassment in the workplace through a widening of the net of responsibility beyond the guilty employees themselves by making all employers additionally liable for such harassment, and then supplying them with the reasonable steps defence [above] which will exonerate the conscientious employer who has used his best endeavours to prevent such harassment, and will encourage all employers who have not yet undertaken such endeavours to take the steps necessary to make the same defence available in their own workplace.[136]

The common law test of vicarious liability has subsequently been modified by the House of Lords, and is now closer to the approach in discrimination and harassment cases.[137] It is clear that it is no defence for the employer to say that the employee was guilty of intentional wrongdoing, or was acting exclusively for his own benefit.

In practice some employment tribunals have accepted the statutory defence where the employer has given express instructions or training on how not to discriminate. In a common law tort case (where no such defence applies), merely giving express instructions not to commit a tort would not enable the employer to avoid liability. In discrimination and harassment cases, tribunals and courts need to investigate carefully whether *all* reasonable steps have been taken, including supervisory and auditing measures.[138]

Principals are liable for anything done by an agent with the authority of the principal.[139] Here the test is whether actual or implied authority was given to the agent to do an act which was capable of being done in a discriminatory manner.[140]

Liability of Employees and Agents

The law has been clarified in relation to the personal liability of the employee or agent in circumstances where the employer or principal is liable, or would have been liable but for the statutory defence of having taken all reasonable steps to prevent the act in question. The employee or agent is liable and it

---

[136] [1997] IRLR 168, para 38.
[137] *Lister v Helsey Hall Ltd* [2001] UKHL 22; [2001] IRLR 472.
[138] *Canniffe v East Riding of Yorkshire Council* [2006] IRLR 555, EAT.
[139] EA, s 109(2).
[140] *Lana v Positive Action Training in Housing (London) Ltd* [2001] IRLR 501, EAT.

is no longer necessary to show that the employee or agent knew that the act was unlawful. The only defence for the employee or agent is to show that he or she has relied on a statement by the employer or principal that the act is lawful and he or she reasonably believes this to be true.[141] An employer or principal who knowingly or recklessly makes a false statement as to the lawfulness of doing something under the act is guilty of an offence punishable by a fine (currently) of up to £5,000.[142]

Instructing, Causing or Inducing Contraventions

The Equality Act clarifies, harmonises and extends the provisions set out in previous legislation regarding the liability of those who instruct, cause or induce someone to discriminate against, harass or victimise someone, or to attempt to do so. Case law had previously allowed the recipient of an instruction to discriminate to sue: for example, a White employee who resigned because she was told to discriminate against Black applicants was found to have been discriminated against 'on racial grounds'.[143] The Act now expressly grants the recipient of the instruction to carry out a prohibited act of discrimination, harassment or victimisation a remedy, provided they suffer a detriment.[144] For the first time, the intended victim who suffers a detriment is allowed to bring proceedings, even if the instruction is never carried out.[145] The EHRC may also bring proceedings.[146]

Aiding Contraventions

Finally, the Act replicates provisions found in previous legislation that make those who aid contraventions of the act liable in their own right. It is unlawful to help a person to carry out an Act which he or she knows is unlawful under the act, unless he or she has relied on a statement by the person being helped that the act is lawful, and it is reasonable to do so.[147] It is an offence, punishable by a fine of up to (currently) £5,000, knowingly or recklessly to make a false statement about the lawfulness of doing something under the Act.[148]

---

[141] EA, s 110.
[142] EA, s 110(4), (5).
[143] *Weathersfield v Sargent* [1999] IRLR 94.
[144] EA, s 111(5)(a).
[145] EA, s 111(5)(b).
[146] EA, s 111(5)(c).
[147] EA, s 112.
[148] EA, s 112(3), (4).

6

Advancement of Equality

CHANGING ORGANISATIONAL
POLICY AND BEHAVIOUR

THE CAMBRIDGE REVIEW, using the insights of modern regulatory theory, designed an 'optimal' form of regulation which could help to reduce, if not eliminate, under-representation, exclusion and institutional barriers to equal opportunities.[1] We described this as 'enforced self-regulation'.

Self-regulation involves three interlocking mechanisms. The first is internal scrutiny by the institution itself to ensure effective self-regulation. The second is the involvement of interest groups (such as managers, employees and service-users) who must be informed, consulted and engaged in the process of change. The third is the Commission, which should provide the back-up role of assistance and ultimately enforcement where voluntary methods fail. These interlocking mechanisms create a triangular relationship among those regulated, those whose interests are affected, and the Commission as the guardian of the public interest. We argued that this broad strategy needed to be developed in specific contexts, in particular (1) a positive duty on public authorities to advance equality; (2) positive duties on private sector employers to achieve employment equity or fair participation; (3) positive duties on employers to introduce pay equity schemes; and (4) the use of contract and subsidy compliance as a sanction and incentive. The only part of this strategy to have been fully embraced in the Equality Act is the first, an enlarged and simplified public sector duty to advance equality, and, to a limited extent, contract and subsidy compliance.[2] The Labour Government also introduced a public sector duty regarding socio-economic inequalities[3] but, this was not brought into force and has been repealed by the Coalition Government.[4] Mandatory employment equity and pay equity schemes

---

[1] Cambridge Review (2000) ch 3.
[2] See p 163 below.
[3] See 1st edn of this book, 141–43.
[4] ERRA 2013.

have been rejected.[5] The new regime is imperfect as a form of 'enforced self-regulation', or what McCrudden describes as 'reflexive' or 'responsive' regulation. But, in his words regarding the *Discrimination Law Review* proposals on which the Act is based, 'it clearly constitutes an important, indeed radical, shift of regulatory philosophy in the area of equality legislation compared with what has gone before'.[6]

Public authorities fulfilling their positive duties, and others seeking to take positive action on a voluntary basis, are limited by the principle of non-discrimination. The use of sex or race or any other protected characteristic as a criterion for more favourable treatment is prohibited, even if this is used to benefit disadvantaged groups.[7] Positive action therefore has to be justified as an exception to the non-discrimination principle, and is allowed only in defined circumstances. There is no provision for 'reverse' or 'positive' discrimination, for example quotas for people who share particular characteristics such as race or sex. Hence it is not lawful under current UK legislation to require quotas of women on company boards of directors. An inquiry for the government by Lord Davies made out a strong business case for increasing the number of women on boards,[8] but unlike many other EU Member States which have imposed quotas of 30–40 per cent, UK governments have resisted statutory quotas. Instead reliance is placed on positive action to reach a target of 25 per cent by 2015. (The proportion of women on the boards of FTSE 100 companies progressed from 12.5 per cent in 2011 to 20.7 per cent in 2014.) Positive action is allowed under the Equality Act in only three circumstances: (1) where it is a proportionate means of achieving a relevant aim; (2) as a 'tie-break' in recruitment and promotion; and (3) in the selection of candidates by political parties for public elections. There are also provisions that allow charities to benefit particular groups.

POSITIVE ACTION

General Exception Relating to Positive Action Measures

The SDA and RRA allowed a limited range of positive action measures to encourage applications and provide special training where women and ethnic minorities were under-represented. The Cambridge Review[9] found that these provisions were little used, and were out of date in at least two

---

[5] See p 120 above.
[6] McCrudden (2007b) 266.
[7] Fredman (1997b) 576.
[8] Davies (2011).
[9] Cambridge Review (2000) paras 2.48–2.49.

respects. First, they were based on a model of training that has changed. Positive action had to be for 'particular work'. This is no longer an appropriate concept because employers' training programmes are linked to giving people specific competencies which may be needed for a variety of positions. Secondly, the provisions did not allow positive action to be taken for all those on work experience and similar programmes.

The provisions were also out of date because they had been overtaken by developments in EU law which permit wider and more flexible use of positive action. Initially, Article 2.4 of Equal Treatment Directive 76/207/ EEC allowed a rather narrow exception to the principle of equal treatment 'to promote equal opportunity for men and women in particular by removing existing inequalities which affect women's opportunities'. The Court of Justice of the EU in the *Kalanke* case[10] held that a tie-break clause in the Bremen Act on Equal Treatment, which required a person of the under-represented sex to be appointed where two or more candidates appeared to be equally qualified, went further than was permissible under Article 2.4, construed as an exception to the equal treatment principle. However, two years later, in the *Marschall* case,[11] the European Court upheld the tie-break provision in the Nordrhein-Westfalen law on civil servants on the ground that there was a savings clause that the rule preferring women applied only where 'reasons specific to another candidate' did not predominate. Provided that there was an element of flexibility in the positive action measure and it removed practical obstacles from career paths, such as lack of work experience or childcare responsibilities, it was not incompatible with Article 2.4. In *Badeck*[12] there was an interview quota, but the selection process started by assessing the candidates' suitability, capability and qualifications, and only if a male candidate and a female candidate could not be distinguished was the female candidate preferred in order to comply with an advancement plan which required posts for academic training to be filled 'with at least the same proportion of women as the proportion of women among the graduates of the discipline in question'. This was upheld as lawful by the Court of Justice. In later cases the Court of Justice has made it clear that the test of proportionality should be applied to all positive action measures.[13] A positive action measure that completely excludes a person from appoint-

---

[10] Case C-450/93 *Kalanke v Freie Hansestadt Bremen* [1993] ECR I-3051.
[11] Case C-405/95 *Marschall v Land Nordrhein-Westfalen* [1997] ECR I-6363.
[12] Case C-158/9 *Badek v Hessische Ministerpräsident* [2000] ECR I-1875.
[13] Case C-407/98 *Abrahamsson v Fogelqvist* [2000] ECR I-5539; Case C-476/99 *Lommers v Minister Van Landbouen, Natuurbeheer EN Visserij* [2002] ECR I-2891; Case C-319/2003 *Serge Briheche v Ministre de l'Intérieur, Ministre de l'Éducation nationale and Ministre de la Justice* [2004] ECR I-8807.

ment or promotion because of a protected characteristic will generally not be regarded as proportionate.

This case law was reflected in the 2002 amendments to the Equal Treatment Directive. Article 3 of the Recast Directive permits Member States to maintain or adopt measures within the meaning of what is now Article 157(4) TFEU, which provides:

> With a view to ensuring full equality in practice between men and women in working life, the principle of equal treatment shall not prevent any member state from maintaining or adopting measures providing for specific advantages in order to make it easier for the underrepresented sex to pursue a vocational activity or to prevent or compensate for disadvantages in professional careers.

Similarly, Article 5 of the Race Directive states that:

> With a view to securing full equality in practice, the principle of equal treatment shall not prevent any member state from maintaining or adopting specific measures to prevent or compensate for disadvantages linked to racial or ethnic origin.

Article 7.1 of the Framework Employment Directive contains an identical provision in relation to religion or belief, disability, age or sexual orientation, and Article 7.2 allows 'measures aimed at creating or maintaining provisions or facilities for safeguarding or promoting [disabled persons'] integration into the working environment'.

The Cambridge Review recommended that UK law should be brought into line with EU law, as interpreted by the Court of Justice. The Equality Act does this through two provisions, one general, and the other applying only to recruitment and promotion. They are permissive and not mandatory, but extend what is permissible. They apply to all protected characteristics. Section 158 provides that the Act does not prohibit a person from taking any action which is a proportionate means of achieving any one of three aims:

(a) enabling or encouraging persons who share a protected characteristic to overcome or minimise a disadvantage connected to the characteristic;
(b) meeting those needs of persons who share a protected characteristic that are different from the needs of persons who do not share it; or
(c) enabling or encouraging participation in an activity where participation by persons who share that characteristic is disproportionately low.

For example, measures can be targeted towards particular disadvantaged groups, including training to enable them to gain employment and health services to address their needs.[14] There is a power to make regulations setting out any action which is not permitted.[15] The courts and tribunals have to

---

[14] EN, para 511.
[15] EA, s 158(3).

decide what is proportionate in accordance with EU law. The Explanatory Notes suggest that relevant factors may be the seriousness of the disadvantage, the extremity of need or under-representation and the availability of other means of countering them.[16] Unconditional quotas or reserved places are clearly not lawful, but it may be possible to give priority to a particular group provided this is based on objective criteria showing why the group is disadvantaged. So a university in which Black students are under-represented may target particular schools and communities, provide access courses and special support for such students, and deal with practical barriers to their recruitment or academic achievement. But the university cannot have a racial quota or reserve places for particular groups. In the case of disability, it is possible to treat a disabled person more favourably than a person who is not disabled.[17] Age discrimination can be justified if this is a proportionate means of achieving a legitimate aim.[18] The positive action provisions allow action to be taken in favour of a group with a particular disability, such as autism or deafness.

Recruitment and Promotion

Tie-breaks in recruitment and promotion have proved to be far more controversial, although they are permitted in EU law within the parameters laid down in Court of Justice case law (above). Section 159 permits an employer to take a protected characteristic into account when deciding who to recruit or promote, where people having that characteristic suffer a disadvantage or are underrepresented. Recruitment is broadly defined, and includes offering a person a partnership, or a pupillage or tenancy in barristers' chambers, and public appointments.[19] An example given during the debates was a primary school with only female teachers. If the school wishes to have a male role model for the pupils, and the female and male candidates are as well qualified as each other, the man may be selected in order to reduce under-representation.[20] The provision can also be used to remedy disadvantage connected with a protected characteristic, such as career breaks for women to have children.

This provision can be used only where the candidates are 'as qualified as' each other.[21] An amendment was moved by the Conservatives to alter

---

[16] EN, para 512.

[17] EA, s 13(3).

[18] See p 77 above. There are also specific exceptions allowing age discrimination, see pp 115 and 136 above.

[19] EA, s 159(5).

[20] PBC (EB) 16th sitting col 6704 (30 June 2009) (Mark Harper).

[21] EA, s 159(4)(a).

this to 'equally qualified',[22] but this was rejected on the grounds that 'the amendments could have the effect of leading employers to interpret the [section] too narrowly by considering the provisions as being solely about the equality of qualifications *per se* ... [or] as a requirement that candidates have identical qualifications'.[23] The Minister said that 'any assessment of candidates' suitability will depend on a number of factors relevant to the job in question, such as experience, aptitude, physical ability, or performance during an interview or assessment. Formal qualifications are only one way in which a candidate's overall suitability may be assessed.'[24] The Explanatory Notes reflect this interpretation.[25] The intention is that if the employer reasonably thinks that the candidates are of a comparable standard, the protected characteristic can be invoked as a tie-break. This is in line with the Court of Justice case law, which has allowed preference to be given where the candidates have 'substantially equivalent merits'.[26]

The employer must not have a 'policy' of automatically treating those who share a protected characteristic more favourably than those who do not have it.[27] There is some ambiguity about the effect of this condition. The JCHR thought that this might prevent an employer from having any fixed policy of adopting positive action measures.[28] The intention, according to the Explanatory Notes, is that each case must be considered by the employer on its merits. It might have been clearer if the Act had avoided the word 'policy' and expressly stated, in line with Court of Justice case law, that candidates must be assessed on their merits up to the point where they are found to have substantially equivalent merits. This is an interpretation that should be adopted by courts and tribunals. Any action taken must be a proportionate means of achieving the aim of overcoming or minimising the disadvantage or under-representation.[29]

Section 158 (general) does not apply to recruitment and promotion; only section 159 does so.[30] It appears that, in practice, little use has been made of section 159 despite its potential to improve diversity without infringing the equal treatment principle.

---

[22] PBC (EB) 16th sitting col 604 (30 June 2009) (Mark Harper); Hansard HL vol 717 col 656 (9 February 2010) (Lord Hunt of Wirral).
[23] Hansard HL vol 717 col 658 (9 February 2010) (Baroness Royall).
[24] Ibid.
[25] EN, para 518.
[26] Case C-407/98 *Abrahamsson v Fogelqvist* [2000] ECR I-5539.
[27] EA, s 159(4)(b).
[28] JCHR (2008–09) para 248.
[29] EA, s 159(4)(c).
[30] EA, s 158(4).

Political Parties

Women have found it difficult to be adopted as candidates by the main political parties, and when they do find a seat, it is likely to be less winnable than those for which men have been selected. The parliamentary franchise was first extended to women in 1918, but it was not until the 1990s that more than 6 per cent of MPs were women. By 2005, 20 per cent of MPs were women; this rose only slightly to 23 per cent (147 women MPs) by 2014. Only five out of 22 cabinet ministers are women. As at April 2014, of the 28 EU Member States, the UK ranked 15th in terms of women's representation in national parliaments, and was 74th in the Inter-Parliamentary Union's listing of 190 countries.[31] Women's representation in local government is somewhat higher than in Parliament but still less than one in three. Black and Asian ethnic minorities are seriously under-represented: following the May 2010 general election just 4 per cent (27 out of 649 MPs) are Black or Asian, compared to about 18 per cent of the UK population who are Black or Asian.[32] Only 4 per cent of local councillors are from ethnic minority backgrounds. The single member, 'first past the post' constituency system contributes to under-representation. If a local party organisation perceives any prejudice in the electorate they will tend to select the candidate who is the 'safest' option. An alternative vote (AV) system, with voters expressing second and third preferences, might lead parties to offer voters a wider choice, particularly if other parties are doing so. It is perhaps significant that in Scotland, where one-third of the members of the Scottish Parliament are women, and Wales, where just under half of those in the National Assembly are women, systems of proportional representation are in operation. Similarly, in the proportionally elected European Parliament, one-third of British MEPs are women.

The Sex Discrimination (Election Candidates) Act 2002 allowed registered political parties to make arrangements for the selection of candidates with a view to improving the representation of women. The Equality Act replicates these provisions and also introduces new provisions for the other characteristics protected under Part 7 (associations). This applies to selection of candidates for Westminster, European, devolved and local elections.[33] A registered political party is allowed to make arrangements in order to

---

[31] Women in Parliament and Government, House of Commons Library, standard note SNO1250, 11 April 2014.

[32] Ethnic Minorities in Politics, Government and Public Life, House of Commons Library, SN/SG/1156, 16 Octobner 2013..

[33] EA, s 104(8).

reduce inequality in the party's representation in the body concerned.[34] For example, a party is allowed to reserve places on a shortlist for people with a specific protected characteristic, such as race or ethnic origin or disability, but this has to be a proportionate means of achieving the purpose of reducing under-representation of that group.[35] This does not permit the use of 'closed' shortlists of persons who share a protected characteristic, except in the case of single-sex shortlists. The latter do not have to be shown to be a proportionate means of reducing under-representation of women.[36] These single-sex closed shortlists are permitted until the end of 2030, by which time it is optimistically expected that greater parity will have been achieved. A minister has the power to extend their use beyond that date.[37] An attempt by Liberal Democrat MPs to extend the positive action provisions to internal party elections was rejected by the Labour Government.[38]

The Speaker's Conference on Parliamentary representation recommended, with all-party agreement, that registered political parties be required to publish anonymised information on the diversity of their selection of candidates. The aim was 'to increase public accountability and act as an incentive for political parties to identify and remove barriers which cause or contribute to the under-representation of certain groups'.[39] A new provision in the Equality Act implements this recommendation by giving a minister the power to make regulations requiring parties to publish data relating to the diversity of party candidates seeking selection.[40] Regulations will specify which protected characteristics are covered, but these characteristics may not include marriage and civil partnership, or pregnancy and maternity.[41] Parties are not allowed to require anyone to provide the relevant information to them,[42] in recognition of their members' rights to privacy.

Charities

The Equality Act replaces and harmonises separate exceptions found in previous legislation allowing charities to benefit people only of the same sex, racial group, religion or belief, or sexual orientation. This has been extended

---

[34] EA, s 104(3)(b). 'Inequality' means inequality between the number of elected candidates who share a protected characteristic and the number of elected candidates who do not share that characteristic: EA, s 101(4).
[35] EA, s 104(3)(c).
[36] EA, s 104(7).
[37] EA, s 105.
[38] PBC (EB) 13th sitting cols 480–85 (25 June 2009).
[39] Hansard HL vol 716 col 1458 (9 February 2010) (Baroness Royall).
[40] EA, s 106.
[41] EA, s 106(6).
[42] EA, s 106(11).

across all protected characteristics.[43] This must be done in pursuance of the terms of the charitable instrument, and the provision of benefits in this way must be a proportionate means of achieving a legitimate aim, or for the purpose of preventing or compensating for a disadvantage linked to a protected characteristic. This does not protect colour discrimination. If the beneficiaries are limited to Black or White people, the charitable instrument will be applied as if the limitation did not exist and benefits can be provided to the whole community. The Act now allows single-sex activities for the purpose of promoting or supporting a charity, such as women-only fun runs.

PUBLIC SECTOR EQUALITY DUTY

Purpose

The vision of comprehensive and transformative equality (see p 1 above) is embodied in the extension and simplification of what is now a single public sector equality duty (**PSED**). The main purpose of the duty is 'to bring about a culture change so that promoting equality becomes part of public bodies' core business'.[44]

The Equality Act contains a new single equality duty which brings together the previous race, disability and sex duties and also covers age, gender reassignment, pregnancy and maternity, religion or belief, and sexual orientation.[45] The duty does not apply to age in respect of functions relating to schools and children's homes[46] because the government believed that there is already adequate provision for this under existing legislation. Nor does it apply to immigration functions[47] or judicial functions.[48]

The General and Specific Duties

Like the earlier legislation, there is a general duty and there are also specific duties. The general duty requires a public authority in the exercise of its functions to have *due regard* to the need to:

- eliminate discrimination, harassment, victimisation and any other conduct that is prohibited by the Act;[49]

---

[43] EA, ss 193, 194; EN, paras 608–13.
[44] Government Equalities Office (2009b) para 3.3.
[45] EA, s 149. See p 14 above for the earlier duties.
[46] EA, sched 18 para 1. See p 40 above.
[47] EA, sched 18 para 2. See p 138 above.
[48] EA, sched 18 para 3. See p 136 above.
[49] EA, s 149(a).

- advance equality of opportunity between persons who share a relevant characteristic and persons who do not share it;[50] and
- foster good relations between persons who share a relevant characteristic and persons who do not share it.[51]

The earlier legislation referred to 'promoting' equality. The change of wording to 'advancing' is significant. It indicates a more proactive approach that focuses on making progress in outcomes. The application of the requirement to 'advance equality of opportunity' to religion or belief proved to be controversial. It seems that this places a duty on public authorities proactively to consider indirect discrimination and to make changes which take account of different needs arising from religion or belief. For example, a hospital must consider the different dietary needs of Muslims and Jews. They could do this simply by avoiding direct discrimination (the first limb of the equality duty), for example by providing vegetarian meals which satisfy all religious or other beliefs. But the duty to 'advance' equality seems to imply that the hospital should make halal and kosher meals available. In the employment context, advancing equality might involve providing prayer facilities for observant employees. Unsuccessful Liberal Democrat amendments at the committee and report stages in the Commons and Lords sought to exclude advancement (but not the other two aims) in relation to religion or belief, on the ground that this duty would put pressure on local and other public authorities to give priority to one religious group over another and could lead to separate facilities being provided for each religion.[52] If segregated facilities were provided for an ethnic group, such as Jews, this would automatically amount to unlawful discrimination;[53] in the case of a non-ethnic religious group such as Muslims, there would need to be evidence that the segregated facilities were less favourable than those provided to another religious group.[54] The Labour Government, with Conservative support, rejected these amendments, arguing that all a public authority is required to do is consider the impact of its policies on the needs of people of particular religions. For example, if Muslim women object to swimming with men, the authority would not have to establish a separate swimming pool for them but could, as many now do, simply arrange different swimming times on certain days for men and women.[55] An authority may, however, have to engage in costly legal action to defend its actions if these do not please a

---

[50] EA, s 149(1)(b). This does not apply to marriage and civil partnership.

[51] EA, s 149(1)(c). This does not apply to marriage and civil partnership.

[52] PBC (EB) 15th sitting cols 554–55 (30 June 2009); Hansard HL vol 716 col 1504 (9 February 2010); Hansard HL vol 717 col 1404 (2 March 2010).

[53] EA, s 13(5).

[54] See p 140 above.

[55] PBC (EB) 15th sitting col 574 (30 June 2009) (solicitor-general).

particular religious group. The inclusion of religion, as Lord Lester said, may encourage 'division, not cohesion'.[56] The duty to advance equality in respect of sexual orientation did not raise similar concerns. The government argued that the duty would not require public authorities to 'promote homosexuality' or devalue the importance of marriage, but it should prompt a local authority or school to take action where there is widespread bullying of gay people.[57]

In addition to the general duty, Regulations place specific duties on specified public authorities to enable them to carry out the public sector equality duty more effectively.[58] These specific duties are intended not as an objective in themselves, but as 'a means to better performance of the general duty'.[59] There were several inconsistencies between the previous specific race, disability and sex duties, and the intention of the Act was to introduce a unified approach for all strands of equality.

There are separate Regulations in respect of public bodies in England,[60] Scotland[61] and Wales.[62] The Scottish and Welsh Regulations go much further than the English ones in prescribing what public bodies must do. The Coalition Government blocked a statutory code of practice aimed at making it clearer what the Act requires, but the EHRC has issued guides in respect of each jurisdiction.[63] In England, the specified authorities, with 150 or more employees, must publish information at least once a year, relating to persons who have the relevant protected characteristics and who are (a) its employees, and (b) other persons affected by its policies and practice. The Scottish and Welsh Regulations go further than the English ones by specifying the information in respect of composition of the authority's employees, and the recruitment, development and retention of employees. Best practice in England also is to collect such information. There are additional requirements in Scotland to publish information on the gender pay gap, and a statement of policy on equal pay and occupational segregation. Collecting and using equality information enables authorities to have a sound evidence-base on which to implement the general duty. After 40 years of race and

---

[56] Hansard HL vol 716 col 1506 (27 January 2010). See, for example, the issue of gender segregation because of religion, p 140 above.

[57] *Discrimination Law Review* (2007) para 5.67.

[58] Made under EA, ss 153, 154, 155. The public authorities are listed in the Regulations.

[59] Government Equalities Office (2009b) para 3.6.

[60] The Equality Act 2010 (Specific Duties) Regulations 2011, SI 2011 No 2260.

[61] The Equality Act 2010 (Specific Duties) (Scotland) Regulations 2012, No 162.

[62] The Equality Act 2010 (Statutory Duties) (Wales) Regulations 2011, No 1064 (W 155).

[63] EHRC, The Essential Guide to the Public Sector Employment Duty: ENGLAND (and Non-devolved Public Authorities in Scotland and Wales), rev 3rd edn (EHRC, November 2012); Essential Guide to the Public Sector Equality Duty (Scotland) (EHRC, 2012); and Essential Guide to the Public Sector Equality duty (Wales) (EHRC, 2012). The Government Equalities Office has also issued 'quick start' guides.

gender legislation it is now relatively easy to gather information about these aspects of identity. The guides stress the importance of 'achieving a culture where employees or service users are ready to be asked about their sexual orientation gender identity or religion'. When monitoring sexuality authorities should be aware of potential conflicts with the right to private and family life under Article 8 ECHR.

The specified authorities must also prepare and publish one or more equality objectives (in Scotland 'equality outcomes') that it thinks it needs to achieve to further any of the aims of the general equality duty. This had to be done by 6 April 2012 in England and Wales (30 April 2013 in Scotland) and then at least every four years after that. The objectives must be specific and measurable. The Scottish and Welsh Regulations require reasons to be given if a set of outcomes does not cover every relevant protected characteristic. The guides say that authorities should take a proportionate approach, which means that larger authorities, such as government departments, are likely to set more objectives across a broader range of issues than a smaller public body with a narrow area of influence such as a primary school. The Scottish Regulations go further than the English ones by requiring the authority to report on the progress made to achieve the equality outcomes not later than 30 April 2015 and subsequently at least once every two years.[64] They also differ from the English Regulations, as do the Welsh ones, by requiring the authority to make an equality impact assessment in respect of any proposed new or revised policy or practice, and it must take account of that assessment when developing a policy or practice.[65] In England, the EHRC guidance has little to say on implementation of the objectives, apart from advising that they need to be embedded into the organisation's business planning and training. The absence of specific obligations in respect of impact assessment and review is a serious weakness of the English Regulations.

The justification given by the Coalition Government for the watering down of earlier requirements in England was the commitment to 'reduce burdens and bureaucracy' on public bodies, and to move away from a process-driven approach to a focus on transparency, in order to free up public bodies to do what is appropriate in their circumstances, to take responsibility for their own performance, and to be held to account by the public.[66] There certainly was a widely held perception that the specific duties under race, gender and disability legislation had led some public bodies to focus on paper exercises and a tick-box approach as to whether they had

---

[64] SI 2012 No reg 5(4)

[65] Ibid, reg 5.

[66] Government Equalities Office, *Equality Act 2010. The Public Sector Equality Duty Reducing Bureaucracy*, Policy Review Paper (March 2011), para 3.

followed the right processes, rather than on whether those processes actually delivered equality improvements.[67]

Engagement

Perhaps the most important function of positive duties is to ensure that internal scrutiny involving all the stakeholders takes place. The specific public sector duty in respect of race, prior to the 2010 Act, required the authority's race equality scheme to state its arrangements for 'consulting' on the likely impact of proposed policies on the promotion of race equality;[68] those relating to gender required the authority to state the actions it had taken or intended to take to 'consult' relevant employees, service users and others (including trade unions);[69] and those in respect of disability went furthest, requiring the authority to 'involve' in the development of an equality scheme disabled persons who appeared to the authority to have an interest in the way it carries out its functions.[70]

The first draft Regulations under the 2010 Act to replace these earlier specific duties, published in January 2011, following consultation, required the listed public bodies to publish details of the engagement they had undertaken when determining their policies. In March 2011, however, there was a volte-face. New draft Regulations for England were published, stripping out the publication details relating to engagement. The requirements are now limited to publication of information collected and the equality objectives. The Scottish and Welsh Regulations, by contrast, provide that in preparing a set of equality outcomes or objectives, a listed authority must 'take reasonable steps to involve persons who share a relevant protected characteristic and any person who appears to the authority to represent the interests of those persons'.[71] The issue is whether transparency as to objectives and outcomes alone will result in adequate internal scrutiny and voluntary action. There are reports that some English public bodies in order to make costs savings are abandoning monitoring and impact assessments and are not consulting interested persons, trade unions and equality representatives or involving disabled persons.

---

[67] See Lord Ouseley, Hansard HL, vol 717, col 1399. See p 174 below.
[68] The Race Relations Act (Statutoy Duties) Order 2001, SI 2001 No 2548, Art 2(b)(i) and the Race Reations Act (Statutory Duties) Order 2003 SI 2003 No 3006, Art 2(b)(i).
[69] The Sex Discrimination Act 1975 (Public Authoirities) (Statutory Duties) Order 2006, SI 2006 No 2930, Art 2(6)(d).
[70] The Disability Discrimination (Public Authorities) (Statutory Duties) Regulations 2006, SI 2006 No 2966, reg 2(2), and information on this had to be included in the scheme: Art 2(3)(a).
[71] SI 2012 No 162 reg 4(2).

Contract and Subsidy Compliance

The Labour government proposed that, when setting out their equality objectives and the steps they intend to take to achieve them, contracting authorities should have to include details of how they will ensure that equality factors are considered as part of their procurement activities. An example given was that an NHS trust which finds that a section of the local community has inadvertently been excluded from accessing a service should consider how procurement could be used to achieve the objective of widening access to all sections of the community.[72] Another proposal was that public authorities should be required to consider the use of equality-related award criteria where they relate to the subject matter of the contract and are proportionate. An example given was that as part of a major estate renovation scheme and in an attempt to redress the local and national under-representation of women in building trades, a local council could include a contract condition that requires 10 per cent of the person weeks required to complete the contract to be delivered by women who have either an apprenticeship, traineeship or employment contract with the contractor or sub-contractor and are engaged in a training programme.[73]

The Coalition Government was not willing to implement detailed obligations of this kind in England, but the Scottish and Welsh governments have done so. The Scottish and Welsh Regulations provide that the authority must have due regard to whether the award criteria and the procurement conditions should include considerations to enable it to better perform the equality duty. Any procurement requirements must be related to and proportionate to the subject matter of the procurement agreement. The English Regulations are silent on this matter but the EHRC guidance says that the procuring public authority may need to include obligations relating to equality in the contract in order to comply with its obligations under the duty. This may include as contract conditions a prohibition on the contractor from any unlawful discrimination, and requiring the contractor to take all reasonable steps to ensure that staff, suppliers and sub-contractors meet their obligations under the Equality Act. This applies to all procurement regardless of the value, but the value may impact on the proportionality of equality considerations. Where public functions are contracted out, the external contractor will itself be subject to the general equality duty. The parties will have to comply with the limits on non-commercial objectives imposed by the EU

---

[72] Hansard HL vol 716 col 649 (9 February 2010) (Baroness Royall).
[73] Ibid.

public procurement regime.[74] The UK must implement by April 2016 a new EU Directive 2014/12/EU on public procurement. Article 18 of the new Directive provides, for the first time that

> Member States shall take appropriate measures to ensure that in the performance of public contracts economic operators comply with applicable obligations in the fields of environmental, social and labour law established by Union law, national law, collective agreements or by the international environmental, social and labour law provisions listed in Annex X.

Among the provisions listed in Annex X are ILO Convention No 111 on Discrimination in Employment and Occupation and Convention No 100 on Equal Remuneration for Men and Women. The Directive states that the relevant measures should be applied in conformity with the basic principles of EU law, in particular with a view to ensuring equal treatment. Contracting authorities must be obliged to create the necessary transparency to enable all tenderers to be reasonably informed of the criteria and arrangements which will be applied in the contract award decision. It is be hoped that the implementing UK legislation will provide that contractors should be excluded from approved lists, not be invited to tender, not be selected against competing bids and be liable to have their contracts terminated if they have been found by an employment tribunal, after a fair hearing, to have committed gross misconduct, including persistent discrimination or any other serious breach of domestic equality legislation and the ILO and EU standards. At present the Act does not contain any explicit provisions on this. The EHRC guidance avoids the issue by simply advising public authorities to seek legal advice before taking remedial steps!

What Is Meant by 'Having Due Regard'?

The Equality Act expressly spells out what is meant by 'having due regard to the need to advance equality of opportunity'. This includes the need to

- remove or minimise disadvantages suffered by persons who share a protected characteristic that are connected to that characteristic;
- take steps to meet the needs of persons who share a relevant protected characteristic that are different from the needs of persons who do not share it; and
- encourage persons who share a protected characteristic to participate in public life or any other activity in which participation by such persons is disproportionately low.[75]

---

[74] The definitive and monumental work on procurement in relation to equality and other social justice objectives is by McCrudden (2007a) 508–66 and see Cambridge Review (2010) paras 3.74–4.77.

[75] EA, s 149(3).

It is made clear that the steps involved in meeting the needs of disabled persons that are different from the needs of those who are not disabled include, in particular, taking account of the disabilities involved.[76] This includes making reasonable adjustments for disabled persons.[77] More generally, complying with the duty might mean treating some people more favourably than others, so long as this is allowed by the Act.[78] This may mean making use of exceptions which permit different treatment or positive action measures. For example, the duty could lead a local authority to provide funding for a Black women's refuge for victims of domestic violence, with the aim of advancing equality of opportunity for women and, in particular, meeting the different needs of women from particular groups; or it could lead a local authority to focus council services on older people; or lead a school to review its anti-bullying policy to prevent homophobic conduct.[79] The Act also spells out what is meant by 'having due regard to the need to foster good relations'. This involves, in particular, the need to 'tackle prejudice' and 'promote understanding'.[80]

There has been fairly extensive case law on the interpretation of this key concept under the earlier race, sex and disability duties, and under the Act of 2010. The interpretation has generally been purposive, and several principles have emerged. One of these is that the duties are concerned with issues of substantive equality, involving active steps and requiring more penetrating consideration than merely asking whether there has been a breach of the principle of non-discrimination.[81] There must be conscious consideration of issues of equality of opportunity, which have now been placed at the centre of formulation of policy.[82] Another principle is that public bodies to which the duty applies must give advance consideration to the issues before making any policy decision that may be affected. This is 'an integral and important part of the mechanisms for ensuring the fulfilment of the aims of anti-discrimination legislation'.[83] At the same time, the court cannot interfere with an administrative decision simply because it would have given great weight to the equality implications of the decision than did the decision-maker.[84]

---

[76] EA, s 149(4).

[77] See p 94 above.

[78] EA, s 149(6).

[79] EN, para 484. The public sector duty applies to this, even though the wrong of harassment cannot be invoked by individuals: see p 101 above.

[80] EA, s 149(5).

[81] *R (Baker) v Secretary of State for the Environment* [2008] EWCA (CIV) 141, para 30 (Dyson LJ); *R (E) v JFS* [2008] EWHC 1535, para 213 (Munby J).

[82] *Bracking v Secretary of State for Work and Pensions* [2014] EqLR 60, para 26.

[83] *Secretary of State for Defence v Elias* [2006] EWCA (CIV) 1293; [2006] IRLR 934, para 274 (Arden LJ).

[84] *R (Hurley and Moore) v Secretary of State fo Business, Innovation and Skills* [2012] EWHC 201 (Admin) per Elias LJ, paras 77–78.

A further principle is that the authority must take a 'substantial, rigorous and open-minded approach' to equality considerations.[85] This includes getting the facts right. So a licensing authority for hackney cabs was not entitled to conclude that the taxi fleet was accessible to 'wheelchair-users as a class' when the evidence showed serious difficulties for some wheelchair-users, depending on the size of the wheelchair and the particular disability.[86] Where there are discriminatory effects, the authority needs to give thought to the steps necessary to avoid those effects, and if the discrimination is indirect it must properly test whether they are legitimate and proportionate.[87] This does not mean that an impact assessment is always necessary, but the authority should at least consider whether an impact assessment, along with other means of obtaining information, is required.[88]

The application of these principles is illustrated by the case of *Bracking v Secretary of State for Work and Pensions*[89] in which the Court of Appeal quashed the decision of the Minister for Disabled People to close the Independent Living Fund (ILF). That Fund operates with local authorities to devise care packages, including services and direct payments, for people such as the disabled needing community care services.. Four severely disabled people challenged the Minister's decision by way of judicial review. The Court of Appeal held that there had been a breach of the duty to have due regard to the PSED. The PSED was said to impose a 'heavy burden' on the authority to show that it had confronted the anticipated consequences of its decision in a conscientious and deliberate way.[90] In this case no evidence had been produced to the Court from which it could be inferred that the minister had more than a vague awareness that she owed duties to disabled persons. Her officials had not drawn her attention to the positive obligation to advance equality. The scope of the PSED in this case was informed by the UK's obligations under Article 19 of the UN Convention on the Rights of Persons with Disabilities 2006 to take effective and appropriate measures to facilitate the right of disabled people to live in the community, which includes, where appropriate, independent living. The Minister ought to have been alerted to these obligations but she was not.

---

[85] *R (Boyejo) v Barnet London Borough Council* [2009] EWHC 3261(admin), paras 58–59 (HHJ Milwyn Jarman QC).

[86] *R (Lunt) v Liverpool City Council and EHRC (Intervener)* [2009] EWHC 2356 (Admin).

[87] *R (Eisai) v National Institute for Clinical Excellence* [2007] EWHC 1941 (Admin), para 93 (Dodds J).

[88] *R (Brown) v Secretary of State for Work and Pensions* [2008] EWHC 3158 (Admin), para 89.

[89] [2014] EqLR 60; an earlier illustration of these principles will be found in *R (Kaur) v London Borough of Ealing* [2008] EWHR 2062 (Admin) where the withdrawal of financial support from Southall Black Sisters was held to be unlawful because of failure to carry out an equality impact assessment.

[90] Ibid, para 74 per Elias LJ.

Which Authorities Are Covered?

The RRA set out a list of authorities to which the race equality duty applied, while the DDA and SDA applied the disability and sex duties to those 'who have functions of a public nature'. The Equality Act combines the two approaches by listing public authorities subject to the duty[91] and, in addition, applying the general duty to anyone who exercises public functions.[92] However, specific duties may be imposed by regulations only on the listed public authorities, and not on the wider category of persons exercising public functions.[93] This significantly limits the scope of specific duties because increasingly public functions at both the local and the national levels are carried out by private and voluntary sector bodies. This is particularly true in education, health, prisons, social care and some aspects of social housing.[94]

Enforcement

The PSED does not give rise to any enforceable private law rights. It is enforceable only by way of judicial review. Judicial review proceedings may be brought by any person with sufficient interest (including the EHRC). Most of the proceedings to date have been brought by non-governmental organisations or individuals, although the EHRC has actively intervened in some cases. Remedies are a matter of discretion. If a decision is reached without due regard to the PSED, then it is an unlawful decision and, subject to any overwhelming discretionary features, the decision should be quashed.[95] There will only rarely be an order for compensation. An interesting development has been the encouragement given by judges to remedy the defect (eg a failure to consult) before the final judgment is handed down.[96] However, it must be remembered that the grounds on which a review can be sought are limited. The usual way of enforcing a specific public sector duty will be by the EHRC issuing a compliance notice; if the authority fails to comply, the EHRC may then seek a court order requiring the authority to do so.[97]

---

[91] EA, sched 19. this includes ministers of the Crown and government departments, the armed forces, the National Health Service, local government, the police, the governing bodies of schools maintained by local authorities, and the governing bodies of further education establishments and institutions of higher education, as well as various Welsh and Scottish public authorities. The list may be amended by a minister (EA, s 150) after consultation (s 150).

[92] EA, s 149(2).

[93] EA, s 153.

[94] Hansard HL vol 717 col 1401 (2 March 2010).

[95] *Bracking v Secretary of State for Work and Pensions* [2014] EqLR 60, para. 69.

[96] Halford (2009).

[97] See p 175 below.

Finally, it may be that a failure to discharge a PSED will provide evidence of discrimination or a rebuttal of a defence of justification of indirect discrimination in proceedings brought by an individual. If a public authority has failed to consider any discriminatory impacts of its policy or any possible justification for the discrimination, it is unlikely that it will be able to persuade a court that its actions were proportionate to a legitimate aim.[98]

Review of the PSED

In the period of austerity in which it has functioned since 2008, the PSED has undoubtedly had an important role in stopping or delaying cuts in public services where it has been possible to show that the authorities failed to give proper consideration to the impact on one or more groups with protected characteristics. Decisions that public bodies had failed to comply with the PSED include: reconfiguring a domestic violence service in a way that would have precluded funding for specialist services for Black and minority ethnic women;[99] school uniform policies with an adverse impact on those with sincere religious or cultural reasons for not complying;[100] care home fees that did not take account of the needs of those with dementia;[101] a planning decision which did not take account of needs of small minority ethnic businesses;[102] licensing of taxis without regard for the needs of wheelchair users;[103] and eviction of tenants without regard to their specific mental health needs.[104] The single unified duty has broadened the coverage of the PSED and has made it possible to deal with intersectional discrimination where two or more groups are disadvantaged by an administrative act. However the focus on specific protected characteristics has meant that wider socioeconomic disadvantage is not targeted and one disadvantaged group may be protected at the expense of another. Section 1 of the Equality Act 2010, now repealed, placed an additional duty on certain public authorities, when making decisions of a strategic nature, to have due regard to the desirability of exercising their powers in a way which would reduce

---

[98] See *Secretary of State for Defence v Elias* [2006] EWCA (CIV)1293, [2006] IRLR 934, para 133 (Mummery LJ); *R (E) v Governing Body JFS* [2009] UKSC 15, paras 100–03 (Lord Mance), 212 (Lord Hope).

[99] *R (Kaur) v London Borough of Ealing* [2008] EWCA 2062 Admin.

[100] *R (Watkins-Singh) v Governing Body of Aberdare High School* [2008] EWHC 1865 (Admin); *R(G) v Head Teacher and Governors of St Gregorory's Catholic Science College* [2011] PTSR 931.

[101] *R (South West Care Homes) v Devon County Council* [2012] EWHC 2967 Admin.

[102] *Harris v London Borough of Haringey* [2010] EWCA Civ 703.

[103] *R (Lunt) v Liverpool City Council* [2009] EWHC 2356 Admin.

[104] *Pieretti v London Borough of Enfield* [2010] WECA Civ 1104.

the inequality of outcomes that result from socioeconomic disadvantage. Although this provision was open to criticism,[105] it aimed to shift the focus from specific identities to wider issues of inequality.

It was hoped that the new unified specific duties would lead to a focus on the outcomes public authorities should be achieving rather than the procedures they should be following. The Government Equalities Office claimed that 'we want to avoid rigid bureaucratic processes or a "tick box" approach resulting in the publication of documents which, once produced, stay firmly on the shelf'.[106] The *Discrimination Law Review* set out four key principles that should underpin the performance of the public sector equality duty: the use of evidence focusing on those areas where the authority can make a real difference; consultation and involvement of employees, service users and other interested parties; transparency, allowing people to see the progress authorities are making; and capability, ie strong leadership and high-level commitment.[107]

In view of these proposals, it is surprising that the Labour government rejected an amendment proposed at the report stage in the House of Lords by Lord Ouseley (former Chair of the CRE), with the support of a wide range of equality and human rights groups, who, Lord Ouseley said, were 'disillusioned and frustrated' by the failure of public bodies to meet their existing duties across all their relevant functions'.[108] The amendment aimed to ensure that the PSED results in more than a paper exercise. It would have required a public authority to 'take all proportionate steps towards' the elimination of discrimination, the advancement of equality, and fostering good relations. The aim was to get public authorities to institute real changes, which could be judged by the EHRC and the courts on the basis of the proportionality principle, in place of the practice of simply piling up a mountain of paper to prove that they have 'had due regard' to equality considerations. In rejecting the amendment, the government claimed that decisions of the courts on the duties had established the need for public authorities to consider the impact 'rigorously and with an open mind',[109] and that if public bodies had to take proportionate steps in relation to all protected characteristics, this would spread their finite resources more thinly 'and some persons with more pressing needs [would] end up with less'.[110]

---

[105] See the 1st edn of this book, pp 141–43.

[106] Government Equalities Office (2009b) para 3.17.

[107] Ibid, paras 3.9–3.14.

[108] Hansard HL vol 717 col 1399 (2 March 2010). The Government Equalities Office and Schneider Ross (2009) reported concerns that impact assessments were overly bureaucratic, although they did say that many organisations had seen improvements in the way decisions were made and resources allocated.

[109] See eg the comment of Moses LJ in *Kaur* (n 89) para 25: '[T]he process of assessment is not satisfied by ticking boxes.'

[110] Hansard HL vol 717 col 1402 (2 March 2010) (Baroness Thornton).

This seems to misinterpret the meaning of the 'proportionality' test, under which the resources of the authority and its priorities, depending on the needs of different groups, would clearly be relevant factors.

The courts have been keen to emphasise that the 'due regard' test is not a duty to achieve a result, and there is no duty to take steps to achieve a particular result. A link between procedures and outcomes could be provided by specific duties to engage with stakeholders. This has been done in Scotland and Wales, but the ideology of removing 'burdens on business' led the government to abandon this requirement in England. Empirical researchers will find it interesting to compare the progress towards equality of opportunity between the three jurisdictions in the light of the different legal obligations. The courts' stress on monitoring, record-keeping and procedure may simply increase.the bureaucratic burden, without changing outcomes. As Fredman points out, 'the courts have been thrust into the very horns of the regulatory trilemma. Impact assessment is highly susceptible to regulatory resistance: indeed, evidence suggests that impact assessment was the issue most susceptible to substituting bureaucratic "form filling" for taking action.'[111]

In May 2012, the Coalition Government set up an Independent Steering Group to assess whether the PSED is operating as intended. The Group reported[112] that there was wide support for the principles behind the PSED, and that some public bodies 'are doing a good job in mainstreaming equality considerations in their work'. But they considered that it was too early to make a final judgment about the impact of the PSED. The Group recommended that clearer guidelines were needed about the minimum requirements on public bodies, that sector regulators, such as inspectors and ombudspersons, have an important role to play in supporting imple- mentation, and that public bodies must take a proportionate approach to compliance and not seek to 'gold plate'. In view of concerns about judicial review it was recommended that the government should consider whether there were quicker and more effective ways of reconciling disputes about the PSED. In its review of government proposals to reform judicial review, the JCHR, welcomed the unequivocal confirmation by the Chair of the Steering Group on the PSED that the PSED should continue to be legally enforce- able through judicial review. This does not rule out the possibility of another quicker and more cost-effective mechanism, but the JCHR recommended that any such mechanism must retain the ultimate legal enforceability of the duty by judicial review rather than be an alternative to it.[113]

---

[111] Fredman (2011) 405, 420.

[112] Government Equalities Office, *Review of the Public Sector Equality Duty*, Report of the Independent Steering Group (September 2013).

[113] Joint Committee on Human Rights, *The Implications for Access to Justice of the Government's Proposals to Reform Judicial Review*.

7

Enforcement

THE EQUALITY AND HUMAN RIGHTS COMMISSION

A Single Commission[1]

T
HE EQUALITY AND Human Rights Commission (EHRC) was
established by the Equality Act 2006[2]and opened its doors on 1
October 2007, taking the place of the CRE, DRC and EOC. It
covers race, sex and disability, and also the new strands of age, religion or
belief, sexual orientation and gender reassignment. The former Commissions
were similar to each other, but were by no means identical, and each chose
to exercise its powers in distinctive ways. The new integrated Commission
has both a more extensive remit, including the promotion of human rights,
and greater enforcement powers (largely modelled on those of the DRC)
than its predecessors.

In order to be able to challenge actions taking place within both the
public and the private sector without fear or favour, the Commission needs
to be independent. Like its predecessors, it is an 'arm's length' non-depart-
mental government body (NDPB), whose Commissioners are appointed by
the Secretary of State, and whose grant and budget are determined by
government. However, the Equality Act 2006 places the Secretary of State
under an obligation to have regard to 'the desirability of ensuring that the
Commission is under as few constraints as reasonably possible in determining' its activities, timetables and priorities.[3] The parliamentary Joint
Committee on Human Rights (JCHR) suggested that it would be more in
conformity with the UN Paris Principles,[4] which set out desirable status,
functions and powers of human rights agencies, if the EHCR were directly

---

[1] See generally, Hepple (2012).

[2] The Act set this up as the Commission for Equality and Human Rights (CEHR), but
the Commission decided to re-brand itself as the EHRC.

[3] EA 2006, sched 1 para 42(3).

[4] *Principles Relating to the Status of National Institutions*, UN General Assembly Resolution
48/134, December 1993.

accountable to Parliament, like the Scottish Human Rights Commission is to the Scottish Parliament, and the National Audit Office and Electoral Commission are to the Westminster Parliament, but this advice was not followed.[5] Responsibility in government for the legislation and the Commissions has been itinerant, at one stage falling under five separate government departments. The Government Equalities Office (GEO) is responsible for equality strategy and legislation across government. Ministerial responsibility shifted after 2010 from the Home Office to the Department for Culture Media and Sport (DCMS). This department currently includes a Minister for Women, responsible for issues of women and the economy and child care, and two parliamentary Under-Secretaries of State, one responsible for the EHRC, legislation and same-sex marriage, and the other for women and growth, women on boards, lesbian, gay and transsexual policy, the PSED and 'body coinfidence'.

The absence of direct accountability to Parliament and the reality of ultimate ministerial control over appointments and budgets could result in a loss of confidence in the credibility of the Commission. For example, the JCHR was strongly critical of the way the Chair of the EHRC had been reappointed in 2009, without open competition, by the then Minister for Women and Equalities. The JHRC reiterated its strong preference for the appointment of EHRC Commissioners to be taken out of the hands of ministers.[6] In 2012, in response to calls for greater accountability to Parliament, the government agreed to pre-appointment scrutiny by the JCHR of the Secretary of State's proposed appointment of Baroness O'Neill of Bengrave as non-executive Chair of the EHRC (which the JCHR endorsed after questioning her.) The JCHR now has an annual session on the work of the EHRC. The independence of the EHRC is crucial to its accreditation as an 'A-status' national human rights institution by the UN International Co-ordinating Committee of National Institutions for the Promotion and Protection of Human Rights (ICC). The ICC has emphasised that 'the most effective national institutions generally have a broad and non-restrictive mandate' and an 'all-encompassing jurisdiction' as well as 'adequate budgetary resources'.[7] In 2013 the EHRC's A-status was questioned because of severe budget cuts and a framework agreement with its then sponsoring department (the Home Office) which appeared to allow the Home Office to exercise undue influence over the operations of the EHRC. A new framework document with the DCMS (April 2013) appears to be in compliance with the Paris Principles. As at January 2014, the EHRC was still accred-

---

[5] JCHR (2005–06) paras 27–30, 126–42.
[6] JCHR (2009–10) para 58.
[7] ICC, *Assessing thr Effectiveness of National Human Rights Institutions* (2005) 8.

ited with A-status. However, accountability has been weakened by requiring the EHRC to make progress reports only once every five years instead of three years.[8]

The pros and cons of a single commission were debated before the 2006 Act. Those who favoured a single commission argued that it would give equality a higher status as a universal principle, would lead to efficiency gains, would be beneficial to employers and other users who wanted consistent information and advice from a single source, and was the best way of absorbing the new equality strands. A single commission would also make it easier to deal with cases of multiple discrimination.[9]

The main disadvantage was thought to be that relatively powerful groups, such as women or ethnic minorities, would swamp other less powerful interests, a point made particularly strongly by disability groups, who wanted to maintain the gains that had been achieved by the DRC in which disabled people themselves played a key role. To some extent, this argument rested on the assumption that a primary function of a Commission is to represent interest groups or to give them a voice. Proponents of a single commission, on the other hand, saw a commission's essential role as being a professional rather than a representational one, to promote equality, to enforce the law, and to ensure that resources are focused on the most important strategic issues.

Structure and Management of the Commission

These differences led to a number of compromises. The Labour government opted for a single commission, and successfully resisted attempts to amend the draft legislation to include fixed quotas of women, and Black and other minority ethnic groups. The Commission consists of between 10 and 15 members, one of whom is appointed by the Secretary of State as Chair, who have experience or knowledge of the matters in respect of which the Commission has functions, in particular discrimination and human rights.[10] The DRC's reluctance to join in was met by providing that the Commission must include a Commissioner who is (or has been) a disabled person, and by establishing a statutory decision-making Disability Committee, which can exercise a number of the Commission's powers relating to disability

---

[8] ERRA 2013, s 64(2) amending EA 2006,s 12(4)(b).

[9] Cambridge Review (2000) paras 2.88–2.89. The issue was raised by the Cabinet Office when consulting on the Race and Framework Employment Directives in 2002, and detailed proposals for a single commission were made in a White Paper; See Department of Communities and Local Government (2004).

[10] EA 2006, sched 1 para 2. The Chief Executive, appointed by the Commission, is an ex officio Commissioner: paras 1(2), 7.

matters.[11] The Chair and at least half the members of the Committee must be, or have been, disabled persons.[12] An independent review in 2014 concluded that the statutory Disability Committee should be replaced by an external high-level strategic advisory committee on disability.

The CRE opposed its absorption into a single commission on the ground that a single commission would 'not be able to focus properly on community relations, extremism and integration issues'. The government was not, however, willing to separate race equality from the core functions of the EHRC, and, with support from the opposition parties and other groups, resisted the setting up of a separate Race Committee and did not prescribe clear ethnic minority representation, although in practice several Commissioners are from Black or other minority ethnic groups. The CRE reversed its position after the government gave its assurances that the powers of the EHRC would not be less than those of the existing Commissions, and that the CRE's racial equality councils could be retained at least in the short term. The CRE received a guarantee that it could continue to operate until 2009, but after Trevor Phillips was appointed first Chair of the EHRC, the merger took place at the same time as the merger of the other Commissions, in October 2007.

General Powers and Duties

The EHRC has a number of statutory duties There is a general duty to encourage and support the development of a society in which there is respect for human rights, dignity, equal opportunities and mutual respect between groups.[13] As we have seen,[14] attempts by the Coalition government to remove this general duty were defeated. A specific duty to promote understanding of the importance of good relations between groups[15] was repealed in 2013.[16] This repeal has raised doubts about the competence of the EHRC to use its powers to support the All-Party Parlliamentary Group's campaign against anti-Semitism or the former CRE's campaign to 'Kick Racism out of Football'. The repeal reflected the view that the EHRC is primarily a law enforcement agency and should leave campaigns of this sort to NGOs. The 'core' duties of the EHRC which remain include promoting understanding of the importance of equality and diversity, promoting awareness

---

[11] EA 2006, sched 1 paras 49–64.
[12] EA 2006, sched 1 para 50(1).
[13] EA 2006, s 3.
[14] Above, p 8.
[15] EA, s 10(1)(4).
[16] ERRA 2013, s 64(1).

and understanding of the rights under the Equality Act, enforcing the Act, encouraging good practice in relation to equality and diversity, and working towards the elimination of unlawful discrimination and harassment.[17]

The former Commissions were largely successful in their task of setting and raising standards. The principal measures by which they achieved this task, aside from general publicity, were through codes of practice. The 2006 Act, as amended in 2010, requires the ECHR to publish proposals and consult appropriate persons before issuing a code. The Secretary of State must approve the draft and lay it before Parliament. If neither House passes a resolution disapproving the draft within 40 days, it comes into force on a day appointed by the Secretary of State.[18] A failure to comply with the provisions of a code does not make a person liable to civil or criminal proceedings, but the code is admissible in evidence and must be taken into account by a court or tribunal in any case in which it appears to be relevant.[19] In place of the separate codes issued by each of the former Commissions, the EHRC has so far prepared new codes of practice on employment, equal pay and the provision of services. The new codes have the virtues of consistency and being up to date, but are too long, over-detailed and prescriptive. There was a high level of awareness of the former employment codes among employers, many of whom were prompted to review their recruitment and selection methods and to take action in accordance with the codes, which resulted in more employment opportunities for ethnic minorities, women and disabled persons.[20] There is a risk that small and medium-sized employers will tend to ignore a lengthy and complex code. The ECHR has powers to monitor the effectiveness of equality and human rights enactments and to advise central or devolved government on them.[21] It must also from time to time identify social changes relevant to its general aims, the outcomes at which to aim, and the indicators by which progress can be measured.[22]

Human Rights

Ever since the passing of the Human Rights Act 1998, many have campaigned for a Human Rights Commission with a wide brief to promote and enforce human rights in general, including the right to equality, as is

---

[17] EA 2006, s 8(1).
[18] EA 2006, s 14.
[19] EA 2006, s 15(4).
[20] Coussey (1992) 40–43.
[21] EA 2006, s 11.
[22] EA 2006, s 12.

the case in several other countries.[23] Others have argued that an umbrella Human Rights Commission, including all the equality strands, would become 'too big and unwieldy and could potentially lose sight of equality issues'.[24] To meet this objection, the Cambridge Review proposed a separate Equality Commission and a Human Rights Commission, as is the case in Northern Ireland, with a memorandum of understanding between the two bodies as to how they would deal with overlapping issues.[25] The Labour Government decided to have a single commission whose objects include the promotion of human ights, but with enforcement powers relating only to equality and not to other human rights. The addition of human rights was welcomed by those who wanted to see equality placed at the centre of a wider human rights culture.

The 2006 Act gave the Commission the task of promoting understanding of the importance of human rights of all kinds,[26] encouraging good practice, promoting awareness, understanding and protection of human rights, and encouraging public authorities to observe rights under the ECHR.[27] In April 2008, the EHRC launched an inquiry to assess progress towards a 'culture of respect for human rights'. The inquiry's report, published in 2009, proposed that the EHRC should assume a leadership role in raising public awareness of human rights and the Human Rights Act, and assisting public authorities to integrate their positive obligations under the Human Rights Act with their public sector equality duty. The EHRC developed a human rights strategy for the period 2009–12, but this was criticised in 2010 by the JCHR for containing 'few indications of timescales, milestones or measures of success or effectiveness'.' The JCHR expressed 'frustration at the EHRC's lack of engagement in major human rights issues',[28] and concluded that the EHRC had 'so far failed to fulfil its human rights mandate' and that its current human rights strategy was 'in need of substantial enhancement'.[29]

The fault may, in part, lie with Parliament itself for failing to give the Commission adequate enforcement powers in respect of human rights in addition to those it has to enforce the Equality Act.

---

[23] Spencer and Bynoe (1998).

[24] ORC Equal Opportunities Group, evidence to Cambridge Review (2000) para 287.

[25] Cambridge Review (2000) para 2.87.

[26] EA 2006, s 10(2). This includes human rights under international instruments which the UK has not incorporated into domestic law, but particular regard must be had to ECHR rights: s 10(3).

[27] EA 2006, s 10(1).

[28] JCHR (2009–10) para 25.

[29] Ibid, para 83.

Enforcement Powers

The drafters of the RRA and SDA envisaged that the Commissions would use their enforcement powers extensively to investigate specific organisations and stop their discriminatory practices. There were two types of investigation. The first was general inquiries which could be carried out, after giving notice, without the Commission holding any specific belief that there may have been breaches of the legislation. These inquiries could not be directed against a named organisation and could result only in a report and recommendations. Subpoena notices compelling witnesses could be issued only on the authority of the Secretary of State. The second type of investigation was the 'belief' or 'accusatory' investigation into suspected unlawful acts by a named person; the CRE and EOC had powers to issue subpoenas and, after a hearing, could issue non-discrimination notices to stop discriminatory practices.

In the early years, the CRE believed that it could act as an inspectorate and investigate a named organisation without any prior evidence of unlawful discrimination, either because there was general evidence of inequality in the sector or occupation or because it was a leading company in the sector. The CRE carried out a number of important investigations which showed how discrimination operates and how to deal with it.[30] However, it encountered judicial hostility, notably from Lord Denning, the Master of the Rolls, who notoriously compared the CRE's powers to those of the Inquisition.[31] In the 1984 *Prestige* case,[32] the House of Lords held that investigations into named organisations were not permissible unless the Commission had already formed a suspicion that the persons concerned may have committed some unlawful act. In the *Hillingdon* case,[33] the House of Lords turned this into a 'reasonable suspicion' test, saying that 'there should be material before the Commission sufficient to raise in the minds of reasonable men, possessed of the experience of covert discrimination that has been acquired by the Commission, a suspicion that there may have been' unlawful acts by the named person.[34]

These decisions, coupled with a lack of adequate resources, placed serious restrictions on strategic enforcement, allowing discriminatory practices to continue unchecked. None of the companies involved in investigations before these decisions had equal opportunities policies in place, and the absence of monitoring meant that there were no records of the ethnic origin of appli-

---

[30] Coussey (1992) 37–40.
[31] *Social Science Research Council v Nassé* [1979] 1 QB 144, CA, 172.
[32] *R v Commission for Racial Equality, ex parte Prestige Group Ltd* [1984] ICR 473.
[33] *Hillingdon London Borough Council v Commission for Racial Equality* [1982] AC 779.
[34] [1982] AC 779, 791 (Lord Diplock).

cants and employees, and other evidence was hard to uncover.[35] Another nail in the coffin of formal investigations was the Court of Appeal's decision in 1982 in the *Amari Plastics* case, where it held that the respondent could challenge the CRE's findings of fact as well as the requirements set out in a non-discrimination notice to stop discriminatory practices.[36] The courts added to the already elaborate procedural safeguards for respondents, for example by imposing a requirement to give the named organisation notice of the proposed terms of reference and the opportunity of a hearing even before the investigation started. Lord Denning candidly remarked that the machinery for investigations and the issuing of non-discrimination notices was 'so elaborate and so cumbersome that it is in danger of grinding to a halt'.[37] Not surprisingly, there was a sharp decline in the use of 'belief' or 'accusatory' investigations against named organisations by the CRE. After 1989, the CRE used accusatory investigations only as a last resort when attempts to persuade organisations to change their practices had been exhausted. At the time, the usual practice was to negotiate an agreement for changes, and then to suspend the formal investigation while the implementation of the agreement was monitored. This approach paid dividends, with major voluntary changes being recorded in organisations such as the RMT Union, the Ministry of Defence (Household Cavalry), the London Borough of Hackney, the Crown Prosecution Service and the Ford Motor Co. The EOC made even less use than the CRE of formal investigations, conducting only 11 from 1977 to 2005, the last of which took place in 1995.

The DRC's powers to conduct formal investigations were framed in a slightly different way, in effect putting the *Prestige* test into statutory form but allowing a non-accusatory investigation into a named person. A useful addition to the powers of the DRC was to provide for 'agreements in lieu of enforcement action'. These were agreements whereby the Commission undertook not to take enforcement action in return for the named person undertaking not to commit any unlawful acts and to take positive action as specified in the agreement. If the undertaking was breached, the DRC could apply for a court order to enforce it. The DRC also had the power to require a person who committed an unlawful act to prepare an action plan for the purpose of avoiding repetition or continuation of the unlawful act.

The Equality Act 2006 gave the EHRC two powers, largely modelled on those of the CRE: one to conduct an inquiry, and the other to conduct a formal investigation. An inquiry can relate to any of the Commission's duties, but leads only to a report and recommendations. These are not

[35] Coussey (1992) 39.
[36] *R v Commission for Racial Equality, ex parte Amari Plastics* [1982] QB 1194.
[37] [1982] QB 1194, 1203.

legally binding, but a court or tribunal may have regard to a finding,[38] and the Commission may use information or evidence acquired in the course of an inquiry for the purpose of a formal investigation.[39]

The Commission has heavily circumscribed powers to obtain information, documents and oral evidence under judicial control.[40] One of the virtues of a single commission is that the inquiry can cut across strands, for example to investigate possible multiple discrimination. The inquiry may relate to a particular sector (the EHRC held such inquiries in 2008–09 in relation to financial services, construction and meat processing),[41] or it may be thematic (eg the EHRC has held an inquiry into human rights), or it may relate to one or more named persons.[42] The EHRC must publish the terms of reference of the inquiry before conducting it and, in particular, give notice of such terms to any person specified in them.[43] The Commission may not investigate whether a named person has committed an unlawful act; it must commence a formal investigation for that purpose.[44] Nor may it state in its report that a person has committed an unlawful act, and it may not refer to the activities of a specified or identifiable person unless it thinks that the reference will not harm the person or is necessary in order for the report adequately to reflect the results of the inquiry.[45] Before settling the report, the Commission must send a draft to any person who is the subject of adverse findings and give them 28 days to make representations on the draft, and consider those representations.[46]

The second power of the EHRC is to conduct a formal investigation. The Commission may do so only if it 'suspects' that the person concerned may have committed an unlawful act.[47] This follows the DRC model, and according to the government sets a 'threshold test' of 'reasonable belief'.[48] This seems to codify the case law (above), but it has been argued that only if the Commission's decision to investigate is irrational or strongly dispropor-tionate should a court interfere.[49] A single complaint of unlawful conduct is unlikely to suffice as the basis for initiating an investigation, but a series of complaints over time might be sufficient. The suspicion may (but need not)

---

[38] EA 2006, sched 2 para 17.
[39] EA 2006, s 16(2)(c).
[40] EA 2006, sched 2 paras 9–14.
[41] Equality and Human Rights Commission (2010).
[42] EA 2006, s 16.
[43] EA 2006, sched 2 paras 2–5.
[44] EA 2006, s 16(2).
[45] EA 2006, s 16(3).
[46] EA 2006, s 16(5).
[47] EA 2006, s 20(2).
[48] *Commission for Equality and Human Rights: The Government's Response to Consultation* (2004) para 38.
[49] O'Cinneide (2007) 155.

be based on the matters arising in the course of an inquiry (above).[50] There are stringent procedural requirements. Before conducting an investigation, the Commission must publish the terms of reference specifying the person to be investigated and the nature of the unlawful act which the Commission suspects. The named person is given at least three opportunities to make representations: first, they must be given notice of the terms of reference and an opportunity to make representations about them;[51] secondly, there must be an opportunity to make representations (which may but need not be oral) regarding the subject of the investigation;[52] and thirdly, before settling a report of an investigation which contains a finding that a person has committed an unlawful act, the person must be given 28 days to make written representations regarding the draft, and these must be considered by the Commission.[53] There are similar powers to those pertaining to inquiries (above) to obtain information documents and oral evidence.[54]

Named person investigations may lead to an unlawful act notice, against which there is a right of appeal to an appropriate court or tribunal.[55] The notice may require the person to prepare an action plan for the purpose of avoiding a repetition or continuation of the unlawful act, and may recommend action to be taken by the person for that purpose.[56] The action plan has to be approved by the Commission,[57] which has the power to apply to a county court (in England and Wales) or sheriff (in Scotland) for an order requiring a person to give the Commission a draft or revised action plan. During the period of five years beginning with the date on which the plan comes into force, an order may be sought and granted requiring the person to act in accordance with the action plan or to take specified action for a similar purpose.[58] Failure to comply with an order without reasonable excuse may lead to a fine.[59] The EHRC also has powers to assess compliance with the public sector equality duty and, where it thinks that a public authority has failed to comply with the duty, the power to issue a non-compliance notice[60] (see p 172 above).

It can be seen that the ECHR remains largely within the enforcement models of its predecessors. In particular, the opportunity to reverse the *Prestige* and *Hillingdon* tests so as to allow named investigations even in the

---

[50] EA, s 20(3).
[51] EA 2006, sched 2 para 3.
[52] EA 2006, sched 2 paras 6–8.
[53] EA 2006, s 20(4).
[54] EA 2006, sched 2 paras 9–14.
[55] EA 2006, s 21.
[56] EA 2006, s 21(4).
[57] EA 2006, s 21(3).
[58] EA 2006, s 21(6).
[59] EA, s 21(9).
[60] EA 2006, ss 31, 32.

absence of evidence of unlawful acts was lost. The EHRC could have been given the power to conduct equality audits in the public and private sectors, like the Irish Equality Authority can do, even in the absence of specific evidence of discrimination.[61] Since 1989, the Fair Employment legislation in Northern Ireland has enabled the Fair Employment Commission (FEC) and it successor, the Equality Commission for Northern Ireland (ECNI), to use the results of triennial reviews that employers are required to submit relating to representation of Catholic and Protestant communities, as well as their investigatory powers, in order to negotiate agreements designed to remedy under-representation of either community. These are affirmative action agreements which usually require undertakings to change the way they recruit, advertise, promote and dismiss, often setting numerical goals and timetables. Most of the agreements reached have been voluntary, but a number are legally enforceable. The voluntary ones usually follow a triennial review, while the legally binding ones tend to follow a formal investigation. Research by Anthony Heath and his colleagues[62] shows that agreements focusing on institutional changes have been more effective in achieving progress towards fair employment than lawsuits which provide financial incentives. Voluntary agreements have been more effective than the legally enforceable ones.

The failure to introduce employment equity and pay audits[63] means that there is little incentive in Britain for employers to enter into voluntary agreements with the EHRC. A step in the direction of legally binding agreements has, however, been made. The 2006 Act gives the EHRC, like the former DRC, the power to make legally binding agreements in lieu of enforcement.[64] It may do so only if it thinks that the person has committed an unlawful act.[65] There are incentives for a person to make such an agreement: the Commission must undertake not to proceed with a formal investigation or unlawful act notice, and the person is not taken to be admitting to the commission of an unlawful act by reason only of entering into the agreement.[66] If the Commission thinks that a party to an agreement has failed to comply or is not likely to comply with an undertaking in the agreement, it may apply to a county court (in England and Wales) or sheriff (in Scotland) for an order requiring the person to comply or take such other action as the court may specify.[67]

The Commission has a number of other enforcement powers. If it thinks

---

[61] O'Cinneide (2007) 157.
[62] Heath, Clifford, Hamill, McCrudden and Muttarak (2009).
[63] See p 155 above.
[64] EA 2006, s 23.
[65] EA 2006, s 23(2).
[66] EA 2006, s 23(1)(b), (3).
[67] EA 2006, s 24(2), (3).

that a person is likely to commit an unlawful act, it may seek an injunction (England and Wales) or interdict (Scotland) to prevent the person from committing that act.[68] The Commission has the capacity to institute or intervene in legal proceedings, whether for judicial review or otherwise, if it appears to the Commission that the proceedings are relevant to a matter in connection with which the Commission has a function.[69] Finally, the Equality Act 2010 amends the 2006 Act so as to allow the EHRC to use its enforcement powers, including conducting investigations and applying for an injunction, in a number of situations where individuals may not be able or willing to take action. This includes cases of direct and indirect discrimination, and making arrangements which, if applied to an individual, would result in direct discrimination. If the Commission uses its powers this does not affect the entitlement of a person to bring proceedings under the Act.[70] An example given in the Explanatory Notes is a bed and breakfast (B&B) which includes a statement in an advertisement that it does not welcome people from gypsy and traveller communities. Even if the EHRC takes action, an individual who is discouraged from staying at the B&B can also bring a claim in their own right.[71] The Commission can act against a suspected discriminatory practice even though it is not aware that any particular individual is affected by it—for example it could take action against a club believed to be operating an informal policy of excluding people from ethnic minorities, even though it is not aware of any particular individual affected by this policy.[72] The Commission can also use its powers when an employer asks job applicants prohibited enquiries about disability and health,[73] and to enforce any diversity reporting arrangements imposed on political parties.[74] These provisions replace those found in earlier enactments relating to discriminatory practices and discriminatory advertisements.

Support for Individuals and the Provision of Conciliation

Individual actions complement and should work hand-in-hand with enforcement by the EHRC. The Equality Act 2006 allowed the EHRC to provide a range of support for individuals and non-governmental equality organisations. The first was a helpline which gave information and general advice The Coalition government stopped funding this helpline but replaced it with

---

[68] EA 2006, s 24(1).
[69] EA 2006, s 30.
[70] EA, sched 26 para 13 inserting EA 2006, s 24a(4).
[71] EN, para 1024.
[72] EA, sched 26 para 13 inserting EA 2006, s 24a(2); EN, para 1024.
[73] See p 96 above.
[74] EA, sched 26 para 13 inserting EA 2006, s 24a; EN, paras 1022–24. See p 162 above.

a generalist advice service run by Siftel (a private sector organisation) working with Disability Rights UK and other partners.. This service can explain legal rights and remedies and options for resolution of disputes. However, it cannot provide legal advice or representation or provide advice on court and tribunal procedures once a claim has been issued or advice on the strength of a case. Second, the EHRC had a legal grants programme[75] that provided awards to voluntary organisations to educate individuals about their rights. It also made grants to advice organisations, such as Citizens' Advice Bureaux and law centres, to provide legal advice and representation,[76] and training for advisers, caseworkers and lawyers. Government support for this grants programme has now ceased. A survey by the Discrimination Law Association of providers indicated that without such grants they would not be able to sustain their services and some might have to close down completely.[77]

Third, the EHRC, like its predecessors, has the power to provide legal advice and representation, facilities for the settlement of disputes, and any other assistance to individuals in proceedings under the Equality Act,[78] under EU law relating to discrimination which confer rights on individuals,[79] and proceedings in which an individual claims to have been disadvantaged by a provision of UK law which is contrary to EU law or a by a failure by the UK to implement EU law.[80] The Commission can support proceedings which relate both to the Equality Act and to other matters. However, if the proceedings cease to relate to a provision of the Equality Act, assistance may not be continued.[81] Following protests that this would prevent continued support for linked human rights cases, a provision was inserted into the Act allowing the Lord Chancellor to issue an order enabling the Commission to continue assistance in a case which started wholly or partly under the Equality Act, and has ceased to do so, but still relates wholly or partly to any Convention rights under the Human Rights Act.[82] There are provisions enabling the ECHR to recoup costs and expenses out of any award of costs and expenses to an individual.[83]

The former Commissions used their powers to provide legal assistance in different ways.[84] The policy of the EOC from the start was to support

---

[75] EA 2006, s 17.

[76] EA 2006, ss 28, 29.

[77] Discrimination Law Association, *Response to the EHRC Reform Consultation* (June 2011) 19–20.

[78] EA 2006, s 28. This does not apply to the public transport provisions of the act: s 28(5) as amended by EA 2010 sched 26.

[79] EA 2006, s 28(12).

[80] EA 2006, s 28(13).

[81] EA 2006, s 28(6).

[82] EA 2006, s 28(7).

[83] EA 2006, s 29.

[84] Hepple (2006a) 109–10.

only selected test cases, and it did so to great effect in various cases which expanded the boundaries of EU sex discrimination law. In 2003 the EOC received requests for assistance in only about 2 per cent of all sex-discrimination and equal-pay cases, and provided full or part assistance in just under half of those. On the other hand, the CRE for many years sought to assist everyone asking for support who had an arguable case, but a new legal strategy was adopted in 2003 which resulted in legal assistance being provided to only 3.2 per cent of those who asked for it. The new strategy confined support largely to test cases, and there was a requirement of a strong prospect of success. Many cases that might previously have been supported directly by the CRE were taken up by race equality councils and other bodies receiving grants from the CRE, as well as by trade unions and other NGOs. The DRC also applied strategic criteria when selecting cases, and had considerable success in clarifying the principles of disability law.

The EHRC has limited resources (see below) but allocated £1.4 million for litigation in the financial year 2013/14. According to its published litigation strategy,[85] the EHRC will identify cases where it is uniquely placed to act or is best placed to work as a partner with others, and assess whether non-litigation options provide more effective and proportionate ways of achieving change. Among the criteria listed are whether the case addresses widespread or systemic equality and/or human rights problems that litigation brought by others has failed to resolve and has the potential to improve equality and/or human rights practices or policies of a strategically significant organisation or sector. There is inevitably a focus on appellate litigation because this is likely to clarify, extend or strengthen compliance with equality and/or human rights law. The case must have good prospects of success or, if not, there must be compelling reasons to become involved anyway. Priority issues, where the EHRC has intervened as a third party in cases taken by others, include the PSED, religious freedom and the protection of exploited migrant workers.

The power of the EHRC to commission a conciliation service in non-employment cases was removed in 2013,[86] a surprising step in view of the Ministry of Justice's commitment to promote conciliation and mediation as a means of reducing the burden on courts and tribunals and reducing expenditure.[87]

---

[85] Crick (2014) .
[86] ERRA 2013, s 64(1) repealing EA 2006, s 27.
[87] In 2010, the EHRC completed 59 mediation cases in non-employment cases with over 86 per cent settled.

Resources

As we have seen, the EHRC has been deprived of some of its powers and been reduced to so-called 'core' functions. It has also suffered a cut of about two-thirds in its budget, with consequent severe staff losses. The single Commission, covering all strands of discrimination and human rights, has had its budget slashed from £70 million in 2010 to a basic grant of £17.1 million plus funding for specific programmes, such as a review of maternity provision, amounting to £7.8 million in 2013–14 and £8 million in 2014–15. Staff numbers have been cut from 368 in March 2012, to 217 in March 2013 and about 190 in May 2014, with further reductions expected. There is an appraisal of the impact of the changes in the legal framework and resources in chapter 8.

INDIVIDUAL ENFORCEMENT

County and Sheriff Courts

The Equality Act continues the jurisdictional separation of employment and non-employment cases. Proceedings in respect of the former must go to an employment tribunal. Those relating to services and public functions, premises, education, associations and some ancillary liabilities must go to a county court (England and Wales) or sheriff (Scotland).[88] The courts also have jurisdiction to make an order to remove or modify a term in a contract or other agreement that is unenforceable because it promotes or provides for treatment prohibited by the act.[89] Immigration cases have to go to the immigration authorities,[90] and education cases relating to disabled pupils go to specialist tribunals.[91]

The Cambridge Review,[92] and a number of organisations responding to the government's *Discrimination Law Review*, recommended that all discrimination cases should be commenced in the employment tribunals; where the matter did not relate to work and equal pay, the tribunal could be called an 'equality tribunal'. This proposal sprang from widespread dissatisfaction with county and sheriff courts, which hear few discrimination cases and

---

[88] EA, s 114.

[89] EA, ss 142, 143; EN, paras 465–71.

[90] EA, s 115. This covers services and public functions (except immigration), premises, education (except relating to disabled pupils), associations, and ancillary liabilities.

[91] EA, s 116 and sched 17. These are the First-Tier Tribunal in England, the Special Education Needs Tribunal for Wales, and an Additional Support Needs Tribunal for Scotland. These cases were previously heard in Scotland in the Sheriff's Court.

[92] Cambridge Review (2000) paras 4.12–4.17.

so do not have the opportunity to develop expertise in this complex field. Moreover, before 2013, unlike complainants in employment tribunals, claimants in the courts had to face the deterrent of paying court fees, and an order for costs and expenses if unsuccessful. There were also more procedural hurdles to jump in courts than in the tribunals. The government rejected these proposals on the grounds that they would 'divert specialist resources from employment tribunals and would create significant jurisdictional problems, for example where claims of discrimination in goods and services are combined with other claims for civil wrongs which would still have to be heard in the courts'.[93] Both of these reasons are unconvincing. Specialisation in a single tribunal would lead to the saving of court resources and gains in efficiency. Jurisdictional problems could be dealt with by giving the President of Employment Tribunals or a regional employment judge power to transfer a case to a court. This argument was lost at the time, but the increasing assimilation of the tribunals with ordinary courts, discussed later, may result in this issue being revived in future. At present the focus must be on more training and specialisation within the courts. In England and Wales several senior salaried employment judges have been appointed as part-time judges in the county courts and employment judges have been promoted to become circuit judges; this provides an opportunity for judges experienced in equality cases to utilise their expertise in both fora.

The very modest concession made by the Equality Act in relation to improving the expertise of courts is a new provision that requires the judge or sheriff to appoint an assessor unless satisfied that there are good reasons for not doing so.[94] Previously assessors had to be appointed in England and Wales only in race discrimination cases, unless both parties agreed otherwise. They could also be used in sex discrimination cases, but there was no provision for their use in cases relating to other protected characteristics. In Scotland they could be used in all discrimination cases in the sheriff court. The new provision creates a presumption that an assessor will be used in all cases. The extension of protected characteristics and the scope of prohibited conduct to cover all areas is likely to increase the caseload of the courts, so providing opportunities for more specialist training and experience.

Employment Tribunals

The employment tribunals have jurisdiction in all work cases. This includes discrimination affecting contract workers, partners, office holders, barris-

---

[93] *Discrimination Law Review* (2007) para 7.23.
[94] EA, s 114(7), (8). it is also possible for a civil court to refer a claim relating to a non-discrimination (pensions) case to an employment tribunal: EA, s 122.

Table 7.1 Claims accepted by employment tribunals

Nature of claim	2007–08	2009–10	2011–12
Sex discrimination	26,900	18,200	10,800
Equal pay	62,700	37,400	28,800
Race discrimination	4,100	5,700	4,800
Religion or belief	710	1,000	940
Sexual orientation	580	710	610
Age discrimination	2,900	3,800	5,200
disability discrimination	5,800	3,700	7,700
All	103,690	75,710	58,850
All excl equal pay	40,990	38,310	30,050

Source: Ministry of Justice: Tribunals Statistics (2013), Table 1 and Tribunals Service, *Employment Tribunal and EAT Statistics (GB)* (2010) Table 1.

ters and advocates, trade unions, trade bodies and professional qualification bodies. They can also deal with the terms of collective agreements that are alleged to be unenforceable because they provide for treatment that is prohibited by the Act, such as an agreement that is indirectly discriminatory against women.[95] The tribunals have jurisdiction to hear complaints regarding the breach of a sex equality clause in a contract, or a sex equality rule in an occupational pension scheme,[96] or a non-discrimination rule in an occupational pension scheme,[97] but the ordinary courts or sheriff may also be able deal with an equality clause[98] or rule or non-discrimination rule.[99]

The overall number of discrimination claims peaked in 2007/08, following the addition of new strands, but there was a drop of about 14 per cent the following year (excluding equal pay cases). This was less than the 20 per cent drop in all tribunal claims (including unfair dismissal) in that year, and only 10 per cent less than in 2006/07. There was a rise in all discrimination claims in 2009/10, particularly in respect of age. In the first full year of operation of the Equality Act (2011/12) there were significant increases in age and disability discrimination claims. The figures for sex discrimination and equal pay claims decreased in 2011/12, but these figures must be treated with caution because they include several multiple claims where a number of people bring cases against one employer on the same or very similar grounds and these are processed together. It must be remembered

[95] EA, s 145.
[96] EA, s 127.
[97] EA, s 120(2)–(5).
[98] EA, s 127(9).
[99] EA, s 120(6).

Table 7.2 Employment tribunal cases: disposals without hearing 2011–12

Nature of claim	Disposed	Withdrawn	ACAS Conciliated	Struck out at hearing
Sex discrimination	14,700	4,900 (33%)	4,500 (30%)	4,200 (29%)
Race discrimination	4,700	1,400 (30%)	1,700 (36%)	400 (8%))
Disability discrimination	7,300	2,300 (31%)	3,300 (45%)	490 (7%)
Religion/belief discrimination	850	260 (31%)	290 (34%)	85 (10%)
Sexual orientation	590	170 (29%)	250 (42%)	56 (9%)
Age discrimination	3,800	1,600 (43%)	1,200 (31%)	500 (4%)
Equal pay	23,800	10,300 (44%)	8,800 (37%)	4,500 (19%)
All excl equal pay	31,350	10,630	12,440	5,731

Source: Ministry of Justice, Tribunal; Statistics Tables 2011–12 (2013). The percentages are those of all claims to tribunals.

that a claim can contain several grounds (so-called jurisdictional cases): for example it may include both unfair dismissal and discrimination.

The early impact of the imposition of tribunal fees from 29 July 2013 (see below) has been devastating. The total number of claims received in the period October to December 2013 was 9,801—79 per cent fewer than in the same period in 2012, and 75 per cent fewer than in the period July to September 2013. The relatively high number in that quarter reflects a last-minute rush to file claims before the new fees regime came into operation.

The outcomes of discrimination cases have remained remarkably similar over the years, despite various procedural changes. Table 7.2 depicts disposals without hearing for the year 2011/12, the first full year the Equality Act was in operation.. Over one-third of cases were withdrawn, and just over one-third were conciliated by the Advisory, Conciliation and Arbitration Service (ACAS). Other withdrawn cases may have been privately settled without ACAS conciliation. Table 7.3 presents statistics of outcomes of cases that went to either full or preliminary hearing. Only 2–3 per cent of all discrimination claims were successful at hearings, compared to 10 per cent of all

Table 7.3 Employment tribunal cases: outcomes of hearings 2011–12

Nature of claim	Successful at tribunal	Dismissed at preliminary hearing	Unsuccessful at hearing	Default judgment
Sex discrimination	341 (3%)	206 (2%)	597 (6%)	44 (0%)
Race discrimination	129 (3%)	236 (6%)	694 (17%)	15 (0%)
Disability discrimination	220 (3%)	250 (39%)	750 (11%)	34 (1%)
Religion/belief discrimination	24 (3%)	45 (5%)	140 (16%)	5 (1%)
Sexual orientation	20 (3%)	29 (5%)	60 (10%)	– (1%)
Age discrimination	48 (1%)	100 (3%)	290 (8%)	201 (9%)
Equal pay	32 (0%)	41 (0%)	35 (0%)	– (0%)
All excl equal pay	1,025	866	2,531	240

Source: Ministry of Justice, *Tribunal Statistics* (2013). The percentages are those of all claims to tribunals.

unfair dismissal claims. A more significant statistic is that of all cases that went to a full hearing (excluding equal pay), only about a quarter succeeded.

Limiting Accessibility

Employment (originally industrial) tribunals were created as tripartite institutions to deal with simple issues of fact and fairness. They were meant to be non-technical, inexpensive and expeditious. However, in practice they have become increasingly formalised, costly and more like the ordinary civil courts.[100] This has happened not only because of the mass of complex legislation, including discrimination laws, which they have to interpret and apply but also because of pressures on public expenditure which have led governments to restrict accessibility.[101]

Race and sex discrimination law in the 1970s could have followed the model in several other countries in which all disputes are dealt with by the ordinary courts. However, the existence of specialist industrial tribunals made them the natural home for disputes about discrimination at work. They held hearings in venues convenient to the parties. Claims and responses could be made without prescribed forms. The proceedings were virtually

[100] Corby and Latreille (2012a).
[101] Hepple (2013) 211–13.

cost-free: there were were no tribunal fees, and costs were awarded against an unsuccessful party only if they or their representative had acted vexatiously, abusively, disruptively or otherwise unreasonably in either bringing the proceedings or the way that they were conducted.

Today tribunals sit in only a limited number of fixed venues in England, Wales and Scotland. (Northern Ireland has its own employment tribunals and Fair Employment Tribunal.) Since 2005 claims and responses have had to be made on relatively lengthy and detailed designated forms and can be rejected if they do not contain all the required information. Since 1980 there have been screening mechanisms to weed out unmeritorious claims; from 1993 there was provision for pre-hearing assessments (PHAs) at which a party with little reasonable prospect of success could be ordered to pay a deposit in order to proceed. A power to strike out claims with little prospect of success was also introduced in 1993, but was subject to a number of procedural requirements. In 2013[102] a much stronger sifting mechanism was introduced. An employment judge must consider all the documents to confirm whether there are arguable complaints and defences within the jurisdiction of the tribunal. If the judge considers that the tribunal has no jurisdiction or the claim or defence has no reasonable prospect of success, he must dismiss it. A party whose case is dismissed on the papers, may then apply for an oral preliminary hearing. If the claim or defence is not dismissed, the judge may make a case management order. In the first full year of operation, about one in ten claims were dismissed after preliminary consideration.

The most devastating obstacle to access was the introduction of tribunal fees from 29 July 2013. Jurisdictions are divded into two levels. Level 1 covers simple claims such as unlawful deductions from wages. Level 2 claims include discrimination cases. At Level 2, claimants are charged an issue fee of £250 and a hearing fee of £950, a total of £1,200. There are higher fees in cases with multiple claimants. There are additional fees for applying to review decisions, for judicial mediation and to lodge a counter-claim There are also fees of £400 to launch an appeal to the EAT and £1,200 for the hearing of an appeal, a total of £1,600. Remissions are available at three levels. At the first level, no fee is payable if the claimant is receiving certain state benefits, such as Income Support. At the second level no fee is payable if the claimant (and partner) have an income below a specified point, ranging from £13,000 for a single claimant with no children to £23,860 for a claimant with a partner and two children. At the third level,

---

[102] The Employment Tribunals (Constitution and Rules of Procedure) Regulations 2013, SI 2013 No 1237. sched 1, rules 26–28. These new rules were drafted following review by Sir Nicholas Underhill. They simplify and clarify the earlier rules but do not make radical changes.

there can be a discount of up to 100 per cent depending on the claimant's monthly disposable income, ranging from £50 for a full discount and a partial discount if the income is between £50 and £250.

The early impact of these substantial fees can be seen from the drop of nearly 80 per cent of claims in the period January–March 2014.[103] Employers may be reluctant to reach a settlement agreement until they have seen whether the claimant has paid the requisite fee. If the claimant is successful in whole or part, the tribunal may make a costs order including the tribunal fee against the unsuccessful party. It has been predicted that once the fee has been paid, claimants will want to recover them as part of any settlement agreement, and this may make it more difficult to reach an agreement.

Decline of Tripartism

The Cambridge Review[104] canvassed the idea of a specialist division of tribunals to handle discrimination cases but found that there was little support for this, partly because of the practical difficulty of separating discrimination claims from other claims raised at the same time (such as unfair dismissal). There is also the danger that specialised judges within the tribunals would become too narrowly focused and jaded. The Review therefore placed its focus on more training in discrimination law and procedure for legally qualified chairmen and non-legal members, but it appears that this training is still limited because of a lack of resources. There is a power in the Employment Tribunal Regulations 2013 to appoint specialist panels of Employment Judges and lay members to deal with proceedings in which specialist knowledge would be helpful, and it was thought that this might be used for such tasks as determining equal value claims.[105] This power has not yet been exercised. It is not to be confused with the practice that started in 1976 of having one member with knowledge and experience of race relations in race cases.[106] Arrangements are in place for employment judges to receive discrimination law training; normally, only after this training are they allowed to chair hearings of discrimination claims. Two or three judges in each region are trained and authorised to hear equal pay cases.

When the tribunals were established, it was expected that all hearings

---

[103] See above, p 194.

[104] Cambridge Review (2000) para 4.6.

[105] Employment Tribunal (Constitution and Rules of Procedure) Regulations 2013, SI 2013 No 1237, reg 8(4).

[106] The Cambridge Review (2000) paras 4.8–4.9 considered it anomalous to confine this to race cases.

would take place before a tripartite bench consisting of a legally qualified chairman (now called an employment judge, following a recommendation by the Cambridge Review)[107] and two non-legal (lay) members drawn respectively from panels appointed after consultation with organisations of employers and employees. The non-legal members were often referred to as an 'industrial jury'. In recent years, however, there has been a tendency to dispense with non-legal members in both the employment tribunals and the Employment Appeal Tribunal.[108] A tripartite panel is still normally required for the hearing of discrimination cases, but an employment judge can sit alone in a wide range of matters (eg in stage 1 of equal value hearings) or where the parties so agree. In addition all preliminary hearings are conducted by an employment judge alone unless the judge thinks it desirable that the hearing be conducted by a full tribunal, or agrees with a request by a party that it be so conducted. These preliminary hearings can give preliminary consideration of a case and the judge can make a case management order. The hearing may be used to determine any preliminary issue, for example whether a person has a disability or a religion or belief and so can bring a claim for discrimination, or whether the claim has been submitted in time. The EAT judges have also been empowered to sit alone.[109] The marginalisation of the non-legal members is likely to result in a loss of specialist knowledge of industrial practice and, in particular, practical experience of discrimination. There are several well-known examples of lay members in both the tribunals and the EAT successfully resisting pressure from the judge to change their majority finding of discrimination.[110]

One respect in which there has been some progress is in improving the diversity of employment judges and the non-legal members who are also judicial officers. Both fee paid and salaried employment judges are appointed following open competition through the Judicial Appointments Commission, while non-legal members are appointed following open competition through the Tribunals Service. The the more transparent and objective appointments process in recent years is enabling the tribunals to better reflect the composition of the workforce they serve, although there are obviously still significant barriers, particularly to the appointment of Black and minority ethnic (BME) candidates.

---

[107] Tribunals, Courts and Enforcement Act 2007, s 48(1), sched 8 paras 35, 36; Cambridge Review (2000) para 4.11.

[108] Corby and Latreille (2012a, 2012b).

[109] ERRA 2013, s 12.

[110] See eg *King v Great Britain China Centre* [1991] IRLR 513, where the lay members were vindicated by the Court of Appeal; Case C-326/96 *Levez v TH Jennings (Harlow Pools) Ltd* [1999] IRLR 36, where the ECJ sustained the lay members' majority decision.

Representative Actions

A change that was strongly pressed by the EHRC, the Women's National Commission, the Citizens Advice Bureaux (CABx) and other groups was the introduction of representative actions, but this was resisted by the government on the basis of the hallowed principle that 'the time is not ripe'.[111] Discriminatory practices affect people because of their membership of a status group. In particular, unequal pay for women is often systemic and requires the whole pay structure to be examined and overhauled. At present, each member of the group has to make a separate claim. The court or tribunal may combine proceedings in certain circumstances, but the individual claimants have to be identified and each one of them has to bring proceedings. The Employment Tribunals Act 1996 already contains a power to make regulations on procedural rules which could be used to permit representative actions, but this power has not been exercised. Liberal Democrats in the House of Commons and Lord Lester of Herne Hill QC in the House of Lords moved an amendment to the Equality Bill to allow the EHRC or a registered trade union to bring a representative action on behalf of a defined class of persons ('the class') who would benefit from the litigation of common issues in relation to rights arising under the Equality Act.[112] The government said that it was unnecessary to include anything on this in the Equality Act because of the existing powers in the Employment Tribunals Act, and that it was premature to make regulations on this topic because an extensive review by the Ministry of Justice with the Civil Procedure Rule committee was underway. Indeed, it has been underway for some years without resolution.[113]

Equal Pay Procedure

A new procedure for dealing with equal value claims was introduced from 1 October 2004, in response to widespread criticism of the inordinate delays involved in processing such claims, and their failure to deliver equal pay.[114] The aims of the reforms were to encourage an early exchange of factual information, setting out an indicative timetable at each stage, utilising independent experts to whom issues are referred more effectively, and restricting the use of expert witnesses. Research by Kate Godwin, published in March

---

[111] Hansard HL vol 716 cols 976–81 (27 January 2010).
[112] The amendment was drafted in terms of equal value claims but could have been applied to all discrimination cases. This was based on the Cambridge Review (2000) paras 4.24–4.26.
[113] Hansard HL vol 716 col 980 (27 January 2010) (Baroness Royall).
[114] Cambridge Review (2000) paras 4.27–4.32.

2009, concluded that 'not only have the [new] Regulations failed to achieve their aims but they represent a retrograde step as cases are taking years to be assigned to an independent expert'.[115]

The new procedure[116] envisages the following:

- A *stage one hearing* (which, since 2009, can be conducted by an employment judge alone) to decide whether or not to refer the matter to an independent expert on a panel maintained by ACAS,[117] to make orders for the disclosure of information, and to order the parties to present a joint agreed statement of job descriptions, relevant facts, and facts about which they disagree.
- A *stage 2 hearing* (before a full tribunal) takes place if the employment judge has decided to appoint an independent expert. The tribunal determines disputed facts, and sets a date for preparation of the expert's report.
- The *independent expert* makes a report on the basis of the facts determined by the tribunal at stage 2.
- A *stage 3 hearing* (before a full tribunal), at which the independent expert's report is admissible in evidence unless the tribunal concludes that it is not based on facts relating to the issue for determination. No other expert may be called by the parties without leave of the tribunal, which may grant such leave when for example the methodology used by the independent expert is challenged.[118] The tribunal must then decide the equal value issue itself, or may order another expert to prepare a report.[119]

Godwin's research[120] found that the exclusion of the independent expert from the fact-finding process has greatly lengthened the procedure, with cases delayed for several years by preliminary issues before the case is assigned to an independent expert. The experience of practitioners is that there are delays because there are not enough experts.[121]

Respondents in Godwin's survey reported that the time taken to determine an equal value claim ranges from 8 to 12 years. Over 90 per cent of equal pay claims to tribunals are withdrawn, usually after the parties have reached a settlement; only a tiny number are resolved by a tribunal hearing

---

[115] Godwin (2009) 16.

[116] Employment Tribunals (Equal Value) Rules of Procedure, sched 3 to the Employment Tribunals (Coinstitution and Rules of Procedure) Regulations 2013 SI 2013 No 1237, which came into force in July 2013, replace the 2004 rules.

[117] s 131 EA empowers the tribunal to require an independent ACAS-designated expert to prepare a report on whether the work of the claimant and the comparator are of equal value.

[118] *Middlesbrough Borough Council v Surtees (No 2)* [2007] IRLR 981, EAT.

[119] Equal Value Rules of Procedure, para 8(2).

[120] Godwin (2009) 16.

[121] From 1983 to 2013 experts were appointed in 732 cases; 68 of these were appointed in 2009/10, but these had declined to 10 cases in 2012/13, at which time the number of experts on the panel had declined from 27 to 24:ACAS (2013).

(see Table 7.2). The procedure may serve a purpose in encouraging settlements, but nothing has happened since the Cambridge Review to change the conclusion that there is not much scope for improving the procedures in individual equal pay claims. The new power of employment tribunals to order equal pay audits[122] may be of some use, but significant changes in the gender pay gap can be brought about only through pay equity plans, changes in the basis of comparison and improved job evaluation.[123]

Legal Assistance

'High quality advice, assistance and representation is essential to ensuring access to justice' for victims of discrimination, harassment and victimisation.[124] Research suggests that a legally represented applicant is more likely to be successful at a hearing than one who appears in person.[125] No current statistics are available as to the extent of representation in discrimination cases. These representatives include not only lawyers but also trade unions, employment consultants and claims advisers, CABx, pro bono units (such as the Bar Free Representation unit), the Civil Legal Advice service and others, but the quality of representation varies greatly. The number of cases in which trade union representatives appear at employment tribunals in all types of case has declined significantly in recent years, and is mainly confined to the public sector. The number of lawyers in all types of case has also decreased.[126].

Lawyers may be funded in a variety of ways: privately, through legal expenses insurance, through the EHRC,[127] trade unions and other organisations., Since April 2013, the new Civil Legal Advice service is the gateway to certain categories of law, including discrimination law. This is a telephone-based service which uses a small, specialist group of advisers.

In some cases lawyers use 'Conditional Fee Agreements' or 'Damages Based Agreements' (DBAs). CFAs and DBAs are commonly referred to as 'no-win no-fee' agreements, but this can be inaccurate because the client may have to pay counsel's fees and other expenses, depending upon the

---

[122] EA, 139A introduced by ERRA 2013, s 98. See p 133 above.
[123] See p 119 above.
[124] Cambridge Review (2000) para 4.34.
[125] See eg Meager et al (1999) in relation to disability cases.
[126] The Tribunals Service's *Employment Tribunal and EAT Statistics*, 1 April 2011–31 March 2012, show that the number of employment tribunal claims with trade union representatives dropped from 29,100 in 2007/08 to 5,500 in 2011/12, while the number with lawyers decreased from 117,600 in 2007/08 to 34,000 in 2011. These figures are not broken down by type of claim.
[127] See p 190 regarding the EHRC's litigation strategy.

agreement. In a CFA the lawyer agrees not to charge a fee if the case fails, but will be able to charge a significant uplift on their normal fee if the case succeeds. CFAs and DBAs were permitted for a limited number of cases from 1995, and their use was extended in 2000 following the abolition of legal aid for most civil cases. They are little used in tribunal discrimination cases because the losing side is only exceptionally ordered to pay costs.

In a DBA the lawyer agrees not to charge if the case fails but will take a proportion of the damages received on success. Such agreements have been allowed for many years for 'non-contentious work', but not for court-based litigation. They are permitted for tribunal work because, anomalously, this is classed as 'non-contentious'. DBAs can provide victims of discrimination with a way of funding their cases with relatively little risk to themselves, and the lawyer has an incentive to achieve the best result for the client. They are particularly suitable for discrimination and equal pay cases with multiple applicants because the total award of compensation is likely to be large enough to make it worthwhile for a solicitor or barrister to take the risk of not earning a fee. Individual awards will rarely be high enough for a lawyer to take the risk. Stefan Cross, a solicitor who has represented many thousands of women in public sector equal value claims, has argued that no-win no-fee lawyers have informed women about their right to equal pay, have challenged discriminatory collective agreements, and have won substantial awards or settlements for underpaid women.[128] However, DBAs have come under a great deal of criticism from trade unions, which claim that some non-win no-fee lawyers 'offer basic advice to low-paid women on offers already made, which the employer will generally not vary, and cream off up to 30 per cent of the women's settlements'.[129] It has been suggested that the lawyer may put pressure on clients to reach an early settlement for less than the true value of the claim, in order to minimise the risk of losing. It is also argued that unfair 'exit' clauses in some DBAs have the effect of inducing clients to accept settlements in order to avoid having to pay for the entire case. Before 2010, there was no regulation of the percentage of damages that could be taken by the lawyer.

The Labour government moved to meet some of the criticisms by introducing the Damages Based Agreements Regulations 2010, which set out the information a DBA must contain in order for the agreement to be enforceable, and limit the fee the representative may charge to 35 per cent, including VAT, of the sum ultimately recovered by the client.[130] The Ministry of Justice cited research by Professor Richard Moorhead in support of the

---

[128] Cross (2008) 18.
[129] McKenna (2008) 16.
[130] SI 2010/1206, reg 5.

proposed 35 per cent cap, but Professor Moorhead himself informed the Merits of Statutory Instruments Select Committee that the research did not support the view that contingency fees generally led to overcharging of clients, and he said that the evidence suggested that contingency fees were generally a better deal for clients than paying on an hourly basis.[131] The Law Society argued against a cap on the ground that there should be some flexibility depending on the complexity of the case. The research showed that fees tended to fall into bands of 5–10, 25–30 and 40–50 per cent according to the complexity of the case.[132] It remains to be seen whether the Regulations will deter meritorious claims.

Burden of Proof

The general legal rule is that it is for the claimant to prove his or her case on the balance of probabilities. This is called the legal burden of proof. The Supreme Court has emphasised that it is important not to make too much of this burden when the tribunal is able to make positive findings on the evidence one way or the other.[133] But where there is room for doubt the courts have recognised that it is unusual to find direct evidence that there was discrimination because of the claimant's protected characteristic. Few respondents would admit to such discrimination; in any event, the treatment of the claimant may be unintentional and based on an assumption or stereotype. The outcome will therefore often depend on what inferences it is proper to draw from the primary facts found by the court or tribunal. The higher courts have from time to time set out guidelines as to how to approach the drawing of inferences, usually avoiding the concept of a shifting evidential burden of proof.[134] The relatively small proportion of race discrimination cases, compared to cases arising under other jurisdictions, in which a tribunal has been willing to draw inferences suggests that the judicial guidelines have been inadequate.

For this reason, many (but not all) employment judges welcomed the statutory rules reversing the burden of proof which were introduced as a result of EU law. This started with the Burden of Proof Directive, which applied to sex discrimination, and was followed by the Race Directive and the Framework Employment Directive, leading to changes in the SDA and

---

[131] House of Lords Merits of Statutory Instruments Committee, Damages-Based Agreements Regulations 2010, appendix: evidence, March 2010.

[132] Ibid.

[133] *Hewage v Grampian Health Board* [2012] EqLR 884, UKSC.

[134] See eg *King v Great Britain China Centre* [1991] IRLR 513, CA; *Zafar v Glasgow City Council* [1998] IRLR 36, HL.

RRA and the Regulations applying to other strands of discrimination. However, because of the limits of the Directives, the burden of proof was not reversed in race discrimination claims based on colour or nationality, claims of victimisation relating to race discrimination, non-work disability discrimination claims, or sex discrimination claims relating to the exercise of a public function.

Section 136 of the Equality Act now extends the reversal of the burden of proof to all claims of direct and indirect discrimination, harassment and victimisation because of a protected characteristic.

> If there are facts from which the court *could* decide, in the absence of any other explanation, that a person [A] contravened the provisions concerned, the court *must* hold that the contravention occurred. ... But [this] does not apply if A shows that A did not contravene the provision.[135] (emphasis added)

Essentially, this involves a two-stage process. At the first stage, the claimant has to prove on the balance of probabilities facts from which the court or tribunal *could* conclude, in the absence of an alternative explanation, that the respondent has committed an act of discrimination, harassment or victimisation. If the claimant does not prove such facts, he or she will fail.[136] It is important to note the word 'could'. 'At this stage the tribunal does not have to reach a definitive determination that such facts would lead it to the conclusion that there was an act of unlawful discrimination.'[137] An example given in the Explanatory Notes is that of a man of Chinese origin who applies for a promotion at work but is not given an interview for the job. He finds out that a number of his White colleagues were given interviews despite having fewer qualifications and less experience than him. These are facts from which the tribunal could draw an inference of unlawful discrimination. The burden of proof would shift to the employer to prove that the reason for the treatment was not because of his ethnic origin.[138] The evidence might simply be that the respondent failed to comply with a provision of the relevant code of practice. Any exculpatory explanation put forward by the respondent is considered not at this stage, but at the next stage.

If such facts are proved, then the burden of proof shifts to the respondent, who must then prove on the balance of probabilities that the treatment 'was in no sense whatsoever' because of the claimant's protected characteristic. The court or tribunal will normally require 'cogent evidence to discharge that burden of proof'. If such evidence is not provided, then, according to

---

[135] This applies to employment tribunals as well as court proceedings.

[136] The tribunal may take the respondent's evidence, as well as that of the claimant, into account at this stage: *Madrassay v Nomura* [2007] IRLR 246, CA.

[137] *Igen Ltd v Wong* [2005] IRLR 258, CA, annex.

[138] EN, para 452.

the President of the EAT, the tribunal need not make an express finding that it does not accept the explanation.

> It must in principle be enough to say (with, of course, such reasons as may be appropriate) 'we were not persuaded that his explanation was right' rather than 'we reject his explanation', that is what the burden of proof is about.[139]

An important aid to proving discrimination was embodied in section 138 of the Equality Act 2010. This enabled a person who thought they may have been unlawfully discriminated against to send a questionnaire on a prescribed form. The questionnaire and answer were admissible in evidence. The court or tribunal could draw an inference from a failure to answer or from an evasive or equivocal answer. Such a provision had been in the law since the SDA 1975 and RRA 1976. The procedure could make it unnecessary to start proceedings, if the answers persuaded the claimant that there was no case. It could also put pressure on the respondent to settle the claim. This provision was repealed in 2013,[140] for no other stated reason than that it was an 'unnecessary burden on business'. In future, claimants will have to rely on a pre-action letter to request information, but this may be less effective than the statutory procedure because of uncertainty as to whether the court or tribunal will draw an adverse inference from a failure to reply or an evasive reply. After a tribunal claim has been lodged, the claimant may seek information and, where appropriate, ask the tribunal to order the respondent to provide the information.

Time Limits

A person must bring a claim in a county or sheriff court within six months of the alleged unlawful act taking place, but this may be extended for such other period as the court or sheriff thinks 'just and equitable'.[141] A new exception allows for a period of nine months where the claim has been referred to a student complaints scheme[142] or to the EHRC for conciliation.[143]

A claim must be brought in an employment tribunal within three months of the alleged conduct taking place.[144] There is an exception relating to armed forces complaints, where the time limit is six months.[145] The tribunal

---

[139] *Pothecary Witham Weld v Bullimore* [2010] IRLR 572, EAT.
[140] ERRA 2013, s 66.
[141] EA, s 118(1).
[142] EA, s 118(3).
[143] EA, s 118(3); see p 207 below.
[144] EA, s 123(1). Where conduct extends over a period the time runs from the end of the period: s 123(3).
[145] EA, s 123(2).

has discretion to extend these limits for such other period as it considers just and equitable. Where the claim is for a breach of an equality clause or equality rule[146] the employee in a standard case must normally present this to a tribunal within six months of the end of the employment contract.[147] More time is allowed where the case is not a standard one, that is where the employer conceals certain information from the claimant or where the claimant has an incapacity. Members of the armed forces have an additional three months to bring a claim.[148]

These periods are substantially the same as under previous legislation. Employment cases remain an anomaly, with a normal three-month period rather than the six months allowed in county and sheriff court claims. There is no apparent justification for distinguishing work and non-work cases in this way, other than a desire to treat discrimination cases in the same way as unfair dismissal, where there is a three-month limit. This can operate harshly on a claimant because an unfair dismissal case is brought at the end of the employment relationship, while discrimination can arise in the course of the employment but the claimant is understandably reluctant to bring proceedings until after the relationship has ended. This is why claimants in equal pay cases are given six months after the end of the employment contract. A similar time limit could have been applied to all discrimination claims.

Equal pay claims that cannot be brought in an employment tribunal because they are outside the time limit can be brought in the ordinary courts within the longer time limit of six years (five years in Scotland). A claim in the ordinary court can be struck out by the court if it could 'more conveniently' be disposed of by an employmentl tribunal.[149] In *Birmingham City Council v Abdullah*[150] the Supreme Court (by a 3–2 majority) decided that a claim can never be more conveniently disposed of by an employment tribunal if it was known that the tribunal would decline jurisdiction because the claim was time barred.

Conciliation and Mediation

Conciliation is a strategy of alternative dispute resolution (ADR), which is designed to reduce litigation. A third party assists the parties in reaching a settlement. This is a voluntary process that can be declined by the parties.

---

[146] See p 121 above.
[147] EA, s 129. There are supplementary provisions in s 130 defining what is not a standard case.
[148] EA, s 129(3).
[149] EA, s 128 (formerly Equal Pay Act s 2(3)).
[150] [2012] EqLR 1147, UKSC

The main provider of this service in the field of employment is ACAS. As we have seen,[151] over one-third of employment discrimination claims are withdrawn following ACAS conciliation. These services are available to parties both before and throughout the tribunal proceedings.[152]

The Enterprise and Regulatory Reform Act 2013 has made it compulsory to refer potential claims to ACAS before issuing tribunal proceedings. The claimant must lodge a form, following which ACAS will contact the claimant and respondent offering conciliation. If the parties agree to this, ACAS will try to help them reach an agreement. If either party refuses to participate, or if they fail to reach an agreement within one month,the early conciliation period comes to an end. ACAS officers can end the period earlier if a settlement appears hopeless or to extend the period for up to two weeks if the parties are close to agreement. Sending the form to ACAS effectively suspends the time period for instituting proceedings.

ACAS conciliation officers have a duty 'to endeavour to promote a settlement'. This may result in a legally binding settlement agreement. The EAT has made it clear that ACAS is not a rights enforcement agency. The ACAS officer has no responsibility to see that the terms of the agreement are fair to the employee, and must never advise as to the merits of the case. A tribunal will not consider whether the ACAS officer correctly interpreted their duties so long as the officer intended and purported to do so in good faith.[153]

Mediation takes many forms, sometimes being used as a synonym for conciliation. Essentially it is 'a process of negotiation, but structured and influenced by the intervention of a neutral third party who seeks to assist the parties to reach a settlement acceptable to them'.[154] At one extreme, the mediator may simply facilitate the parties' own efforts to reach a settlement; at the other extreme, the mediator may give a view as to the merits of their respective cases and make a recommendation. It is a flexible, open-ended process and much can depend on the personality and techniques of the mediator. The process is voluntary but can result in a legally binding settlement agreement. In practice a claimant may find mediation helpful if he or she is still in employment and wants to continue the employment relationship.

Hunter and Leonard argued for a 'rights-based' model of mediation in sex discrimination cases which would 'prioritise legal rights and the elimina-

---

[151] See p 194 above.
[152] Between October 2004 and April 2009 there were fixed periods for conciliation, but these did not apply to discrimination and equal pay claims.
[153] *Clarke v Redcar & Cleveland Borough Council* [2006] IRLR 324, EAT.
[154] Mackie, Miles, Marsh and Allen (2005) 11.

tion of discrimination'.[155] The mediator would redress the power imbalance between the parties by ensuring that the eventual settlement does not undermine the legal rights of the parties. There have not been the public resources or the willingness to provide facilities for this type of mediation. Mediation today is largely confined to privately funded services used in high-value sexual harassment and discrimination claims, where large organisations wish to avoid the cost or publicity attached to litigation.

A scheme providing for Mediation Case Management Discussions' (CMD) was extended to all regions in England and Wales from 2007. This is facilitated by a trained employment judge, who remains neutral and tries to assist the parties in resolving their dispute. The judge helps to identify the issues but does not make a decision or give an opinion on the merits of the case. The CMD is held in private and is confidential. If mediation fails, the hearing of the case takes place before a different judge. An evaluation of the use of judicial mediation of discrimination cases starting between June 2006 and March 2007, published in March 2010, concluded that, although employers and (less discernibly) claimants valued the process, it was expensive to administer and it had no statistically significant impact on the rates of cases settled or resolved without a hearing. Outcomes following judicial mediation were not significantly better (statistically) than those following unmediated cases.[156] Fees are payable for the use of judicial mediation.

Compensation

The main remedies for the statutory torts of discrimination, harassment and victimisation in the county and sheriff courts are a declaration of the rights of the parties, damages, including damages for injured feelings, and an injunction.[157] There is no power to make a recommendation. The employment tribunals may make a declaration, award compensation, including for injury to feelings, and make an appropriate recommendation.[158] In a case where unintentional indirect discrimination is proved, a court may not make an award of damages without first considering whether to make any other disposal, and a tribunal must first consider whether to make a declaration or recommendation.[159] There is no power to order engagement of a

---

[155] Hunter and Leonard (1997) 312. The Cambridge Review (2000) para 4.64 recommended a pilot project along these lines for mediation in sexual harassment claims, but this has not been acted upon.

[156] Ministry of Justice (2010) 57–58.

[157] EA, s 119. In Scotland these remedies are a declaration, reparation and an interdict.

[158] EA, s 124(2).

[159] EA, ss 119(5), (6), 124(4), (5). Previously there were differences in this respect between the various strands: Cambridge Review (2000) para 4.44. See p 86 above.

person refused employment on discriminatory grounds, and re-engagement or reinstatement of an employee is possible only if the case is also one of unfair dismissal.[160]

The principles on which damages or compensation are assessed are well established.[161] The main elements are loss of earnings and pension loss. Compensation should, as far as possible, put the claimant in the same position he or she would have been in but for the unlawful act. Unlike unfair dismissal, as a result of the case law of the Court of Justice of the EU there is no upper limit on the amount of the award that can be awarded.[162] Table 7.4 shows that the median award of compensation in recent years has remained under £10,000. and has declined slightly since 2010. (This is more informative than the average award, which went up to £20,910 in 2009, because a few very large awards can distort the picture.)

Table 7.4 Median awards of compensation by employment tribunals 2010–12

Jurisdiction	2013	2011	2010
Age	£5,809	£8,000	£7,250
Disability	£7,700	£7,646	£8,000
Race	£5,000	£4,000	£7,865
Religion	£2,875	£1,000	£56,976
Sex	£8,000	£8,986	£8,000
Sexual orientation	£4,000	£4,500	£4,000
Combined jurisdiction	£7,450	£12,000	£14,423
All awards	£7,700	£7,518	£8,000

Source: *Equal Opportunities Review* 249 (July 2014) Table 1.

In theory, exemplary damages are available in England and Wales in the law of tort where compensation is insufficient to punish a defendant for oppressive and arbitrary conduct.[163] Although punitive damages go beyond 'compensation', some tribunals have been willing to consider making such an award in discrimination and harassment cases.

As far as is known, no such award has been upheld on appeal.[164] However, courts and tribunals have been willing to award aggravated damages, which

---

[160] The Cambridge Review (2000) para 4.49 recommended such a power for tribunals.

[161] *Ministry of Defence v Wheeler* [1998] IRLR 23; *Ministry of Defence v Cannock* [1994] IRLR 509. The *Equal Opportunities Review* contains a valuable detailed annual analysis of compensation awards.

[162] Case C-271/91 *Marshall v Southampton and South West Area Health Authority (No 2)* [1993] ECR I-4367; [1993] IRLR 445.

[163] *Kuddus v Chief Constable of Leicestershire Police* [2001] UKHL 29; [2002] AC 122.

[164] *Equal Opportunities Review* 201 (July 2010) 11, Box 3, 16, Box 4.

compensate the victim for mental distress in circumstances where the injury was caused or exacerbated by the manner in which the defendant committed the wrong. This focuses on the effect on the victim rather than on punishment or deterrence. Guidelines given by the Court of Appeal[165] updated by presidential guidance indicate three bands of award for injury to feelings:

- in the *top band* (£19,800 to £33,000) are the most serious cases, such as where there has been a lengthy campaign of discriminatory harassment;
- the *middle band* (£6,600 to £19,800) is for serious cases which do not merit an award in the highest band;
- the *bottom band* (£660 to £6,600) is for less serious cases, such as where the act of discrimination is an isolated or one-off occurrence.

Table 7.5 indicates that the median award for injury to feelings (including aggravated damages) remains well within the bottom band. Nearly two-thirds of all awards fell into this band in 2012 and 2013. In a very limited number of cases aggravated damages are given as a separate award from injury to feelings. In 2013 such awards ranged from £1,000 to £7,000.

Table 7.5 Injury to feelings median awards (including aggravated damages) by employment tribunals 2010–13

Jurisdiction	2013	2011	2010
Age	£2,500	£3,500	£4,250
Disability	£5,250	£5,000	£6,000
Race	£4,500	£4,000	£4,500
Religion	£2,875	£1,000	£5,500
Sex	£5,000	£6,000	£5,000
Sexual orientation	£4,000	£5,000	£4,000
Combined jurisdiction	£6,000	£12,000	£10,500
All awards	£5,000	£5,000	£5,000

Source: *Equal Opportunities Review* 249 (July 2014) Table 2.

Recommendations

The employment tribunals have long had the power to make a recommendation that an employer take certain action to obviate or reduce the adverse effects of the discrimination on the claimant. In practice this power is rarely

---

[165] *Vento v Chief Constable of West Yorkshire Police (No 2)* [2003] IRLR 102, CA; updated to take account of inflation in *Da'Bell v National Society for the Prevention of Cruelty to Children* [2010] IRLR 19 and in *Simmons v Castle* [Practice Note] [2013] EWCA Civ 1288, [2013] 1 WLR 1239.

used.[166] It has been restrictively interpreted: for example, the Court of Appeal held that the tribunal cannot recommend that the employer promote the claimant to the next available vacancy as this would prevent consideration of other candidates.[167] Moreover, many discrimination claims are brought after the employment has ended, making it unlikely that a recommendation could benefit the claimant personally. However, many claimants want their case to benefit others in the future and in reaching a settlement are willing to trade a high injury to feelings award for the respondent's agreement to accept recommendations that might help others.

The Equality Act, following the precedent of the Northern Ireland Fair Employment Treatment Order, widened the tribunals' powers so as to enable them to make a recommendation that within a specified period the respondent takes specified steps for the purpose of obviating or reducing the adverse effect on both the complainant and 'any other person'.[168] For example, the tribunal could recommend training in good equality practice, or that reasonable adjustments be made for disabled persons. If the respondent failed without reasonable excuse to comply with a recommendation relating to the complainant, the tribunal could award additional compensation.[169] However, if the respondent failed to comply with a recommendation relating to 'any other person', there was no legal sanction. This power has been used on over 30 occasions, but the Dergulation Bill 2014 proposes to repeal it on the ground that it is an 'unnecessary burden on business' despite the fact only 12 per cent of those consulted wanted the provision to be removed.

---

[166] In 2013 recommendations were made in 30 cases, 8 of these relating only to the individual claimant. The remaining 21 contained wider action recommendations: *Equal Opportunities Review* 249 (July 2014) 11.

[167] *British Gas v Sharma* [1991] IRLR 530, CA.

[168] EA, s 124(3).

[169] EA, s 124(7).

8

An Appraisal

T HE OVERRIDING AIM of the Equality Act is to achieve the harmonisation, simplification and modernisation of equality law. There are striking parallels between this harmonisation and the harmonisation of health and safety legislation in the 1970s. The traditional British view of legislation was expressed in 1882 by WS Jevons, a leading economist and logician, who said that there were no principles of legislation—'legislation must proceed on the grounds of experience, legislation must be Baconian'.[1] That view was shared by many early twentieth century social thinkers, such as Sidney Webb, who described a 'century of experiment in factory legislation' as a 'typical example of English practical empiricism'.[2] The implication that there was some kind of process of 'trial and error' is now generally regarded as mistaken.[3] Instead,

> it is in the ebb and flow of struggle by unions and reform groups inside and outside Parliament, and the resistance by powerful groups of employers and the intellectual supporters of *laissez-faire* that the key must be found to the patchy character of the still influential protective legislation which began with the Regulation of Chimney Sweepers Act of 1788 and the Health and Morals of Apprentices Act of 1802.[4]

The history of equality legislation in Britain, too, is the story of struggles inside and outside Parliament against those who are prejudiced or fearful of 'outsiders', powerful business and political interests who have to

---

[1] Cited by Tillyard (1936) 16. The Baconian method is the investigative method developed by Sir Francis Bacon and put forward in his book *Novum organum* (1620), and is a forerunner of the scientific method. The method consists of procedures aimed at isolating the causes of phenomena through the use of inductive reasoning.

[2] Webb (1926) ix.

[3] Kahn-Freund (1977) 33; Wedderburn (1971) 238; See generally Wedderburn (1986) 385 *et seq.*

[4] Hepple (1983a) 405.

be persuaded that equality can improve economic and social performance,[5] and intellectual supporters of deregulated markets who seek to rationalise elitism, exclusion, prejudice, greed and social pessimism.[6] The campaigns were focused on racial discrimination in the 1960s, sex discrimination in the 1970s, disability discrimination in the 1980s and 1990s, and age, sexual orientation, and religion or belief in the 2000s. The victories were always partial and resulted in fragmented, patchy and inconsistent legislation, creating a history of bits and pieces.[7]

Surveying the scene of health and safety legislation in 1972, an official Committee of Inquiry under the chairmanship of Lord Robens found that there were some nine main groups of statutes controlling different industrial activities, and these were supported by over 500 subordinate statutory instruments. This was a situation not dissimilar to the state of equality legislation before 2010. The earlier health and safety laws, like anti-discrimination laws, contained a mass of intricate and ill-assorted detail. They showed neither internal logic nor consistency and were far from comprehensive—over 5 million of the 23 million workers in Britain were not subject to any occupational health and safety legislation. As a result of recommendations put forward by the Committee, a comprehensive Health and Safety at Work etc Act was enacted in 1974, extending coverage to the whole workforce and others. The Equality Act too is comprehensive, covering nearly all aspects of work, services and public functions, premises, education and associations. The protected characteristics effectively cover nearly the entire population.

The basic philosophy of the new health and safety system was self-regulation in place of the old patchwork which 'encourage[d] rather too much reliance on state regulation and rather too little on personal responsibility and voluntary self-generating effort'.[8] This 'self-regulation' was supported by workers' safety representatives, safety committees, and positive legal duties placed on line management, as well as by the integration of various inspectorates under the policy direction of the Health and Safety Commission and the administration of the Health and Safety Executive. This too has parallels with the new equality framework of responsive regulation, positive duties (although here confined to the public sector) and a single integrated Commission.

There can be no doubt that the comprehensive system has been one of factors leading to a vast improvement in health and safety standards in

---

[5] The attacks on the evidence produced by Wilkinson and Pickett (2009) that reducing inequality 'is the best way of improving ... the real quality of life for all of us' illustrate the continuing battle of ideas in this field (see www.equalitytrust.org).

[6] These are seen by Dorling (2010) 5 as the 'five faces of social inequality'.

[7] See p 11 above.

[8] Robens (1972) para 28.

Britain over recent decades. The question discussed in this chapter is whether the newly harmonised legal framework of the Equality Act, enforced by a single Commission, is capable of delivering substantive and transformative equality. Or is it simply an improvement in 'lawyer's law'—which is of little relevance to the victims of discrimination and disadvantage?

The initial issue is whether the Act is sufficiently comprehensive in its coverage to make a difference for ordinary people. One way of assessing this is against the benchmark of internationally recognised equality standards. The Equal Rights Trust's (ERT) *Declaration of Principles on Equality*, drawn up in 2008, represents 'a moral and professional consensus among human rights and equality experts'.[9] The *Declaration* proclaims the right to equality of all human beings (principle 1), equal protection from discrimination regardless of the grounds concerned (principle 6), and the obligation on states to give 'full effect' to the right to equality in all activities of the state (principle 11). There must be no hierarchy of equality. The same rule should be applied to all strands unless there is a convincing justification for an exception. To a large extent, the Act achieves these aims, but in some respects it does not go far enough, so reducing its effectiveness; in others it stretches harmonisation too far, with the risk of undermining the credibility of the law.

Broadly speaking, the drafters have managed to limit the exceptions to the general principles of equality. The defence of justification of direct discrimination has been allowed only for age discrimination[10] and discrimination arising from disability.[11] Outdated and inflexible exceptions, for example in respect of occupational requirements,[12] have been modernised, but there is bound to be argument at the margins. Continuing pressure resulted in one of the most controversial exceptions—the mandatory default retirement age of 65—being dropped by the Coalition government even before it could come into force.[13] But others remain, for example the exclusion of children from protection against age discrimination;[14] the exclusion of immigration decisions which discriminate because of disability, nationality and national or ethnic origins, and religion or belief;[15] and the absence of protection from harassment on grounds of religion or belief or sexual orientation outside work contexts. Exceptions in respect of age discrimination in the provision of services, added by secondary legislation, are unnecessarily wide and

[9] Equal Rights Trust (2008) 2.
[10] See p 78 above.
[11] See p 91 above.
[12] See p 110 above.
[13] See p 113 above.
[14] See p 38 above.
[15] See p 138 above.

ambiguous,[16] particularly because direct age discrimination can already be justified if the means are proportionate to a legitimate aim.

A particularly welcome aspect of harmonisation is that the concept of indirect discrimination—an increasingly important tool in the struggle for substantive equality—applies across all protected characteristics, including disability.[17] The essence of this wrong is whether a provision, criterion or practice which puts a group at a particular disadvantage can be justified. A standard defence that the provision is a 'proportionate means of achieving a legitimate aim' now applies across the board. This has enabled the judiciary to continue the standards of strict scrutiny laid down in the *Elias* case.[18] Is the legitimate objective sufficiently important to justify limiting the fundamental right to equality? Are the measures rationally connected to the objective? And are the means no more than necessary to accomplish the objective? The mainstreaming of equality in both the private and public sectors is encouraged by the Supreme Court's insistence in the *JFS* case[19] that a decision-maker must always consider the discriminatory impact of a provision, criterion or practice and whether there are less discriminatory ways of achieving the objective.

There are three main areas where harmonisation has not gone far enough. First, equal pay. The distinction remains between sex-based pay inequality and claims for pay discrimination because of other protected characteristics. If the matter is one regulated by the contract of employment, women, unlike other protected groups, cannot bring an ordinary claim for direct or indirect discrimination. Despite a concession to allow women to bring an ordinary discrimination claim where a sex equality clause has no effect—for example because there is no male comparator in the employer's undertaking—the legislation remains unnecessarily complex and has continued to be ineffective.[20] Repealing the special provisions on equal pay for women would actually improve enforcement by allowing all protected groups to utilise the statutory discrimination tort and straightforward contractual claims. It would remove the baffling rules on comparators, avoid the 'all-or-nothing' approach which prevents a woman from claiming 'proportionate' pay to that of a man where her work does not have exactly the same value, and allow full compensation in respect of back-pay.[21]

A second respect in which the Act is not sufficiently comprehensive is

---

[16] See p 136 above.

[17] See p 97 above.

[18] *R (on the application of Elias) v Secretary of State for Defence* [2006] IRLR 934, CA. See p 88 above.

[19] *R (on the application of E) v Governing Body of the JFS* [2009] UKSC 15. See p 89 above.

[20] See p 122 above.

[21] Newman (2012).

the coverage of protected characteristics. A unitary human rights perspective demands that all forms of status discrimination be outlawed, as is the case with Article 14 ECHR, which lists a number of specific characteristics and then adds 'or other status'. Instead, the Act simply brings under one statute the nine characteristics covered in earlier legislation, to which 'caste' is soon to be added as an aspect of race. The Act does not add any of the other characteristics that are mentioned in human rights instruments, such as genetic features, birth, social origin, political opinion and language. Nothing has been done to reverse restrictive judicial interpretations of 'national origin' which prevent the law from being used to restrain egregious direct discrimination and harassment against people because they are ambiguously categorised as 'born abroad' or are 'immigrants' 'asylum-seekers' or 'foreigners'.[22] Discrimination against non-EU nationals in respect of the exercise of immigration functions is sanctioned and legitimated by the Act.[23] Although marriage by same-sex couples is now recognised, single persons and those who cohabit without being married or civil partners are largely unprotected.[24]

Whenever pressed to improve protection in respect of other status, the response of successive governments is that there is 'no evidence' of significant discrimination against the particular group. Nothing could better illustrate the 'practical empiricism' of the British approach. This stands at odds with the principle of equality that all invidious classifications that impair the dignity of individuals because of attributes or characteristics attaching to them should be prohibited. The principle does not mean that differential or unequal treatment is never permissible, but this inequality must be justified as being proportionate to a legitimate aim.

A third respect in which the process of harmonisation is not complete is that of full compliance with international and European human rights standards. This book has mentioned some provisions of the Act that, arguably, are in conflict with specific obligations of the UK. These include: the exclusion of children from protection against age discrimination, which may prevent them from enjoying their rights as set out in the UN Convention on the Rights of the Child;[25] the medical definition of 'disability', which is at variance with the 'social' model set out in the UN Convention on the Rights of Persons with Disabilities;[26] the absence of a defence of justification of direct religious discrimination, which may be in conflict with Article 9(2)

---

[22] See p 49 above.
[23] See p 138 above.
[24] See p 63 above.
[25] See p 40 above.
[26] See p 43 above.

ECHR;[27] the exclusion of single persons and those who cohabit but are not married or in a civil partnership from protection, which may violate Articles 8 and 14 ECHR;[28] the absence of specific protection for carers, which may conflict with EU law;[29] the repeal of provisions on intersectional discrimination and third-party harassment, contrary to the requirements of EU law;[30] the exemption of the armed forces, which may be incompatible with the UN Convention on the Rights of Disabled Persons;[31] and the exclusion of immigration functions, which may violate Articles 8, 9 and 14 ECHR, and also the UN Convention on the Rights of Persons with Disabilities.[32] Other gaps in compliance may emerge, and eventually will have to be closed by fresh legislation.

On the other hand, an area in which harmonisation may have gone too far is that of religion or belief. There is a potential for conflict between the absence of a defence of justification of direct religious discrimination in the Equality Act, and the availability of such a defence in respect of limitations on the freedom to manifest one's religion under Article 9(2) ECHR. When negotiating a new EU Directive which will prohibit religious discrimination in respect of goods, services and other non-work areas, the government should ensure that there is a defence of justification, and the opportunity should be taken to propose amendments to the Framework Employment Directive in this respect. This should have been coupled with a duty to make reasonable accommodation for a person's religious observance or practice where this could be done without undue hardship to others.[33]

Similarly, the extension of all aspects of the public sector equality duty to religion or belief is problematic. It was important to iron out the inconsistencies between the separate race, sex and disability duties and bring them together in a single duty. The extension to age does not create particular problems and is significant because of the key role that public authorities play in setting priorities for health care and social services for older people; nor should the extension to sexual orientation cause disquiet, provided that the right to private and family life is respected.[34] Clearly there must be a duty on public authorities to eliminate discrimination and harassment because of religion or belief, and also to foster good relations between different groups. But the 'advancement' of equality in respect of religion or belief may encourage segregation and division rather than integration. It

---

[27] See p 55 above.
[28] See p 63 above.
[29] See p 76 above.
[30] See p 77 above.
[31] See p 137 above.
[32] See p 138 above.
[33] See p 56 above.
[34] See p 57 above.

is also likely to come into conflict with other rights, such as those relating to freedom of expression.[35]

Despite these limitations, the Act can help to bring about a change of approach, from identity politics to a unitary human rights perspective. To a significant extent, this depends on the willingness of practitioners and judges to embrace and apply universal human rights principles. As is well known, systemisation and the codification of principles has been regarded as alien to the spirit of the English common law, which functions on the basis of case-by-case precedent, and is fashioned by the needs and habits of practitioners seeking practical remedies for their clients. These methods are part of a broader political heritage of subordination to the will of Parliament, and reflect the 'English practical empiricism' to which Sidney Webb referred.

On the other hand, a number of factors have led to more purposive interpretations and application of equality legislation by the judiciary in recent decades. These include the recognition by the Court of Justice of the EU of a fundamental right to equal treatment to which national courts must give effect; a series of judgments in the House of Lords and Supreme Court, particularly those delivered by Lady Hale, clarifying the meaning and scope of direct and indirect discrimination;[36] the development by academic lawyers of legal principles relating to equality, several of whom now cross the once impenetrable boundaries between theory and practice; and the growth of a university-trained judiciary willing to refer to living academic authors. However, there are still scandalously few women in the higher judiciary: only one in the Supreme Court, and 8 per cent of Court of Appeal judges. The Judicial Appointments Commission is trying to improve the position: there has been an increase of female High Court judges from 12 in 2008 to 21 in 2014, and 23 per cent of district judges are women. But until the judiciary is more representative of the population, and of the increasingly feminised legal profession, there will be a lack of public confidence in the capacity of the judiciary to understand and enforce equality law. The same applies to the paucity of Black and Asian judges (currently 2–4 per cent).

Since the enactment of the Human Rights Act 1998, lawyers have increasingly become used to thinking in terms of human rights. One has only to compare the decision of the Court of Appeal in 1913, based on the venerable authority of Coke, that a woman was not a 'person' within the meaning of the Solicitor's Act 1843, and so could not be admitted as a solicitor,[37] with modern case law interpreting anti-discrimination legislation to see that there has been a wholesale transformation of judicial attitudes. Examples of this

---

[35] See p 164 above.
[36] See p 91 above.
[37] *Bebb v Law Society* [1914] 1 Ch 286, CA. This had to be reversed by the Sex Disqualification (Removal) Act 1919.

are the invocation of international human rights treaties to which the UK is a party and customary international law against racial discrimination by Lord Steyn and Lady Hale in the *Prague Airport* case,[38] and the reliance on decisions of the UN CERD committee and academic literature on descent-based discrimination in the *JFS* case.[39] This increased judicial sympathy for the objectives of equality legislation may be seen by comparing the obstacles that the Court of Appeal and House of Lords placed in the 1980s on the exercise of the powers of the CRE, notoriously likened by Lord Denning to the Inquisition,[40] with the purposive interpretation of the new public sector equality duty in recent years.[41] The task of the judges would have been made simpler had the Equality Act contained an explicit statement of purposes. In the absence of such a statement they must resort to the purposes of the EHRC set out in section 3 of the Equality Act 2006, which, despite the Coalition government's unsuccessful attempt to repeal this section, embody the values of respect for individual human rights, dignity and worth of the individual, equal opportunity to participate in society and mutual respect.[42] The 2010 Act mirrors those purposes. When in doubt about the intent of detailed provisions of the Act, the courts and tribunals should have recourse to these underlying values. They also need to have regard to the standards in international and European human rights law.[43]

CHANGING ORGANISATIONAL POLICY AND BEHAVIOUR

The vision of *transformative equality*[44] is supported by the widening of the possibilities for positive action in both private and public sectors and in the selection of candidates by political parties,[45] and by the extension of a single public sector equality duty to all protected characteristics.[46] However, these are the only measures in the Act that reflect the model of 'reflexive regulation'[47] or 'enforced self-regulation' which the Cambridge Review advocated.[48] There is no private sector duty to advance equality. The outdated provisions on positive action have been replaced by section 158 of the Act,

---

[38] *R (European Roma Rights Centre) v Immigration Officer at Prague Airport* [2004] UKHL 55; [2005] 2 AC 1, HL, paras 44–47, 98–103. See p 70 above.
[39] [2009] UKSC 15; [2010] IRLR 136, para 82 (Lord Mance). See p 49 above.
[40] See p 183 above.
[41] See p 170 above.
[42] See p 17 above.
[43] See p 18 above.
[44] See p 1 above.
[45] See p 156 above.
[46] See p 163 above.
[47] McCrudden (2007b) 255.
[48] See p 155 above.

based on EU law, which recognises the legitimacy in respect of all protected characteristics of positive action that is a proportionate means of achieving any one of three legitimate aims: minimising disadvantage, meeting special needs, and encouraging participation by under-represented groups. Section 159, which the Liberal Democrats persuaded the Conservatives to bring into force despite earlier opposition, allows tie-breaks in recruitment and promotion but it appears to have been little used in practice—it would be particularly helpful, for example, in making senior appointments. One may confidently predict in the light of binding EU law that UK law will not move in the direction of quotas or job or educational reservation for particular status groups. When positive action is taken in favour of a broadly defined status group, there is a risk of giving preference to what in India has been called the 'creamy layer', ie members of the group who are not themselves at a particular disadvantage.[49] For example, a university that targets a broadly defined group such as all Black and other minority ethnic groups might end up with a high proportion of Indian or Chinese-origin students, who are already over-represented in the student body, but fail to attract Bangladeshi women or Afro-Caribbean men, who are seriously under-represented. Precise targeting which takes account of relative socio-economic disadvantage is essential.

Another risk is that status-based positive measures, if not carefully designed, could reinforce stereotypes. An example is a decision of the Court of Justice of the EU[50] that to provide childcare facilities for working mothers and not working fathers was legitimate and proportionate. Fredman comments:

> Genuinely transformative change can only occur when both parents are equally responsible for child-care. Special measures for women, however well-intentioned, run the risk of reinforcing their primary role as child-carers and therefore perpetuates their disadvantage. This does not mean that there should be no special provision for parents. That would revert to formal equality. ... Instead such measures will only achieve real change if they refer to both parents.[51]

Judicial scrutiny of positive action measures should be aimed at supporting measures which genuinely seek to achieve substantive equality, provided that the decision-maker can show that the aim is legitimate and the measures are proportionate.[52] Greater diversity, for example in an educational institution or company boardroom, can itself be a legitimate aim. This is because it

---

[49] Sankaran (2010) 296.

[50] Case 476/99 *Lommers v Minister van Landbouw, Natuurbeheer an Visserij* [2002] ECR I-2891; [2002] IRLR 430.

[51] Fredman (2010a) 28–29; See too Browne (2006) 129–34 for a critique of an earlier decision upholding 'mother-only' benefits.

[52] Fredman (2010a) 27.

brings into those environments the perspectives of excluded groups such as women and disabled people, and may lead to incentives for structural change. Greater representation—of women, disabled persons and other disadvantaged groups—provides role models for those who have been excluded in the past.[53] Sections 158 and 159 thus provide an opportunity to achieve change. The public sector equality duty will encourage public bodies to adopt positive action measures; it is potentially an important vehicle for transformative equality.

Much will depend upon how effectively the Commission uses its enforcement powers. Contract and subsidy compliance, facilitated by a new EU Directive in 2014,[54] will be one way in which public authorities can improve the practices of their suppliers. Unfortunately, the scope of specific duties will be undermined by the increasing outsourcing and privatisation of public services, particularly in health, social care and education. Although the general duty applies to anyone (including private bodies) exercising public functions, the specific duties may be imposed only on listed public authorities.[55]

The public sector equality duty has proved to be a useful weapon to stop or delay cuts in public services where it can be shown that the public authority failed to consider adequately the impact of their measures on disadvantaged groups.[56] However, the duty suffers from two main defects: lack of provision in the primary legislation for engagement with stakeholders, and a low standard of judicial scrutiny. First, the absence of such a provision in the Act itself, has meant that separate Regulations have been made for each of England, Scotland and Wales. In England a crucial gap is a mechanism for public authorities to engage with interest groups, particularly those who stand to benefit from positive action. For example, there are many thousands of equality representatives appointed and supported by trade unions who give advice and support to members on equality issues in the workplace. Their effectiveness is dependent on the willingness of employers to recognise and consult with them. The TUC estimates that only 36 per cent of equality representatives have an employer who automatically consults with them frequently, only 26 per cent of employers negotiate with equality representatives, and 22 per cent of employers never involve the representatives.[57] There is no legal duty to consult these representatives. The Labour Government rejected an amendment, promoted by the TUC,

---

[53] Ibid, 35–37.
[54] See p 169 above.
[55] See p 165 above.
[56] See p 173 above
[57] These statistics were quoted from a TUC briefing by Baroness Gibson of Market Rasen, who moved the amendment: Hansard HL vol 716 col 984 (27 January 2010).

to allow these representatives paid time off work to carry out their functions and to receive training. The government's reason was the familiar one: a lack of 'sufficient empirical evidence that the time off should come through the law'.[58] This contrasts with regulations that require employers to consult safety representatives, who are elected by employees, and to ensure that these representatives receive training and are given paid time off to perform their functions.[59] Information, dialogue and balanced participation of employees and other interest groups on equality matters is key to effective regulation. This appears to have been recognised in Scotland and Wales where, under devolved powers, there is provision in the Specific Duties Regulations for 'engagement'.

The second major defect in the public sector duty is the failure to adopt Lord Ouseley's proposed amendment which would have required the public authority to take all proportionate steps towards the statutory objectives. The courts have stressed that the 'have due regard' test is not a duty to achieve a particular outcome. In practice it substitutes bureaucratic form-filling and compliance with procedures for taking action.[60]

The biggest failure in terms of adopting a responsive regulation approach is in relation to the private sector. There is no positive duty on private firms to advance equality. One way to overcome this to some extent would be for the EHRC to invoke its investigatory powers where the Commission reasonably suspects discrimination, and then seek to negotiate a legally binding positive action agreement in lieu of enforcement.[61] But in the absence of a legal duty on employers to conduct employment and pay equity audits, there is unlikely to be a sufficient incentive on employers to take positive action to improve employment opportunities for disadvantaged groups and to reduce the pay gap between women and men. In McCrudden's words, 'the rejection of proposals to introduce compulsory monitoring ... [is] the single greatest blow to the likelihood that reflexive regulation will be successful in the British context'.[62]

The general approach of governments of all complexions to the private sector has been that only if voluntary methods do not work will legislation be considered at a 'later date'. This evolutionary approach is, as the Cambridge Review pointed out,[63] profoundly mistaken. It has always failed in the past, an example being the voluntary procedures under the RRA 1968.[64] There

---

[58] Ibid, col 986 (Baroness Thornton).
[59] Deakin and Morris (2012) para 9.46.
[60] See p 174 above.
[61] See p 172 above.
[62] McCrudden (2007b) 265.
[63] Cambridge Review (2000) para 3.4, from which this text is drawn.
[64] See p 12 above.

is no reason to believe that purely voluntary guidance or codes will fare any better in the future in a technologically complex society, in which organisations have flatter and less hierarchical structures than before, so reducing the effectiveness of 'command and control' methods. Moreover, the antithesis between 'soft' and 'hard' regulation is a false one. One form of regulation (voluntarism) is not an alternative to another (legal enforcement). A voluntary approach may work in influencing the behaviour of some organisations (eg a leading edge company whose markets are among ethnic minorities will readily want to project an equality policy), but not others who for social or economic reasons are resistant to change. Regulation needs to be responsive to the different behaviours of various organisations. Although regulators start with attempts to persuade those subject to them to co-operate, they need to be able to rely on progressively more deterrent sanctions until there is compliance. There must be a gradual escalation of sanctions and, at the top, sufficiently strong sanctions to deter even the most persistent offender.

IMPROVING ENFORCEMENT

It was not until the arrival of the third generation of anti-discrimination legislation, the SDA 1975 and RRA 1976, that administrative enforcement by the Commissions and a right for individuals to bring civil proceedings became the normal method of enforcement. This is the model that has been continued by the Equality Acts 2006 and 2010. In principle this provides the best approach to enforcement. The decision to establish the single Commission before the enactment of a single Equality Act complicated the transition process. In 2007, a House of Commons select committee said that 'indecision, instability and delays in government's management of the transition have also undermined the ability of the Commission to deliver from day one'.[65] An investigation by the JCHR in March 2010 concluded that the first three years of the Commission's work had been marred by management failures, lack of adequate financial controls, and conflicts of interest.[66] Perhaps these transitional difficulties could have been avoided by keeping the three old Commissions in operation and simply expanding their remit to embrace the new strands. But this would have meant sacrificing the potential of a single Commission to become more than the sum of its parts.

Doubts have been expressed about whether the Commission is still fit for purpose. Since 2010, the Commission has been restricted to its so-called 'core' functions and its budget has been cut by more than two-thirds. There

---

[65] Department of Communities and Local Government Select Committee (2007).

[66] JCHR (2009–10) para 82; for the EHRC's account see Equality and Human Rights Commission (2009) and (2010).

is a need to recognise that we have moved away from 'command and control' by the Commission towards a model of enforcement that rests on 'reflexive self-regulation'. The role of the EHRC is to inform and persuade, and where necessary enforce the law. This involves education and monitoring and the stimulation of voluntary action by organisations, investigation if there is a belief that discrimination is occurring, and then enforcement by compliance notice, judicial process and sanctions.

The EHRC also has a wider role. The government failed in its attempt to repeal the general duty in section 3 of the 2006 Act, but the EHRC's duty to monitor progress has been confined to specific human rights duties set out in sections 8 and 9 of the 2006 Act. The 'communities' duty in section 10, the legal basis for work against racism in sport and similar activities, has been repealed. Despite these limitations, the EHRC can still be more than a think-tank. It can establish itself as the key guardian and enforcer of equality and human rights. There are welcome signs that, under new leadership, the EHRC is adjusting to its more limited funding, while not neglecting its wider role. There have been successful interventions in a significant number of high-profile cases. Most importantly from the view-point of reflexive self-regulation, the EHRC is developing partnerships, such as working with police forces to reduce race disproportionality in stop and searches. But more use could be made of its powers by following up indi-vidual cases with formal investigations. This is one way to overcome the removal of tribunal powers to make wider recommendations for organisa-tional change. The EHRC has given guidance on various matters such as the public sector equality duty. It should, however, lead in this respect rather than wait upon events: for example, why did the EHRC fail to act sooner to halt religious extremism by preachers who would speak only to gender-segregated audiences in universities?

The Equality Act did not make any significant changes in individual enforcement procedures, apart from a welcome clarification and extension of the provisions on the burden of proof.[67] The power to make regulations to permit representative actions in employment tribunals have not yet been utilised, and the equal pay procedures, revised in 2004, have failed to achieve their aims. Mediation, including the scheme relating to judicial mediation in employment tribunals, has had only a limited impact and the effect of new provisions for early conciliation is uncertain. The most significant change has been the limits on accessibility. This is partly because of the increasing formalisation of procedures and screening mechanisms making employment tribunals more like ordinary courts. The most serious blow to accessibility have been the introduction of tribunal fees, which have so far led to an 80

---

[67] See p 203 above.

per cent drop in claims, and the virtual disappearance of public support for legal assistance. Together, these factors mean that individual rights are less likely to be enforced.[68]

The Equality Act left the remedial powers of courts and tribunals unchanged, except for a new power for employment tribunals to make recommendations that benefit persons other than the claimant. This little-used power has been repealed after only three years in operation.[69] In practice tribunals continue to make relatively modest awards of aggravated damages (including injury to feelings), and do not in practice exercise the power they now appear to have, as a result of case law, to award exemplary damages. Apart from exceptional cases, such as those of senior women harassed in city firms, it is only in equal pay cases with multiple claimants that a respondent has to fear substantial monetary awards. This is an obvious reason for the reluctance of employers to accept representative actions.[70]

LIMITS OF LAW: POVERTY AND DISADVANTAGE

There is extensive evidence that a high level of income inequality persists in Britain and that deep-seated and systemic differences in economic outcomes exist between men and women, between different ethnic groups, between social class groups, and between those living in disadvantaged and other areas.[71] Social disadvantage is a complex, multidimensional problem with many causes, including lack of opportunities to work or to acquire education and skills, childhood deprivation, disrupted families, inequalities in health, poor access to social housing, and also discrimination on grounds of age, gender, disability, ethnicity and religion.[72] The National Equality Panel, set up by the Labour Government, provided detailed evidence which supports this analysis.[73] The Panel showed that social class differs from fixed characteristics such as gender, disability and ethnicity, because it is 'both an outcome of the labour market and part of the transmission mechanism that affects how people's lives develop'.[74] In particular, 'people's occupational and economic destinations in early adulthood depend to an important degree on their origins'.[75]

In 1999, the Labour Government promised 'an integrated and radical

---

[68] See p 195 above.
[69] See p 211 above.
[70] See p 199 above.
[71] National Equality Panel (2010); Hills, Sefton and Stewart (2009).
[72] Hills, Sefton and Stewart (2009) 11.
[73] National Equality Panel (2010) esp ch 9.
[74] Ibid, 243.
[75] National Equality Panel (2010) 393.

policy' response to the combined sources of disadvantage.[76] The public sector equality duty is confined to specified strands of status equality. Its origins lie in Northern Ireland legislation and in the finding of 'institutional racism' by the Stephen Lawrence inquiry. The desirability of reducing socio-economic disadvantage more generally has increasingly been on the agenda of public debate. For example, the *New Opportunities* White Paper in 1999[77] proposed a duty on public authorities to reduce socio-economic inequality. Section 1 of the 2010 Act introduced such a duty but it was never implemented and has now been repealed. But the social problem with which it purported to deal remains.

A truly comprehensive and transformative approach to equality obviously does not mean that all aspects of socio-economic disadvantage have to be dealt with by a single duty or in a single statute. It certainly would have been possible to extend the public sector duty regarding status equality by including in that duty the advancement of equality of outcomes for people regardless of 'social origin', which is already recognised as a protected characteristic in European and international human rights law.[78] But the fixed status of 'social origin' does not exactly correspond with the mobile characteristic of socio-economic status. Far more important than the section 1 legal duty would be a range of other socio-economic measures in respect of schooling and education, the labour market, the distributional effect of taxes and spending, and providing resources for groups such as pensioners. These vital socio-economic measures lie beyond the scope of status equality law.

The Equality Act represents only one form of response to socio-economic disadvantage. It is not a cure-all. There are at least two reasons why the cycle of disadvantage and social exclusion cannot be remedied solely by legislation relating to status equality, a point I tried to make some years ago:

> The first reason is that ... [l]aw, as Ehrlich and others have pointed out, demands specificity. Legal concepts have to be relatively clear and they can be enforced only against identified persons. Put another way, the legal process can operate only by individualizing conflict between specific parties. ... Secondly, the law is directed at only one element in the many causes of disadvantage, namely 'discrimination'. The demand for specificity has led to a narrow and technical definition of this concept. ... Whether we rely on negative concepts like direct or indirect discrimination or a broader positive notion of 'equal opportunity', or even 'fair opportunity', it would be illusory to believe that these can be translated into legal terms of art which will lead, without more, to the promised land of [transformative] equality. ... Law is both too *specific* and too *selective* in its choice

---

[76] Department of Social Security (1999) 23; see generally Hills, Sefton and Stewart (2009) 8–16.
[77] Department of Social Security (1999).
[78] See p 36 above.

of the causes in the 'cycle of disadvantage' to be capable in itself, of delivering real substantive equal rights.[79]

These limits of law apply to policies such as 'social inclusion' and 'solidarity', and the duty to have regard to the desirability of reducing socio-economic disadvantage. We need to see the Equality Act as simply one element in the processes of social change. The law cannot be expected to remove the power that privileged elites exercise over disadvantaged groups, 'but it can help to direct that power into legitimate procedures which recognize their interests'.[80]

It has been argued that discrimination against individuals because of their poverty—eg the exclusion of someone who is from a poor area, or unemployed—should be made unlawful. If the individual is from a disadvantaged status group, this may constitute indirect discrimination. But poor people who do not have a recognised protected characteristic have no such protection. While it is generally acknowledged that the law cannot deal with the primarily economic manifestations of poverty, it has been suggested that the law could prohibit stigma and hostility and affirm the dignity and worth of people regardless of their means.[81] There are problems with defining poverty as a status,[82] even if it is long-lasting and passed on from generation to generation in deprived families. Unlike race or gender, for example, it is possible at least in theory to escape from poverty to relative affluence. Poverty or socio-economic class is not an essential attribute or characteristic of a person. The law on status equality can deal with stigma and recognise individual worth, but it is generally not effective in bringing about redistribution between rich and poor. It may do so indirectly because poverty is often associated with membership of a disadvantaged social group, and this may lead to redistribution within a status group, with those who use the opportunities won through status equality law progressing more successfully than those who fail to get or use those opportunities. Redistributive aims have to be achieved through welfare legislation, taxation and similar measures. These measures may be reinforced by social and economic rights, for example to access to health services, or to vocational training and work, or to social welfare. But status equality law on its own is generally not a suitable vehicle for this.

---

[79] Hepple (1992) 20–27.
[80] Ibid, 31.
[81] Fredman (2010a) 39.
[82] The South African Promotion of Equality and Prevention of Unfair Discrimination Act, Act 4 of 2000, s 34(1) includes 'socio-economic status', in terms that include poverty, as a potential ground of unfair discrimination, although this is yet to be activated.

LAW AND POLITICS

A theme of this book has been that the Equality Act marks a significant shift from the politics and law of single identities to the politics and law of equality as a fundamental human right. This ideal has not yet been fully achieved, as we have seen from a detailed analysis of the exceptions and exclusions, and from the limitations of the EHRC's enforcement powers in respect of human rights violations.[83] But the Act, like its predecessors, is a compromise between conflicting social and political groups. Those opposed to extensions of the law will continue to exaggerate differences between groups, and some on the other side will still use differences to strengthen their own power relative to other groups. The relative social and political power of those advocating change and those resisting it has been the decisive element in the making of equality law. In order to understand the Equality Act, a purely functional approach is less instructive than one that emphasises power. Indeed, legislation is often a symbolic focus for emerging ideological and political conflicts—this is why the debate over the proposed repeal of section 3 of the 2006 Act assumed such significance. The Equality Act symbolises the growing ascendancy of human rights values in our politics. This is my view as a democratic pluralist who sees these values as the social and political ideal that can best bind our society together.

The struggles for equality have resulted in the gradual recognition of the legal rights of a wider range of disadvantaged groups, and in the expansion of the law to deal not only with individual acts of direct discrimination but also subtler forms of indirect discrimination. The new, fifth generation, now embodied in the Equality Act, is based on the premise that members of disadvantaged groups will not have equal life chances or enjoy respect for their equal worth unless institutions take proactive measures to ensure equality. Progress to date has been piecemeal, patchy, and often bureaucratic. The Act provides an enormous opportunity to raise the status of the equality principle within a wider culture of human rights beyond the confines of equal treatment and equal worth. No one should pretend that all inequality can be remedied by law. But the single Commission and the single Act are less likely to be seen as representing only sectional interests, particularly since issues affecting White men—such as age, religion or belief, and sexual orientation—are included. The EHRC can speak with a strong voice on the basis of an overarching modern principle of transformative equality that recognises the need to develop the capabilities of individuals and groups if they are to enjoy genuine human rights in the civil, social and economic spheres.

---

[83] See p 181 above.

It is all too easy to allow the setbacks of the past few years—deregulation of useful anti-discrimination measures, the disempowerment of the EHRC and the limits on accessibility to justice—to lead one to indulge in facile pessimism about the prospects for equality law. Instead, I would argue for a positive and more nuanced approach. I have suggested there are ways around the removal of some of the rights under the Equality Act, such as third party harassment,[84] intersectional discrimination[85] and the repeal of the questionnaire procedure.[86] There are new rights which can be used creatively, such as the power to order a pay audit by a firm that is found to have discriminated in respect of women's pay.[87] There are several new 'family-friendly' rights, such as to shared parental leave and pay and a new simplified right to request flexible working. The public sector equality duty still offers possibilities for transformative action. The imposition of tribunal fees and the absence of legal aid means that alternatives to legal action have to be developed by NGOs and trade unions, including publicity about and boycotts of firms with discriminatory practices.

It is becoming increasingly clear that the promotion of equality cannot be separated from the wider issue of protecting all vulnerable individuals from exploitation. General measures that guarantee decent standards are required. For example, the national minimum wage needs to be raised for the five million workers (the majority of whom are women) who earn below the 'living' wage, and enforcement of the minimum wage law needs to be made more effective. Then there is the problem of agency workers recruited abroad. The Temporary Agency Workers Regulations 2010, which transposed the Temporary Agency Workers Directive 2008 into UK law, needs to be revised so as to prevent abuse. The jurisdiction of the Gangmasters Licensing Authority should be extended to care homes and the construction industry and the Authority needs more resources to ensure enforcement. The law on trafficking and forced labour needs to be extended and more vigorously enforced.

Any pessimism about the future of equality law should be short-lived. There are many ways in which those who are committed to equality can use existing and new legal rights, can revitalise the EHRC, can develop new forms of dispute resolution, strengthen NGOs and trade unions, and campaign for the re-regulation of open labour markets to protect vulnerable individuals. This is not the end of the struggle for equality but a new beginning.

[84] See p 102 above.
[85] See p 76 above.
[86] See p 205 above.
[87] See p 133 above.

References

Advisory, Conciliation and Arbitration Service (ACAS) (2010) *Annual Report and Accounts 2009/10* (London, ACAS).

Albertyn, S (2006) 'Substantive Equality and Transformation in South Africa' 23 *South African Journal of Human Rights* 253.

Alldridge, P (2006) 'Locating Disability Law' 59 *Current Legal Problems* 289.

Ashtiany, S (2014) 'Caste Discrimination in the UK' 247 *Equal Opportunity Review* 14.

Barnard, C (2004) 'The Future of Equality Law: Equality and Beyond' in C Barnard, S Deakin and G Morris (eds), *The Future of Labour Law. Liber Amicorum Sir Bob Hepple* (Oxford, Hart Publishing) ch 10.

—— (2012) *EU Employment Law*, 4th edn (Oxford, Oxford University Press).

—— and Hepple, B (2000) 'Substantive Equality' 59 *Cambridge Law Journal* 562.

Barrett, B (2010) 'When Does Harassment Warrant Redress?' 39 *Industrial Law Journal* 194.

Bell, M (2002) *Anti-Discrimination Law and the European Union* (Oxford, Oxford University Press).

Bercusson, B (1996) *European Labour Law* (London, Butterworths).

Bingham, T (2010) *The Rule of Law* (London, Allen Lane).

Browne, J (2006) *Sex Segregation and Inequality in the Modern Labour Market* (Bristol, Policy Press).

—— (2011) 'O'Neill and the Political Turn against Human Rights' *International Journal of Political Science*

Cambridge Review (2000): see Hepple, Coussey, Choudhury (2000).

Cheung, SY and Heath, A (2007), 'Nice Work if You Can Get It: Ethnic Penalties in Britain' 137 *Proceedings of the British Academy* 507.

Choudhury, T (2000) *Discrimination on Grounds of Religion or Belief*, Independent Review of the Enforcement of UK Anti-Discrimination Legislation, Working Paper No 6 (Cambridge Centre for Public Law).

Cohen, G (2000) *If You're an Egalitarian, How Come You're So Rich?* (Cambridge, MA, Harvard University Press).

Collins, H (2003) 'Discrimination, Equality and Social Inclusion' 65 *Modern Law Review* 16.

Commission for Racial Equality (2005) *Citizenship and Belonging: What is Britishness?* (London, CRE).

Corby, S and Latreille P (2012a) 'Employment Tribunals and the Civil Courts: Isomorphism Exemplified' 44 *Industrial Law Journal* 387.

—— (2012b) 'Tripartite Adjudication: An Endagered Species' 43 *Industrial Relations Journal* 94.

Cornford, F (1908) *Microcosmographia Academica: Being a Guide for the Young Academic* (Cambridge, Bowes and Bowes).

Coussey, M (1992) 'The Effectiveness of Strategic Enforcement in the Race Relations

Act 1976' in B Hepple and EM Szyszczak (eds), *Discrimination: The Limits of Law* (London, Mansell).

—— (2002) *Tackling Racial Equality: International Comparisons,* Home Office Research Study 238 (London, Home Office).

—— and Jackson, H (1991) *Making Equal Opportunities Work* (London, Pitman).

Creighton, WB (1979) *Working Women and the Law* (London, Mansell).

Crick, M (2014) ' EHRC's Litigation Strategy' 245 *Equal Opportunities Review* 8

Cross, S (2008) 'What Good Are No-Win No-Fee Lawyers?' 174 *Equal Opportunities Review* 18.

Davies, Lord (2011) *Women on Boards: Review* (Department for Business, Innovation and Skills).

De Marco, N (2004) *Blackstone's Guide to the Employment Equality Regulations 2003* (Oxford University Press).

Deakin, S and Morris, GS (2012) *Labour Law,* 6th edn (Oxford, Hart Publishing).

Department for Communities and Local Government Select Committee (2007) *Equality,* Sixth Report, 2006–07 session.

Department of Communities and Local Government (2004) *Fairness for All: A New Commission for Equality and Human Rights,* Cm 6185 (London, The Stationery Office).

—— (2007a) *Fairness and Freedom: The Final Report of the Equalities Review* (London, DCLG).

—— (2007b) *Discrimination Law Review: A Framework for Fairness. Proposals for a Single Equality Bill for Great Britain* (London, DCLG).

Department of Social Security (1999) *Opportunity for All: Tackling Poverty and Social Exclusion,* First Annual Report, Cm 4445 (London, The Stationery Office).

Department of Trade and Industry (2001) *Towards Equality and Diversity: Implementing the Employment and Race Directives,* Consultation Papers (London, DTI and Cabinet Office).

Discrimination Law Review (2007): see Department of Communities and Local Government (2007b).

Dorling, D (2010) *Injustice: Why Social Inequality Persists* (Bristol, Policy Press).

Doyle, B (1995) *Disability Discrimination and Equal Opportunities: A Comparative Study of Employment Rights of Disabled Persons* (London, Mansell).

—— (1999) *Reform of the Disability Discrimination Act,* Independent Review of the Enforcement of UK Anti-Discrimination Legislation, Working Paper No 4 (Cambridge Centre for Public Law).

Dworkin, RM (2000) *Sovereign Virtue: The Theory and Practice of Equality* (Cambridge, MA, Harvard University Press).

—— (2002) 'Paternalism' in *Stanford Encyclopedia of Philospohy,* available at http://plato. stanford.edu/entries/paternalism.

—— (2006) *Is Democracy Possible Here?* (Princeton, NJ, Princeton University Press).

Ellis, E (1998) *EC Sex Equality Law,* 2nd edn (Oxford, Clarendon Press).

—— and Watson, P (2012) *EU Anti-Discrimination Law,* 2nd edn (Oxford, Oxford University Press).

Equal Rights Trust (2008) *Declaration of Principles on Equality* (London, Equal Rights Trust).

Equalities Review (2007): see Department of Communities and Local Government (2007a).

Equality and Human Rights Commission (2009) *Annual Report and Accounts 2006–8,* HC 632 (London, The Stationery Office).

—— (2010) *Annual Report and Accounts 2008–9,* HC 232 (London, The Stationery Office).

Equality Commission for Northern Ireland (2008) *Section 75—Keeping it Effective: Final Report* (Belfast, ECNI).

European Commission against Racism and Intolerance (1998) *Legal Measures to Combat Racism and Intolerance in the Member States of the Council of Europe,* Report prepared by the Swiss Institute of Comparative Law, Lausanne (Strasbourg, Council of Europe).

Feldman, D (1999, 2000) 'Human Dignity as a Human Value' [1999] *Public Law* 682–702; [2000] *Public Law* 61–76.

Fredman, S (1997a) *Women and Law* (Oxford, Oxford University Press).

—— (1997b) 'Reversing Discrimination' 113 *Law Quarterly Review* 575.

—— (1999) *A Critical Review of the Concept of Equality in UK Anti-Discrimination Law,* Independent Review of the Enforcement of UK Anti-Discrimination Legislation, Working Paper No 3 (Cambridge Centre for Public Law).

—— (ed) (2001) *Discrimination and Human Rights: The Case of Racism* (Oxford, Oxford University Press).

—— (2004) 'The Ideology of New Labour Law' in C Barnard, S Deakin and G Morris (eds), *The Future of Labour Law. Liber Amicorum Sir Bob Hepple* (Oxford, Hart Publishing) ch 1.

—— (2008) *Human Rights Transformed* (Oxford, Oxford University Press).

—— (2010a) 'Facing the Future: Substantive Equality under the Spotlight' in O Dupper and C Garbers (eds), *Equality in the Workplace* (Cape Town, Juta).

—— (2010b) 'Positive Duties and Socio-Economic Disadvantage: Bringing Disadvantage on to the Equality Agenda' *European Human Rights Review* 288.

—— (2011) *Discrimination Law,* 2nd edn (Oxford, Oxford University Press).

—— and Spencer, S (eds) (2003) *Age as an Equality Issue* (Oxford, Hart Publishing).

Godwin, K (2008) 'Bullying and Harassment: EOR Survey 2008' 176 *Equal Opportunities Review* 17.

—— (2009) 'Equal Value: Justice Denied?' 186 *Equal Opportunities Review* 16.

Government Equalities Office (2008) *The Equality Bill—Government Response to the Consultation,* Cm 7454 (London, The Stationery Office).

—— (2009a) *Equality Bill: Making it Work. Ending Age Discrimination in Services and Public Functions* (London, GEO).

—— (2009b) *Equality Bill: Making it Work. Policy Proposals for Specific Duties* (London, GEO).

—— (2010) *The Equality Bill: Duty to Reduce Socio-Economic Inequalities—A Guide* (London, GEO).

—— (2011) *Building a Fairer Britain: Reform of the Equality and Human Rights Commission* (London, GEO).

—— and Schneider Ross (2009) *Equality Duties: Assessing the Cost and Cost Effectiveness of Specific Race, Disability and Gender Equality Duties* (London, GEO).

Halford, J (2009) 'Paying Attention to Inequality: The Development of Positive Equality Duties' 14 *Judicial Review* 21.

Hardy, ST (gen ed), *Sweet & Maxwell's Encyclopedia of Employment Law* (London, Sweet & Maxwell).

Harris D, O'Boyle, M, Bates, E and Buckley, C (2009) *Law of the European Convention on Human Rights,* 2nd edn (Oxford, Oxford University Press).

Heath, A, Clifford, P, Hamill, H, McCrudden, C and Muttarak, R (2009) 'The Enforcement of Fair Employment Law in Northern Ireland: The Effects of Commission

Agreements, MacBride Agreements and Fair Employment Tribunal Cases', unpublished paper.

Heath, AF and Cheung, SY (2006) *Ethnic Penalties in the Labour Market: Employer and Discrimination* (London, Department for Work and Pensions Research Report No 341).

Hepple, B (1968) *Race, Jobs and the Law in Britain* (London, Allen Lane/Penguin), 2nd edn (1970) (Harmondsworth, Penguin).

—— (1983a) 'Individual Labour Law' in GS Bain (ed), *Industrial Relations in Britain* (Oxford, Basil Blackwell).

—— (1983b) 'Judging Equal Rights' 36 *Current Legal Problems* 71.

—— (1992) 'Have Twenty-five Years of the Race Relations Act in Britain been a Failure?' in B Hepple and EM Szyszczak (eds), *Discrimination: The Limits of Law* (London, Mansell) 19.

—— (2000) 'Freedom of Expression and the Problem of Harassment' in J Beatson and Y Cripps (eds), *Freedom of Expression and Freedom of Information: Essays in Honour of Sir David Williams* (Oxford, Oxford University Press) 177.

—— (2002) 'Enforcement: The Law and Politics of Co-operation and Compliance' in B Hepple (ed), *Social and Labour Rights in a Global Context: International and Comparative Perspectives* (Cambridge, Cambridge University Press).

—— (2004) 'Race and Law in Fortress Europe' 67 *Modern Law Review* 1–15.

—— (2006a) 'The Equality Commissions and the Future Commission for Equality and Human Rights' in L Dickens and AC Neal (eds), *The Changing Institutional Face of British Employment Relations* (The Hague, Kluwer Law International) 101.

—— (2006b) 'The European Legacy of *Brown v Board of Education*' *University of Illinois Law Review* 605.

—— (2008) 'The Aims of Equality Law' 61 *Current Legal Problems* 1.

—— (2009) 'Equality at Work' in B Hepple and B Veneziani (eds), *The Transformation of Labour Law in Europe: A Comparative Study of 15 Countries 1945–2004* (Oxford, Hart Publishing) ch 5.

—— (2012) 'Agency Enforcement of Worplace Equality' in L Dickens (ed) *Making Emplpyment Rights Effective:Issues of Enforcement and Compliance* (Oxford, Hart Publishing) ch 4.

—— (2013) 'Back to the Future: Employment Law under the Coalition Government' 42 *Industrial Law Journal* 203.

—— and Choudhury, T (2001) *Tackling Religious Discrimination: Practical Implications for Policy-Makers and Legislators* (London, Home Office Research Study 221).

—— and Szyszczak, EM (1992) *Discrimination: The Limits of Law* (London, Mansell).

——, Coussey, M and Choudhury, T (Cambridge Review) (2000) *Equality: A New Framework. Report of the Independent Review of the Enforcement of UK Anti-Discrimination Legislation* (Oxford, Hart Publishing).

——, Lord Lester of Herne Hill QC, Ellis, E, Rose, D and Singh, R (1997) *Improving Equality Law: The Options* (London, Justice and the Runnymede Trust).

Hills, J, Sefton, T and Stewart, K (2009) *Towards a More Equal Society? Poverty, Inequality and Policy since 1997* (Bristol, Policy Press).

Hindley, G (1990) *The Book of Magna Carta* (London, Constable).

Hunter, R and Leonard A (1997) 'Sex Discrimination and Alternative Dispute Resolution: British Proposals in the Light of International Experience' *Public Law* 298.

JCHR (Joint Committee on Human Rights) (2005–6) *Legislative Scrutiny: Equality Bill* 4th

Report of Session 2005-6, HL Paper 89, HC Paper 766 (London, The Stationery Office).

—— (2008–9) *Legislative Scrutiny: Equality Bill*, 26th Report of Session 2008–09, HL Paper 169, HC Paper 736 (London, The Stationery Office).

—— (2009–10) *Equality and Human Rights Commission*, 13th Report of Session 2009–10, HL Paper 72, HC Paper183 (London, The Stationery Office)

Kahn-Freund, O (1977) *Labour and the Law*, 2nd edn (London, Stevens).

Kenner, J (2003) *EU Employment Law: From Rome to Amsterdam and Beyond* (Oxford, Hart Publishing).

Le Grand, J (1991) *Equity and Choice: An Essay in Economics and Applied Philosophy* (London, HarperCollins).

Lester, A (Lord Lester of Herne Hill QC) (2001) 'Equality and United Kingdom Law, Past Present and Future' *Public Law* 77.

Lester, A and Bindman, G (1972) *Race and Law* (Harmondsworth, Penguin).

Mackie, K, Miles, D, Marsh, W and Allen, T (2005) *The ADR Practice Guide*, 2nd edn (Haywards Heath, Tottel).

McColgan, A (2005) *Discrimination Law: Text, Cases and Materials*, 2nd rev edn (Oxford, Hart Publishing).

—— (2009) 'Class Wars: Religion and (In)Equality in the Workplace' 38 *Industrial Law Journal* 1.

McCrudden, C (1986) 'Rethinking Positive Action' 15 *Industrial Law Journal* 215.

—— (2004a) 'Equality and Non-Discrimination' in D Feldman (ed), *English Public Law* (Oxford, Oxford University Press) ch 11.

—— (2004b) 'Affirmative Action: An Empirical Assessment' 24 *Oxford Journal of Legal Studies* 363.

—— (2007a) *Buying Social Justice: Equality, Government Procurement and Legal Change* (Oxford University Press).

—— (2007b) 'Equality Legislation and Reflexive Regulation: A Response to the Discrimination Law Review's Consultative Paper' 36 *Industrial Law Journal* 255.

—— (2008) 'Human Dignity and the Judicial Interpretation of Human Rights' 19 *European Journal of International Law* 655.

McKenna, B (2008) 'The Union Perspective on Equal Pay' 174 *Equal Opportunities Review* 13.

McClaughlin, C (2014) 'Equal Pay. Litigation and Reflexive Regulation: th Case of the UK Local Authority Sector' 43 *Industrial Law Journal* 1.

Ministry of Justice (2010) *Evaluating the Use of Judicial Mediation in Employment Tribunals* (London, Ministry of Justice Research Series 7/10).

Modood, T (1992) 'Cultural Diversity and Racial Discrimination in Employment' in B Hepple and EM Szyszczak (eds), *Discrimination: The Limits of Law* (London, Mansell) ch 13.

Monaghan, K (2013) *Equality Law*, 2nd edn (Oxford, Oxford University Press).

Napier, B (2014) 'Equal Pay in 2013' 246 *Equal Opportunities Review* 8.

National Equality Panel (2010) *An Anatomy of Economic Inequality—The UK Report of the National Equality Panel* (London, Government Equalities Office).

Newman, D (2012) 'Repeal the Law on Equal Pay' 223 *Equal Opportunities Review* 8.

Nuffield Council on Bioethics (2007) *Public Health: Ethical Issues* (London, NCOB).

O'Cinneide, C (2007) 'The Commission for Equality and Human Rights: A New Institution for New and Uncertain Times' 36 *Industrial Law Journal* 141.

—— (undated) *Taking Equal Opportunities Seriously: The Extension of Positive Duties to Provide Equality* (London, Equality and Diversity Forum).

O'Neill, O (2005) 'The Dark Side of Human Rights' 81 *International Affairs* 427.

Parekh, B (chair) (2000) *The Future of Mutli-Ethnic Britain: Report of the Commission on the Future of Multi-Ethnic Britain* (London, Profile).

Political and Economic Planning (1967) *Report on Racial Discrimination* (London, PEP).

Race Relations Board (1966–7) *First Annual Report* (London, HMSO).

Rawls, J (1971) *A Theory of Justice* (Cambridge, MA, Harvard University Press).

Robens, A (Lord) (1972) Committee on Safety and Health at Work, *Report of the Committee 1970–2*, Cmnd 5034 (London, HMSO).

Robinson, J (2003) 'Age Equality in Health and Social Care' in S Fredman and S Spencer (eds), *Age as an Equality Issue* (Oxford, Hart Publishing) 97.

Rose, EJB and associates (1969) *Colour and Citizenship: A Report on British Race Relations* (Oxford, Oxford University Press for Institute of Race Relations).

Rubenstein, M (2007) 'What Is the Next Frontier for Discrimination Law?' 166 *Equal Opportunities Review* 31.

—— (2008) 'Sex Discrimination Act (Amendment) Regulations 2008: an EOR Guide 176 *Equal Opportunities Review* 25.

—— (2009a) 'The EOR Guide to the Equality Bill: Part I—General Principles' 189 *Equal Opportunities Review* 22.

—— (2009b) 'The EOR Guide to the Equality Bill: Part 2—Protected Characteristics' 190 *Equal Opportunities Review* 28.

—— (2010) 'Default Retirement Age to Go' 204 *Equal Opportunities Review* 20.

Sankaran, K (2010) 'Towards Inclusion and Diversity: India's Experience with Affirmative Action' in O Dupper and C Garbers (eds), *Equality in the Workplace* (Cape Town, Juta).

Schiek, D (2005) 'Broadening the Scope and the Norms of EU Gender Equality Law: Towards a Multidimensional Conception of Equality Law' 12 *Maastricht Journal of European and Comparative Law* 427.

Schuller, T and Watson, D (2009) *Learning through Life: Inquiry into the Future of Lifelong Learning* (Leicester, NIACE).

Sen, A (1992) *Inequality Re-Examined* (Oxford, Clarendon Press).

—— (1999) *Development as Freedom* (Oxford, Oxford University Press).

—— (2006) *Identity and Violence: The Illusion of Destiny* (London, Allen Lane).

—— (2009) *The Idea of Justice* (London, Allen Lane).

Spencer, S and Bynoe, I (1998) *A Human Rights Commission: The Options for Great Britain and Northern Ireland* (London, IPPR).

Stephen Lawrence Inquiry (1999) *Report of an Inquiry by Sir William MacPherson of Cluny*, Cm 4262-I (London, HMSO).

Street Report: Street, H, Howe, G and Bindman, G (1967) *Anti-Discrimination Legislation* (London, PEP).

Tawney, RH (1931) *Equality, with an Introduction by Richard M Titmuss* (London, Unwin Books, 1964).

Thane, P (2000) *Old Age in English History* (Oxford University Press).

Tillyard, F (1936) *The Worker and the State*, 2nd edn (Tillcoultry, NCLC Publishing Society).

Uccellari, P (2008) 'Multiple Discrimination: How Law Can Reflect Reality' 1 *Equal Rights Review* 24.

Webb, S (1926) 'Preface' in BL Hutchins and A Harrison, *A History of Factory Legislation*, 3rd edn (London, King and Son).

Wilkinson RG and Pickett K (2009) *The Spirit Level: Why Equal Societies Almost Always Do Better* (London, Allen Lane).

Women and Work Commission (2006) *Shaping a Fairer Future* (London, Women and Work Commission).

—— (2009) *Shaping a Fairer Future: A Review of the Recommendation of the Women and Work Commission Three Years On* (London, Women and Work Commission).

Wedderburn, KW (Lord) (1971) *The Worker and the Law*, 2nd edn, (1986) 3rd edn (Harmondsworth, Penguin).

Index